Major Characters in CASTLE OF DECEPTION

Tanithia. A witch, and a very talented and well-trained adept. Formerly ruler of a fair-sized country, she had been overthrown in a political/religious revolution. At the time of this book, she has been in hiding for two or three years. Gifted with considerable beauty and magnetism, she has used her mastery of the arcane arts to maintain herself at the peak of her powers. A very sensual and loving person, her sexuality is both the source of much magical power (see essay on "Sex Magic" in the back of this book) and a cause of some severe misjudgements and dangerous risks on her part.

Count Waldmann. A middle-aged nobleman who, because he supported Tanithia before the revolution, is now largely confined to his own lands by the current government. A very strong and intelligent person, and a just and courageous ruler, he is rich in years of experience and understanding.

Lyia. A sorceress of considerable power who has devoted herself to the "left-hand path," but recently badly overstepped herself and made some catastrophic blunders. Unknown to those whom she meets in this book, she is now the abused puppet of the dark forces she once controlled. To maintain her beauty, and her life, she has become vampiric. Even so, she feels deeply about her essentially hopeless situation and is strong-willed enough to try to win back something of her inner worth.

Swordsman Gort. A young, highly-skilled and idealistic fighter. He is of solid country stock and quite conventional even for his era, although he is sympathetic with the ancient Pagan ways. He falls in love with Tanithia, but her wanton ways are a challenge to his conservative temperament.

Deacon Elijus. An officially-sanctioned witchfinder during the recent revolution, Elijus was dismissed after its success for being over-zealous in his inquisition. He is fully devoted to his warrior-god, even to feeling totally justified in using *any* means required to advance his new religion. He has some magical talents himself, which he firmly channels to the benefit of his religion.

The Demon King. Sentient, alien, and totally inimical to human life, this being is basically a para-normal creature. Brought forth originally (probably) by Lyia's demonological experiments, he now controls her! There are numerous similar demons in this story, though this one is the largest, oldest, most intelligent, and the leader of its kind here.

Longrunner and Grey Lady. Wolves! Leaders of the wolf-pack who are capable and intelligent individuals in their own right—with their traditions, histories, and even their own variety of magic. In many ways they are non-human parallels to Waldmann and Tanithia.

About the Author

"Ed Fitch" isn't his real name! The ideas in this book, even presented as fiction, are too fantastic and yet entirely too real to reveal his identity. Under his "real" identity, he is an ex-Air Force officer currently employed by a major defense contractor working as a space scientist. In the Air Force, he served in the Far East and in Southeast Asia, and while there studied oriental philosophy and magic, and the martial arts. He has also traveled, and studied, extensively in Northern Europe.

As "Ed Fitch" he is well known as the editor of Crystal Well, a neo-romantic journal of modern Paganism. He is the author of many articles on Witchcraft, Paganism, and magic, and several short stories of science fiction and fantasy.

He is knowledgeable in the themes developed in this book of fiction. He is a High Priest of Gardnerian Wicca (15 years) and a Master of Sciences in the Society for Creative Anachronism, a medieval society in which swordsmanship and all the elements of medieval Europe are a cultivated play of interest and achievement comparable to the oriental martial arts.

About the Artist

Bill Fugate was born September 3, 1954, at his maternal grandmother's home in Morehead, Kentucky, and spent his "wonder years" in the nearby city of Lexington. An early interest in comic books, macabre fiction and horror movies led him to begin a checkered career as a cartoonist/illustrator in the early 1970's. He has been a contributor to the critically-acclaimed *Gay Comix* magazine & is currently involved in a number of projects, including a folio based on the works of M.R. James.

To Write to the Author

We cannot guarantee that every letter written to the author can be answered, but all will be forwarded on to him. Both the author and the publisher appreciate hearing from readers. Please write to the author,

Ed Fitch
c/o Llewellyn Publications
P.O. Box 43383-COD, St. Paul, MN 55164-0383, U.S.A.

Please enclose a self-addressed, stamped envelope for reply, or $1.00.

The world of fiction is, itself, the realm of magic: in it an author's private world is made alive and sent forth into the "real" world that is shared with the rest of us. Fantasy is just one step further by which the author leaps the limits and boundaries ordinarily accepted in the real world and carries the reader with him into other worlds and other realities.

That doesn't mean that these other realities are untrue, nor that they are "un-real" to the world we live in. It just means that most people we know don't believe in them sufficiently to live their daily lives by them. But—some of these things not ordinarily recognized as part of familiar reality today have been intrinsic to it in other times, and some are still part of it for people living in cultures not yet fully dominated by our present nearly world-sized culture.

And some of these things are now being discovered and re-discovered, and are being explored by pioneers within the dominant culture. For these New Age people, the whole realm of the "occult" is no longer merely a vehicle for entertainment but is rapidly becoming seminal to exploding new directions of the physical and psychological sciences—including new appreciations and applications of such things as Out-of-Body Experiences, Psychic Healing, Past Life Recall, Suggestive Therapeutics, Dowsing, etc., not to overlook those areas that were not long ago considered part of the occult and today are fully, or nearly so, accepted: Hypnosis, ESP, Accupuncture, etc. Combined with this is a new appreciation for the beliefs and practices of other cultures: Yoga, Meditation, Witchcraft, Shamanism, Tantra, Zen, etc., including those from our own past—older medical lore, agricultural practices, folk beliefs, the Pagan world view of Nature Aware and Earth Alive.

Today, the dominant culture is more open and less threatened by the exploration of other possibilities. Indeed, many people see such explorations of "alternative" values and sciences as vital if we are to find answers to the present predicament of a world in which nuclear holocaust is a real possibility, where the poisoning of land and water and air is brought sickenly home to one community after another, and where values and judgements derived from the past no longer seem adequate in a world without boundaries in which personal computer power has replaced horsepower.

Through the world of fiction we can explore these other realities, and through fantasy experience them. In the process of being entertained we may learn things and become open to new perceptions about the real world in which we live. We may be stimulated to look harder at other values, to try other disciplines, to explore other answers—and find ways to change our world to meet the dark challenges of the moment.

Carl Llewellyn Weschcke, Publisher

Other Works from the Author

Forthcoming:
  Crystal Rites: The Crystal Well Grimoire of Pagan Rituals

Tapes:
  Fantasy Journeys: Narrated Quests for the Mind and Spirit —
  Tape 1: *The Armor of Light*
      Audience with the Sea Queen
  Tape 2: *Journey to the Land of Yesod*
      Dragon Ride
  Tape 3: *Visit to the Elvish Hills*
      Throne of the Golden Ages
  Tape 4: *Building an Astral Temple*
      Visit to the Cave of Aphrodite

Also forthcoming:
  a series of books and tapes on various matters of serious and
  lighter aspects of Magick, "Hi-tech" metaphysics, and further
  novels of other-worldly fantasy with lessons for this world.

  Write for full list of forthcoming works
  and current information on related topics.

  LLEWELLYN PUBLICATIONS
  P.O. Box 43383-COD, St. Paul, MN 55164-0383, U.S.A.

CASTLE OF DECEPTION

A Novel of
Sorcery and Swords
and Other-worldly Matters

by
Ed Fitch

with
Seven Short Essays
On the Reality of Matters Supernatural

Illustrated by
Bill Fugate

1983
Llewellyn Publications
St. Paul, Minnesota, 55164-0383, U.S.A.

International Standard Book Number: 0-87542-231-4
Library of Congress Catalog Card Number: 83-080166

First Edition 1983

Cover Art:
Drawing by Bill Fugate
Painting by Greg Guler

Produced by Llewellyn Publications
Typography and Art property of Chester-Kent, Inc.

Published by
LLEWELLYN PUBLICATIONS
A Division of Chester-Kent, Inc.
P.O. Box 43383
St. Paul, MN 55164-0383, U.S.A.

Printed in United States of America

To the true Tanithia
And the true Lyia:
I beg your forgiveness
For the liberties taken
In weaving this tale,
Yet I would have others
Know of you.

E. F.

 HE girl moved softly through the dappled glade. She was alone and obviously at home in the forest. Her peasant dress was not quite so coarse as one might expect, nor did her finely-chiselled features bespeak those of a peasant. Honey-golden hair tumbled free to her waist, and her close-laced bodice was cut low to display her round fullness.

She paused at a fresh, lively brook and set aside the basket she carried which was half-filled with berries and wild flowers. Balancing delicately, she tested the coolness of the water with one bare toe, then hitched the long dress up around her smoothly-sculptured thighs and waded out into the stream, enjoying the refreshing feel of the swift water. Yet her eyes, as she looked about, were those of a wild creature.

Her eyes were compelling and hypnotic, reflecting her every mood. Like the delicate features of her face, they indicated not a wandering peasant girl, but someone of considerable depth and perceptiveness, with levels of understanding that went remarkably far. Yet now, despite all else, they gave the impression of a hunger within her . . . a desperate yearning that made her reckless, in spite of the counsels of good sense.

Her body was tense and expectant . . . as though she sensed something near. The wood-scented air was soft with the sound of forest birds, and the water was cool about her feet and legs. For a moment the sylvan setting relaxed the tightness within her, and for a brief while she was at ease.

Indulging in a long moment of justifiable vanity, she admired her own comeliness, examining the full length of her well-shaped leg and ankle, then running a slender finger gently along the low-cut bodice . . . testing the softness of her breasts and, perhaps, weaving some whisp of a fantasy.

Then . . . alert once again; for the forest had fallen silent . . . the silence portending more than any random noise. With seeming casualness, yet with her eyes darting to and fro about her, she eased toward the bank of the stream.

There! The sound of a twig cracked . . . as if under a foot! Quickly now, tense and trembling, she stepped lightly up onto the mossy bank. Her breath came rapidly, and it seemed to her that her heart pounded loudly enough to echo through the suddenly ominous dark wood. The path . . . there was only one path out!

Quickly, or she would be trapped, or caught painfully in the dense tangles of the thickets about her. Gathering her skirts high about her hips, she dashed down the path on silent bare feet.

Sounds were in the brush behind her . . . something or someone in pursuit. She redoubled her pace, full breasts bouncing against her bodice top, almost out of the thin cloth that only partially enfolded them. Her long hair streamed behind her like the flowing mane of some wild creature as she fled.

She ran to the narrow road and paused, breathless, uncertain which way to turn. The yearning within her body contended with the cool wisdom that indicated the way of escape.

The men stepped out of the forest from either side. Large, coarse-looking rogues, eyeing her appraisingly as they, with studied casualness, cut off her path of flight. She heard another approaching up the path she had taken.

"Well met, boys," said the largest of the brown-clad ruffians, rubbing his grizzled chin speculatively as his eyes lingered on her heaving breast and her slender bare legs. Flushing, she pulled down her skirts quickly. A useless gesture, for their passions were aroused, and her chance for escape had vanished.

"What have we here?" he rasped, "A lovely wench and all alone in these dim woods. Tch, Tch. Lass, ye shouldn't be wandering alone out here . . . especially clad so lightly. Who knows . . . there may be some random rogue who just might desire to sample the round and ripe fruit that ye so beauteously display." He and his comrades chuckled nastily, edging closer about her. Touching her hand to the deep cleft between her breasts in a futile (yet unconsciously provocative) gesture of shielding herself, she backed away, eyes wide.

"No!" she whispered.

"Aye," said another. She turned to look at him, absently sweeping her long, tumbled hair back from her face. "Perhaps even your maidenhood could well be in danger from such scum as those, girl."

The third nudged his comrade. "Rob, methinks perhaps her maidenhead may already have been ta'en from her.." He chuckled, moving closer to her.

"Oh? D'ye think so?" grinned the first through his bristling beard. "I can't say. But perhaps we can find out." They stepped in closer about the girl. Like a trapped creature, her eyes darted from one to the other, and to yet the other.

"No! Please . . . " she whispered beseechingly, her hands cupped over her breasts, as if to shield them from those who had captured her. "No . . ." she barely shaped the word, breathing harder, uncertain . . . expectant. Yet here eyes were bright, and her face showed no fear.

She backed away as best she could, until her bare heel hit a gnarled root. She felt her tumbled mass of hair and then her smooth back pressed against the large tree. Her cheeks burned as she realized that they had backed her exactly where they wanted. She dug her toes into the soft, cool loam, as if to draw strength from the very ground itself.

The three, their eyes gleaming, moved in about her. She shuddered as a coarse hand ran along the side of her face. "She has smooth skin. Fine, like some noble lady." Another coarse hand ran over her bare shoulder, and she tried to pull her dress back over it, but could not. "Nice shoulders . . . round and soft." Rough hands ran through her hair, as through a stream of tumbled honey-gold. She closed her eyes for a moment, trembling. Within her, the rising hunger seemed to sear her very soul.

Their breath was strong, and the smell of sweat about them was like that of rutting animals. Rough fingers played lightly on her shoulders, down over the softness of her full breasts. A small, trapped sound came from her throat.

"Oh, don't fear, pretty wench," said the bearded one. "We merely like the feel of such warm, sweet, and inviting fruit."

"Aye", said another. "And look at this. They're tipped

in the purest of rose." The cloth over her breasts was pulled down and the coarse hands, harder and harder, kneaded their round fullness. Gasping, with sweat starting from her forehead, she writhed as if to flee.

"Ah, come now, little one. You're with friends! Friends, d'ye hear?" Rough hands cupped her breasts, now bare completely, and a massive body pressed close as heavy lips sought hers, crushing her cruelly against the tree.

"Aye, this is a fine one. But what of her maidenhood?" leered one, lifting her skirt and caressing her soft ivory thigh, then pressing his hand higher yet until he cupped the soft cleft. She gasped, protesting wordlessly, her skin flushing still more deeply.

"Why, methinks she likes our attentions, me lads." And verily, almost shamefacedly, her own expression belied her struggles, for animals though they were, the place, the time, the manner, and the inevitability of her rape had aroused an even higher passion within her. A passion that overcame fear . . . a passion, as she writhed beneath the indignities of their probing hands, that disregarded even the possibility of murder once they had finished using her.

Massive, eager hands hastily unlaced her low bodice, and bristle rimmed lips sought her flower-red nipples, erect now in her own desperate desire. She closed her eyes, trembling with anticipation.

"Who'll be first, boys?" came the hoarse, almost whispered words.

"The dice, Rob, the dice. We'll throw, and the winner gets her first." There was the sound of a dagger being drawn from its sheath, and the point pressed gently but firmly against the base of her throat. "Don't move, wench. Or you'll not leave this glade alive." Then to another, "Loop the rope around her . . . just enough to keep this pretty bird from trying to fly. It'd be a shame to have to cut that soft throat before we've had our tumbles with her." She felt the rasp of a coarse hempen line about her, and in a moment she was bound to the tree, her arms pinned behind against the rough bark and the equally rough loops of rope over and under her soft breasts. She lowered her head, as in dispair, and unbound hair tumbled down over the naked roundness of her bosom.

Somewhere deep within, conscience and wisdom berated the wanton folly of getting into so perilous a situation, and a gnawing fear began building a panic within her, But her very blood seemed afire with the blind yearning that consumed her.

Hair dishevelled, her skirts caught up by the rope as if to display the sleekness of her limbs, she awaited the outcome of the dicing.

"Five." "Seven." "Twelve!" came the triumphant call. "I takes her first!"

"Ah, you were always lucky, Rob," came the disappointed mutter. "But make it fast! She's too good to wait for long." Eyes glittering, Rob advanced on her, tugged loose the rope, and crushed her in his powerful arms, his mouth pressing hers and his firmness moving hard against her yielding body, as he began to tear her clothes . . . those which remained . . . from her.

There was a roaring in her ears. She gasped in fear and in overwhelming passion . . . her hips grinding back against his and, in spite of herself, her lips avidly seeking those of her conqueror. She was forced roughly down onto the ground, his heavy fetid body pressed down atop her own white form.

Hoofbeats. The sound of a horse. "Hold there!" came a loud cry. "What's going on?" Shouts of rage and frustration from the three rogues. The one atop the girl ceased forcing himself on her, snarled, and stood erect.

"Get out! Away, damn ye! Be you a lord or not, this woman is ours!"

She scrambled back against the tree, pulling at the bodice to at least partly conceal her nakedness, and trying somehow to cover bare limbs with her rumpled and tangled skirts. Hair disheveled and tumbled in a golden cascade over her bare shoulders and breasts, she breathed hard, feeling confusion, fear, and yes . . . bitter frustration . . . all intermixed.

Somewhere wisdom whispered relief, but passion shrieked loud fury. She looked at the elegant figure astride the chestnut bay that pranced like a dangerously eager warhorse before them. Steel sang against steel and a sword glittered in the dappled sunlight.

"Out!" commanded the rider, gesturing menacingly with his blade. "Off these lands. Now! Or there'll be three new souls in hell!"

Muttering sullenly and uncertainly, and not wanting to relinquish the girl who was their prize, the three ruffians backed slowly away. Clearly unwilling, yet fearing the deadly intent of the rider, they peered apprehensively behind him for signs of the retainers they knew would be near.

Suddenly, one jumped quickly for the girl, seizing her roughly by a slender white arm. She gasped in sudden pain as he thrust her before him as a shield, and her garment again fell away. Silently, appealingly, she glanced over a white shoulder at her rough captor and then at the powerful grey-tipped figure on the horse before her. His eyes glanced momentarily down at her form, then, narrowed, back to the one who shielded himself with her body.

"We take this 'un with us!" her captor snarled defiantly. "She comes with us, or ye'll have her skewered body!" He fumbled for just a moment at his dagger. A sudden thrust by the nobleman, and his sword bit into the man's arm. With a howl he hurled her from him and jumped back, suprised and shocked at the sudden agony and the fast-swelling of blood from his arm.

The girl pulled herself to the bole of a nearby tree, crouching there, and with smouldering eyes, covering herself as best she could.

"Out! Leave these lands and don't come back! Begone, scum!" The nobleman urged his steed forward and swung, catching the nearest rogue soundly with the flat of his blade. With howls in unison, the three took to their heels, running, shouting in anger, pain, and frustration. The horseman cantered leisurely after them for a short few hundred paces, swinging the flat of his blade to impel them onwards, chuckling, as he made certain that they continued on their way. Rounding a bend in the road, he caught sight of a band of his retainers, attracted by the sound of the shouting, and motioned significantly at the three fleeing ruffians. The grinning peasants, with hoes and cudgels, took up the chase themselves as he reined in his steed and watched smiling as they disappeared down the road.

Then he turned back to where the woman had pulled herself up onto her finely-shaped feet, standing, statuesque and subtly defiant, against the tree. She had slowly begun to don her torn and dishevelled dress, though it concealed little, and her honey-colored cascade of wild hair tumbled invitingly over bare shoulders and breasts. The look in her grey eyes was not of fear or even of relief, he noted, but of challenge as she stood provocatively (that was the only word, he thought to himself) before him.

Her deep eyes were on his, burning with barely suppressed passion. "I thank you, my lord," she said in a throaty voice. "You saved me from certain rape and possible death at the hands of those coarse rogues." Again, she tugged at the remains of the bodice that scarcely covered the rosy tips of her full breasts.

He smiled at the manner in which her formal words spoke one meaning, while all else about her spoke a very different message . . . quite deliberately . . . it seemed to him. Even so, h⁓ was subtly surprised at the implications of unexpected sophistication given by her manner of speech.

Savoring the moment, the grey-templed nobleman relaxed in the saddle and let his eyes roam leisurely over the rich fullness of her form, so ineffectually clad before him. Her bold eyes and her very demeanor invited him to come closer and to perhaps complete a conquest.

He eased himself down from the saddle and casually tied the reins over a convenient tree branch. Removing his embroidered leathern gloves, he slapped them against his hand as he eyed her appraisingly, an interested smile behind his grey moustache. He placed his hands over hers and drew them away from where they were so invitingly covering the roundness of her breasts. For a long moment he gazed at her naked beauty, then abruptly seized her and drew her in, smothering her with kisses and caresses . . . to which she responded with passionate eagerness.

Fondling her ripe breasts and pulling the remains of the clothes from her trembling body, he drew her down onto the ground. She cried out with delight as he took her.

A seeming infinity of pleasure coursed through her body as she responded to this nobleman's sophisticated and knowledgeable caresses and lovemaking . . . far more readily and far more passionately than to the crude pawing to the odiferous oafs who had all but taken her before.

Finally . . . spent, they lay as in a slowly draining pool of passion and pleasure, on his cloak and the tattered remnants of her clothes.

She was at ease, relaxed and carelessly graceful in her naked beauty. He, still muscular and firm and maturely handsome, looked at her, at the face which, lovely and perfectly shaped, with full lips and a delicate chin, was familiar somehow. Not being immersed in passion, he now looked more closely at her features. She seemed unaware of his scrutiny as she drowsed, reclining on his cloak. This lovely woman . . . seemed to be someone he . . . knew. He looked at her more closely. It seemed almost as if her features altered and changed slightly.

He gasped and drew his breath in suddenly. "Lady Magda!" he exclaimed. "It's you!"

Smiling, she opened her eyes and made made a soft purring sound.

"You are . . . I mean . . . " he stammered. "By the Old Ones . . . I had no idea! I never realized . . ." Confused, he paused.

"Oh come now," she said, stretching lithely and rolling into his arms again, "Of course you didn't. And you enjoyed it as much as I did." Her eyes closed, her lips sought his as she pressed against him. "And I thank you, milord."

"But, you looked . . . unfamiliar!" he said haltingly.

"Of course," she replied. "To control one's features is not particularly difficult. It's just . . . that I forgot to hold the changed face while I was relaxing after my hm . . . pleasant conversation . . . with you."

"My Lady Magda," he began . . .

"Please," she interrupted, touching her soft fingers to his lips, "I now call myself 'Tanithia'. Magda," she said stretching, "is no more."

"But my Lady Ma . . . Tanithia, they said that you were burned at the stake when the revolutionaries took the capital of Valoria more than two years ago. It was definitely you."

She sighed, pulling herself up into a sitting position and resting her chin on her knees. "Fanatics," she said with a hint of cynicism, "see what they want to see. It wasn't I who perished when they brought their cult of the desert war-god into power. But they thought it was I, for as you've just found, appearances can be changed."

"Then who . . ."

"Hush," she interrupted, again placing a soft hand to his lips. "It wasn't . . . I, though . . . " Her voice trailed off as her eyes became distant for a moment, and her expression changed to one more somber. When she spoke again, there was a trace of sadness and of bitterness in her voice. "There's a story to be told of what happened on that terrible night, but this is neither the time nor the place for relating it."

"Yes," he said after a pause. "It was said by many that you had been stoned and burned by the mob, and that your lover had fled in the night. Where is he?" asked the nobleman.

Again a slight shadow crossed her otherwise perfect features. "I have no idea," she said. "It was a night of fire, a night of chaos. Where he is and what's become of him, I have no idea. I don't know whether he's alive or dead."

Count Waldmann looked at her, as for a moment she stared off into space, lost in her own reminiscences. She seemed not to have aged, even though she had ruled these lands as an enlightened monarch for some years. In spite of the stresses of those years, her face was as young and unlined as those of a girl scarce more than eighteen summers. And, he observed with some interest, her body was still the essence of perfection.

He got up briefly, fetched a flask and goblets from his saddlebag, and returned to pour sweet liqueur for the two of them. Sitting down again beside her, he passed her a goblet, eyed the obvious beauty of her unclad body and flowing hair, then looking deeply in her eyes, tapped his cup to hers, smiling. "To beauty, to magic, to times that were good. And to a truly magnificent witch-queen!"

They drank deeply. After a few moments he leaned back against the tree, toyed idly with a lock of her long hair, and then asked, "But how did you come here, and what brought you to the situation that I rescued you from?"

"Ah yes," she smiled, "I thank you, milord, for saving my virtue." She chuckled. "And it was a delight to lose it again, immediately." She reclined her ivory body against him, though her thoughts were obviously far from their recent lovemaking. "No, I knew that the revolt was coming. One didn't need magics and divinations to see that new and discouragingly harsh patterns and forces were building in Valoria. I knew that sooner or later I'd be overthrown and I prepared accordingly." She stretched and curled her toes in the folds of his cloak, enjoying the warmth of his arms for a few more moments. "The old estate beyond the river to the north of your lands. Remember it?"

"Oh yes", he said, "Why that place has been abandonded for years, and it's so remote that even my huntsmen seldom go near it."

"Indeed," she murmured. "That's the very reason I chose it as one of my refuges. I dwell there with a handful of aged retainers, my books, and my magical tools. It's quiet and a good place for contemplation and study."

"Contemplation . . . and study . . . milady?" he exclaimed with mock surprise, tousling her hair playfully. "Why, you were scarce known for that when you ruled from the palace!"

"Ah yes," she said with a reflective smile. "Those were the days. Yet scandalous though I may have been, I did study much when I was there. It's just that the needs of statecraft and the presence of my lover kept me from fully devoting myself to the study of the magical arts."

He chuckled, for she had indeed been notorious for her lack of discretion concerning her frequent escapades. A good ruler, yes. None would honestly say otherwise, for the land had prospered under her gentle though firm and well-organized rule. But her succession of lovers gave constant gossip and continued even when she settled down with her sturdy and handsome Captain of the Guard, a mercenary from the steppes beyond the distant eastern marches.

He noticed that her eyes were on him. The demeanor of a frightened peasant girl had dropped from her as something no longer needed, and again she was a woman who was beautiful, intelligent, and shrewd, eyeing him as though she could see his very thoughts. She smiled at him as if catching this thought as well.

"But my lady," he said, gesturing at the road, the forest, the glade, and the tattered remnants of her scattered clothes. And yes, a few drops of congealed red, spilled from the wounded arm of the rogue who had assaulted her. "Why do you do this?"

She sipped on the sweet liqueur from her cup. A drop fell on her breast, and she idly drew her finger around in a spiral where the drop had fallen. "I get lonely . . . desperately lonely. And as you well know, I'm a creature of strong passions. I now devote myself to study and an almost completely monastic style of life." Her eyes sparkled up at him as she cozied her body against his, for the afternoon was late and the forest was becoming cool. "A very radical change for me, as well you know. For after all, I don't dare take the chance of being recognized by agents of the current regime, or especially their blood-handed priests. Stray lovers tend to talk, and to be treacherous; rogues committing crimes never prattle . . . it's a matter of professional caution." She sipped once again at her goblet. "Since losing my love I don't really want anyone else permanently . . . not for now." A look of soft pain crossed her delicate features. He pulled her close to comfort her.

"After all, I'm human. Only a fool would say that you can devote yourself to books or to a god and remain continent in mind and body." She turned toward him in his arms, almost assuming a crouched position, her breasts trembling slightly in her intensity as she looked at him . . .

again for a moment with passion.

"I go for as long as I can, milord. But there are times when all meditations, all books, all conjurations can't hold back my need . . . my yearning. I like men." She smiled. "And yes, women too. And I can't do without them completely. There are times I seek to be conquered . . . and violently so, as you saw today. I come from another land, remember, where women are at least equal and where one can sleep with whom and where she wishes. The idea of rape holds no terror for me. I'd only dislike a man's attentions if they were forced on me against my will. If someone could force me . . . and yet live to boast of it!" She smiled wolfishly and, though he did not fully understand her meaning, the look of her face and the tone of her voice left no doubt as to her confidence and resolve.

"But it's dangerous", he said, caressing her cheek. "You might have lost your life."

Smiling, she eased back to him and held his hand against her cheek. "There is danger, yes. But I like the danger . . . and I feel my Arts, in the final analysis, will have protected me.

He stroked her tumbled hair. "You take a terrible chance, my pretty one." He looked around, noting the lengthening shadows. "But the day is wearing on, and you should get some clothes on that comely form of yours. Also there isn't time to reach your own estate before sunset, even on horseback. Would you sup with me this evening? My servants are all very discreet . . . after all, I was known as one of your retainers, and thus I'm not at all favored by the theocrats who now rule the country.

"Yes," she said, drawing his cloak about her, "I'm impressed at how well you've managed to get along, when so many of my nobles had to flee the country . . . or worse."

He gathered her scattered clothes and bundled them under his saddlebag. "I tread a delicate line, milady." He knelt and held out his hands for her soft foot. She eased onto the saddle, the flowing cloak covering her golden body gracefully as she seated herself sidesaddle. Yet, viewing her, it would seem clear to any observer that, in spite of the cape, she was still totally unclad.

He settled into the saddle behind her. "I have, for the sake of appearances, accepted their religion of the 'one, true, and only god'," he grimaced. "And further, I and my people stay on my own lands. Essentially I'm in exile on my own fiefdom. They need the food which my lands produce so well, and they're content to let me retain my own domains. And probably," he said, snapping the reins so that his horse started ahead, "Probably they'll continue to let me do so." Tanithia pressed herself back comfortably into his arms as they trotted off towards his manor house.

An older man, certainly, she thought. But one rich in warmth and dependable for protection.

HE servants were surprised by the touseled, golden-haired lass that Count Waldmann brought back with him, for since the death of his wife some years before he had enjoyed the company of few women. Perhaps he vanished for an evening or so to a hut in the forest or to a villa in the small town nearby, but never had he entered his courtyard bearing so lovely and even so self-assured a beauty as he did now.

As guest and as lover she was given free rein of his house and grounds. And with the nobility borne of the position she once had, she confidently accepted it. First a hot bath, in which she luxuriated for an improbable long period of time. Count Waldmann had the women search through the trunks and locate various gowns which Lady Tanithia could use, and laid them out for her.

With interest and with amusement he noted that her taste in clothing was as . . . interesting . . . now as it had been when she ruled from the palace, for she chose only the richest and most revealing of the gowns. And, rather than slippers, simply arrayed her delicate feet with fine jewelry. He gathered that her current estate was austere, for she revelled quite obviously in the modest luxury of his halls.

The dinner that evening was rich and formal, with many candles, excellent silver, fine wine, and a cut of beef prepared in so tasty a manner that they both agreed that the cook had completely outdone himself.

The excellence was such that the count had not thought possible from the shelves of his buttery. Yes, he mused as he looked across the table at Lady Tanithia, soft and very female in the glistening light, she had served to inspire not only himself but his retainers as well. The men all seemed to be fascinated by her almost arrogant beauty, though it seemed that none of the women disliked her, for she was to them both mysterious and glamorous, and the force of her personality was such that all were encompassed in her aristocratic, intense, sensuality.

She sipped from her crystalline goblet, looking at him. Jewels glistened in her hair and from her ears. She wore a pendant of diamonds about her ivory neck, the largest stone hanging between her full breasts. The full roundness of her bosom was well displayed by the rich, dark velvet of the gown she wore.

"A coin of silver for your thoughts, Count Waldmann," she smiled.

"Tanithia . . . Lady Tanithia . . . you needn't ask what's obviously on my mind." he said, gazing at the golden array of curls which framed her face and which tumbled over her bare shoulders. "Yet . . . I've wondered. No one ever seemed to know where you had come from, when

you appeared in our country some years ago. It was as though you had simply walked out of the forest. You went from being the mistress of a minor noble, very rapidly, to the very throne itself. Where, pray tell, did you come from?"

She smiled and touched a jewelled finger to her lips. "Ah . . . that is the question, my love. Somewhere far beyond the mountains is a valley of some great size, where people follow the ancient gods, and the lovely Witch-Goddess. Things were bad in the outside lands, and I was groomed well for the task, then sent thus to Valoria. I'm sorry, but I must keep the location of my birthing-place a secret, even from the dearest of my friends, for so have I given my word and pledged my honor. But I did the best that I could for as long as I could, and though the god-men have brought back their patriarchal ways, I think the land is better now by far than when I came." She looked, unseeing, at the glass she held, her finger tracing the outline of the dragon pattern etched into the crystal. Then she brightened and looked up at him.

"But milord, enough of this. You're probably lonely from time to time. I remember that your wife was particularly gracious and very dear to you. It's been quite a while since you lost her, hasn't it?"

"Yes, " he said, "I had many good years with her, which I enjoyed greatly; and probably I'll never know her like again." He was quiet for a while . . . smiling, but with a sadness in his eyes. He smoothed his graying moustache. "I've kept a few of her things . . ."

Tanithia cocked an eyebrow at him, feeling that it would be better if the count were kept cheerful. "Including this gown, my lord? Really, I hope I can do it justice," she said smiling, touching her fingertips lightly across the low neckline.

The count reddened somewhat, and his smile was sheepish. "Well, no . . . that particular gown belonged to

. . . well . . . someone else." He paused, embarrassed for a moment, then threw his head back and laughed aloud.

"All right, you pretty vixen, I confess! The past was as fine as good wine, but one must live in the present. I'll admit it . . . I'm only human!" She raised her glass to him, joining his laughter with her own.

"Whoever this particular lover was, I like her taste in garments. The cloth is of fine quality and the jewels are rich," she said, touching the single large diamond that hung between her breasts. She looked at him, her hand still at her breast. The mood was light and jovial. Holding back a smile she looked at him with wide, innocent-seeming eyes and feigned a breathless, imploring expression.

"Do you favor me, milord?" she asked. "As a man of polish, grace, and dignity you must view me almost as a coarse trollop."

He looked at her for a long moment, still smiling, though a new and more pleasingly different tension was in the air.

"Oh no, my lovely lady," he said, coming around the table to her and putting his hands on her soft shoulders. "You are . . . you're different. You're like some primal force . . . a power from a time and a place that is far gone."

She leaned back, her scented hair against his elegant doublet. He caressed her cheek, very much aware of the deep cleft between her breasts, their warm roundness covered only at the very tips by the heavy velvet of her gown.

"Thank you," she said softly, holding his hand firm against her cheek. "I so need the company of someone like you. Perhaps it can't be for long. I'm a wild creature, I warn you, but I appreciate your care and your tenderness."

His face bent to her perfumed hair and his hands eased around to feel the warm fullness of her breasts. She purred softly and held his hands closer to her as he fondled her round warmth. She looked up at him, and his lips found hers. He swept her up into his arms, and held her in a long, passionate kiss.

"Shall I dance for you, my love?" she asked huskily.

"No, not now", he whispered as he touched her further, and she gasped with pleasure. "Let's go to my chambers . . . we've got a very good night of lovemaking before us."

"Indeed," she murmured, kissing him long with her open mouth, and their tongues darted in boldly, each at the other. His hands roamed over her body. The few lacings on the gown came undone easily, and the soft velvet began to fall from her ivory-gold body as he caressed her more and more passionately.

A cunning wench, he thought, and an eager one. Tonight definitely will be magic. Together they walked to the stairs, still whispering and caressing as they went. The jewels on her toes twinkled as she raced kittenishly up the stair ahead of him. He followed her into the chamber as she danced ahead, smiling her invitation.

She stood with her back to the bed, proudly, bare breasts jutting out over the folds of the long velvet gown which just barely clung to her body.

"Take me," she said, her eyes challenging his. "Take me now!" The gown fell from her, and he swept her up in his arms to bear her down onto the bed.

And for the rest of the long night they tasted, again and again, the most exquisite of pleasure.

The dalliance continued for a fortnight or more. Count Waldmann enjoyed the company of Lady Tanithia and she, on her part, was happy for a while to forget the hard regime of studies to which she had dedicated herself for these last three years. The count was witty and urbane; a man who had travelled much in his earlier years, learned much, and seen much of the known world.

However, an afternoon came on which this idyllic liaison was to change.

Tanithia, relaxing in an afternoon gown, was browsing through the count's library when she heard the clatter of a hard-ridden horse coming in through the front gate. The arrival of a messenger was rare enough, in these isolated times of the count's self-imposed exile, to warrant more than a passing curiosity.

She made her way to his study and found him engrossed in a letter, the messenger waiting nearby. The young man's tired eyes lightened as he saw Tanithia step softly into the chamber. She liked the glint in his eye, and indeed found him to be pleasingly handsome . . . if in a somewhat saddle-weary way. She fluffed her hair and drew in her breath for his benefit as she turned to the count, being sure that the young messenger had at least a brief view of the deep-cut V of her neckline.

"My lord?" she queried. "You seem concerned . . . is there news?"

The count was indeed somewhat worried. His brow was creased as she had not seen it since her arrival, and there was the look of, perhaps, apprehension in his eyes. He noticed the messenger and motioned to him. "Please . . . go to the kitchen and get something to eat. Then the majordomo will find you a room for the night."

The messenger's departing footsteps echoed down the hall as the count sat rapt in concern and immersed in the missive before him. On silent toes Tanithia stepped gracefully around behind his chair, draped her arms over his shoulders, and pressed the fullness of her breasts against him.

His mood broken, he looked around with a smile and felt for her hand. "Most interesting, my dear. And somewhat disconcerting. Something rather strange and unsettling has been happening at one of my more distant fiefdoms."

"Oh?" With narrowed eyes she scanned the letter, peering over his shoulder.

He held the second page of the letter for her to read, saying, "A number of people have died there, a distressingly large number. The peasants are more than a little frightened, and some have even been fleeing. Can't say that I blame them . . . somehow I feel that there are not . . . natural . . . forces in effect here." Engrossed in the letter, she nodded silently.

"Since my liegeman, the baron who administers those lands for me, has disappeared so suddenly as of a moon ago, the problems have gotten worse. And this letter from his overseer seems written in haste and in fear."

"May I see the letter more closely?" she asked, frowning slightly. She re-read it completely, then folded the parchment and held it to her forehead, eyes closed, to test for psychic impressions of what else may have been unsaid. Purposefully she cleared her mind and the relaxed conscious control so that the deeper realms of her being could become active.

Darkness. A feeling of unease, growing stronger and ever yet stronger. Eyes in the darkness, gleaming a baneful, unnatural scarlet. Running in wild fear through a haunted wood. Coming face to face with . . . terror. Then . . .

She opened her eyes and looked at the count. "My love, there is more amiss in your land than swords can set aright. I sense a truly demonic presence, and perhaps vampirism! In all it has an entirely evil feel to it. Your fiefdom has become infested with something . . . un-healthy. It wreaks agony and horror upon your subjects."

"Is that what you saw?" he asked. He knew of her second sight, and knew it to be accurate even on far distant events, for so he had seen in the past.

She looked at him with a level gaze. "It's more than your people can handle, and I feel that many will soon follow the few who've fled, until the land is empty of any living beings."

"My lady," he spoke, "I haven't any particular talent or strength in this area of magics and demons, and I don't trust the clerics of the new rulers of this land." He looked at her for a long moment. A charming and kittenish sensualist no more, Tanithia seemed now to have iron within her, for she sensed, obviously, danger and a challenge. When she had reigned from the palace, he had seen this side of her often, and knew her to be firm, capable, and courageous . . . and far more shrewd than any man he knew. He considered for a moment.

"Of course, milady, you realize that I must ask for your assistance in this."

"Indeed," she said, rising to her toes to kiss him softly and quickly. "I was expecting nothing else. When do we leave?"

On Tanithia's suggestion the count chose eleven of his very best men-at-arms, including the young messenger who had brought the tidings of trouble to them. He was, so it proved, excellent with broadsword as well as with horse.

Tanithia herself required certain implements. Old ones: a sword, well suited to her slender hand, certain herbs, and certain elixirs which the Count's own people had not know were stored in his cellars.

"**S**O SHE uses the high tower," said the young messenger, wonderingly. "What is she doing there, on this night before we depart?"

"Come now, young Gort," said the Sergeant of Swords, with a hearty slap on the shoulder. "Surely ye've divined it by now. Or have you been too taken with the beauty of that lady to think straight, eh?"

"How's that?" Gort asked, rousing himself from gazing at the window. For indeed he had found himself intrigued and aroused by the comeliness of one whom he had learned was called "Lady Tanithia." Gort considered. "I . . . well . . . she oftimes has the bearing of a noble-woman, but . . . but then . . ."

"Aye," said the sergeant, with a crooked grin. "She dresses the part of a forest wench. And she is indeed a wild one. Did ye not see the signs, even though our laird doesn't speak of it; She's a witch, boy . . . a witch!"

"Oh?" commented the younger man, "I had thought that all had been burned or driven from the land over these last three years."

"Hardly," chuckled the grizzled old soldier. "They'd like to have you believe that. But those who follow the Old Ways still dwell in the forests and in the high mountains. I don't know who this 'Tanithia' might have been, though she must have been noble. But she has all the signs of magic about her. And mind you," he said, putting a gnarled finger towards the young man's face, as if to instruct him, "Say nothing of this when away from here. Remember . . . It's the Count's wish that she be here, and that she accompany us on this mission."

"Yes," said the younger man, his face shadowing, "We'll need all the help we can get. Things are bad at home . . . very bad. And getting worse."

"Were there none of the clerics of the True One God to try and deal with this plague of hellspawn?" asked the older man.

"Aye," said the younger. "There were two or three sent more than a year ago to oversee that the fiefdom had divested itself of the Old Ways. One night one of them disappeared. The next night the other was found, his throat torn open. The third night . . . the night of the dark moon, I think it was . . . the third went raving insane, and finally threw himself from a precipice. They claim to have the undefeatable power of all righteousness, but they fall all too easily . . ."

A light flared in the windows of the high stone tower above them, and both looked up at the sound of a woman's voice chanting something strongly in a tongue which neither knew.

"Then we'll try other ways to deal with it," said the

Sergeant of Swords. He rubbed his grizzled chin. "The Old Ways were always better." Then he caught himself and looked sharply at the young man.

"You can trust me, friend," said the other, clasping the sergeant by his arm. "I have my word of honor, which I gave to my liege lord before he died. And also," he looked up at the tower, "Also . . ."

"Use care," said the older man. "For you know she beds with the Count himself!"

"I don't care with whom she couches," said the younger man, looking yearningly upwards. "I'd like nothing better than to give my fealty to the Lady Tanithia . . . even though she might not know it."

It was well after midnight when finally Tanithia decended the winding stone staircase that led down from the high tower. In the darkness of the great stone structure she felt, rather than saw, the way down, groping with delicate toes for each cold stone step, and running a hand along the cold wall. Her implements, left behind in the upper chamber until dawn, were properly charged. Her work finished, the ritual complete; she felt exhausted by the power which had been drawn from her slender frame. She paused and smoothed back her long hair as she stepped out into the moonlight of the courtyard. With the power gone for the night, she felt tired and cold. Her single, netlike garment, near transparent even in the moonlight, seemed no protection at all against the evening chill.

Footsteps echoed from the corridor that led to the courtyard.

"Lord Waldmann", she stated rather than asked.

"Aye, milady," he replied, and paused for a moment, goblet in hand. "I saw the lights in the tower fade, and felt that you may have need for something to warm that lovely body of yours, now that the rite is complete."

"Ah yes," quoth she, swaying towards him in the moonlight. "Is it brandy that I smell?" She eagerly took the brass cup and drew deeply from it, for a moment looking like a finely sculptured statue in the moonlight. Then, with a sigh she lowered the goblet. "Ah . . . that's good. Especially now. My feet are chilled and my nipples are so cold they feel like brittle porcelain."

"What did you learn?" he asked, holding his arms out to her. She melted into his arms, her body pressing closely against his.

"Hmmm . . . you're warm," she murmured. "I know fairly well what it is that we are up against, and that we should be able to meet and to destroy it without too much danger."

His hands ran through her hair, and for a long moment her mouth sought his in a lingering, increasingly amorous kiss. He drew back chuckling, imprisoning her slender hands in his massive ones.

"Now pretty one," he smiled, "You are only passionate because the night is chilly, and I'm warm."

"Milord," she said softly, rubbing her head against his hands, "Is there a better reason?"

"Well, among other things, you lovely vixen, my boots are only large enough for my own feet. So you needn't try to get those pretty toes of yours into them as well."

"So, my lover," her eyes sparkled in the moonlight. "Then perhaps I'd best get you out of . . . your boots." She drew back for a moment, his hands about her slender waist, arched her full body back, and drank deeply. Draining the cup, then laughing, placed it on a low cornice nearby.

"Ahh . . . that was nearly as good as another way which I know to be warmed on a night like this." His hands reached for her white throat and undid the one fastener to her thin garment. She shrugged out of it, lithe and silvery in the moonlight, and danced about on silent white feet, running her hands over her waist, along the smooth curves of her hips, and then momentarily cupping her breasts before sweeping out her hands and whirling, her cascade of light hair tumbling like liquid moonlight.

"Am I not beautiful, my lord? Do you not wish to possess me? To have me be yours?"

An animal rumble escaped from the count's throat and he reached for her bare flank. Laughing, she danced out of his way. Again he came for her and she danced aside, white teeth sparkling momentarily in the moonlight as she smiled widely. Then again, and again. "My lord, have you not the ability . . . mighty warrior that you are . . . to capture one girl of the forest? — Oh!" she yelped, for her buttocks had come hard against cold, unyielding stone. "You have me trapped. You've been driving me towards this corner like a hunter would a deer!"

"Indeed, pretty one," he laughed, pinning her expertly into a closed doorway. "An now we shall see who is the cleverer." His hands roamed over her body and his lips sought hers as she gasped in desire.

"The wall is so cold, milord," she murmured. Then, as his hands almost brutally roamed over her naked body, he was suddenly gentle and tender as he cupped her white face in his hands and kissed her mouth, her cheeks, her eyes. Then to her throat and her breasts, caressing and touching.

"Let us go, lover," she panted. "Please . . . let's go."

Half leading her, half dragging her as she sought more caresses and more kisses, he led her from the courtyard to his chamber. The sound of their passionate voices died away to echoes.

From the far side of the courtyard, out of the deep shadows, stepped Swordsman Gort. In spite of the chill, he wiped the sweat from his face and stiffly walked across the courtyard, looking off into the direction into which the lovers had vanished. His foot caught on something, and he bent to pick up the fine net garment which she had shed. His eyes burning, he ran his hands through the soft cloth and clasped it to him.His gaze, like fire itself, fixed on the direction into which she had gone. Then, for a moment he buried his face in the folds of gossamer cloth . . . and quickly walked off into the shadows.

ARLY on the following morning a column of riders rode out from the main gate of the count's estate. In a leisurely manner they made their way off into some of the lesser-used trails and back roads that would lead, after several days, to Castle Drakenstane. The route, which led through the deep forest and into the mountains, had been carefully chosen, for Tanithia had no desire to be seen by, possibly, the wrong people.

Grey cloaks for all, well-equipped saddle packs bulging with supplies, swords strapped to harnesses . . . all appearances were of a small detachment of men-at-arms on some long-distance errand. Perhaps detailed to another fief for protection of the populace against brigands, or, less enviably, assigned to collect taxes.

And so they appeared when passing through the

various villages in the first few leagues of travel. Once apart and away from habitation, however, Tanithia shed her cloak and boots, and unbound her honey-red hair to fall free almost to her saddle. She preferred a pair of men's short breeches and a loose peasant shirt, gathered at the waist by a sash.

"Tanithia, my dear," smiled the count, "There is no possible way that you could masquerade as a man, or pass as a soldier, clad as you are."

"Oh?" she looked at him quizzically. "I think I fit rather well into men's clothing."

"All too well," he replied, eyeing her appreciatively. "You fill the breeches as none of us could. And likewise the shirt."

"I wondered if anyone would notice," she smiled at him wickedly, inhaling deeply of the cool forest air so that her breasts pressed out against the thin fabric. "Do you think it's laced too low?" she asked.

"Most definitely, my lady. But please . . . don't lace your shirt any higher than it is now. You certainly keep the men awake and alert in the saddle. You'll notice they're all riding behind you . . . the better to enjoy their view of the forest, I'm certain."

"But seriously," he continued, "When we passed through that small village an hour or so ago it was well-nigh impossible to tell that there was a woman among us. But it's now most obvious indeed, in every possible way, that you are most exquisitely female. It seems that you have the ability to alter more than just your face."

"A part of my craft, milord," she said. "The mind will see what it expects to see. Although I enjoy being very much a woman, I can make myself, for a period of time, appear quite different to the casual observer."

"We shall be traveling on these forgotten trails for several days, shall we not?" she asked.

"Yes Tanithia, you wished to make the journey in silence and without being seen. This, I feel, is the best way. Two days out from Castle Drakenstane we'll come to a small and quite remote inn. There we can pick up additional supplies and prepare ourselves for the final work which must be done. Afterwards, of course, we can reprovision ourselves from the castle stores themselves, once we have cleansed that fortress."

They rode on in silence for a while. Tanithia, tilting her head slightly, smiled and then looked sidelong at the count. "I've noticed that Swordsman Gort has been looking at me from time to time." She smiled teasingly. "Do you think he likes me?"

The count snorted. "Likes you? His eyes have been devouring you ever since we started. Nay, from the very first time he laid eyes on you. Yes, I daresay that he's noticed you. I would mark his sheep-eyed gaze as infatuation complicated by a good bit of sheer lust. You are, after all, a very attractive female."

She looked back over her shoulder. Briefly . . . for Gort's gaze had immediately met hers. In a slightly calculating manner she nudged her mount closer, so that her leg occasionally brushed the count's. "Milord . . . might I have your permission sometime to have a brief . . . shall we say . . . dalliance . . . with Swordsman Gort? I think he's very handsome."

The count smiled at her. "My lovely little vixen, I couldn't prevent you from doing your wish even if I tried. And although I dearly would like to have you entirely to myself, I know enough of women to know that it can't be. Go ahead, you may share his blankets tonight, if that's your desire."

"No," she said unexpectedly. "I shan't be sleeping with anyone on this journey. I'm working a spell of power, and the magic demands that I remain continent. And yet, since I feel we may be contending with very strong demonic forces, I wish to have the strength of your men as well as my own. I doubt that any of them know it, but they all have considerable psychic power potential within them . . . that was the primary reason I insisted on your picking this particular eleven. So I'm weaving them into my enchantment. I wish to have you . . . I wish to have all of them . . . desiring me, and in love with me. If this can be managed, then I can call forth great powers if I need them. It's simply a matter of changing one kind of force into another which is not really too different in its basic nature."

"Hm." The count looked at her. "Eleven plus myself makes twelve, and with you it is thirteen. Pretty witch, you have your coven, don't you?"

She smiled, but said nothing more as they continued on the old road.

The day passed apace as they slowly wended their way further back into the high country. When at long last the sun was near to cutting the far horizon, they halted and pitched camp for the night. The evening rations of mutton, wine, and hardtack were served out and, after a while, nothing remained but the routine work of rubbing down the horses, mending harness, and maintaining their weapons.

Tanithia produced a small harp from her saddlebag,

and wrapping herself in a cloak against the chill of the evening, settled down near the fire; she tuned the instrument, and began to sing. The men listened, for the music was much to be desired in this wilderness. Further, both the songs and the style of singing were of considerable beauty.

She sang of old lands, of old ways . . . of times and places long past. Some of the music was strange to them, and in keys which were unfamiliar, for the music came from a time when songs were sung differently . . . in strange and haunting minor keys, and with different rhythms. And so, late into the night, they continued.

The next day they proceeded further, passing only very small and scattered settlements. And as before, the count and Tanithia rode at the head of the column.

As the day was nearing noon, Waldmann glanced across at her. "My dear, pray tell . . . what's happened to your shirt? Yesterday it was a full garment, but now the sleeves have been nearly cut away and you've trimmed away the lower part to display a lot of that slender middle of yours. Even the sash is slung lower. Is it that you want to show a cleavage in the back for the benefit of the troops? If so, you're doing admirably well. And I can assure you that they appreciate it. Or is it that you want to make my life more difficult by the way you bob so esthetically in front as you ride? Really, those open lacings and that slashed shirt really conceal very little."

She glanced at him wickedly. "You state things so crassly, lover. But of course. That's exactly what I want to do . . . I'm weaving further with my spell, in many ways." She brushed back her mane of honey-colored hair with one hand. (Two troopers who had been dozing in the saddle came suddenly alert, to the amusement of their comrades.) "And of course the day is warm. It's more comfortable this way."

"Aren't you running something of a risk?" he asked. "After all, you're the only woman here. Nay . . . the only one we're likely to meet, other than a few wizened drabs in the various settlements. You may get more than you bargained for, with this troop of healthy lads."

There were a few moments of silence as they jogged on, side by side. "I'm playing a very careful game, milord. I want to entice you and the men. I want to tantalize you. But not . . . not too far. Oh, I'll admit that it might be quite diverting indeed to be raped by a whole troop of lusty soldiers; that idea had occured to me. But crass sensuality isn't my intent—there's a magical principle involved. The desire of woman for man . . . and of man for woman . . . can be the root of very powerful magics, if it can be aimed and channeled properly. And this, of course, is what I'm doing. and I.ll continue, because I want to have a lot of sheer, raw power available for our cleasing of the castle. Afterwards? We shall see." She looked at him, and glanced briefly back at the troops. Her smile, he thought to himself, was entirely like that of a fox. She dug her bare heels into her horse's flanks and urged him on ahead, her eyes sparkling.

The footlhills grew steeper and more rugged as next day they ascended into the high country. The afternoon sun slanted down with a lazy warmth as the column of horses plodded further on up the little-used road. The forest was thick to either side and rocky promontories rose sheer at infrequent intervals, wrapped about with greenery.

A few of the men talked quietly about matters of trivial importance, though for most the boredom of a long, uneventful ride had set in. Some dozed in the saddle while others were wrapped in thought or in reminiscence. One or two passed the time by watching Tanithia, and weaving fantasies.

Tanithia herself sat daydreaming. A bit tired and a bit bored, she was lulled by the steady, slow clip-clop of hooves in a steady, never-ending rhythm. Without particular interest she noticed that they had reached the top of a rise, and that the old road dipped down for a few hundred paces before slowly following the rise in the terrain. Well up ahead the road passed between two steep, forested hills.

Suddenly she sat bolt upright in the saddle and stared ahead, and abruptly reined in. Waldmann halted his horse also and looked quizzically at her as the entire column came to an unexpected halt behind, the men coming awake.

"What's the matter?" Waldmann asked curiously.

"I don't know," she said, her eyes searching the scene ahead. "But I had a flash . . . a vision. There are people ahead, close. And they're not friends . . . there's something dangerous!"

Count Waldmann motioned for the rest of the column to hold their positions, and rode forward a short ways to the high point in the road and stopped, carefully scanning the terrain ahead. For a short while he sat quietly in the saddle, absently stroking his grey moustache as he contemplated the road and the forested hills, considering.

He turned and called, though not loudly. "Swords Sergeant. Gort. Up front!" The two rode up next to him, and he pointed to the two knolls that were ahead. "There's a good chance that someone has set an ambush for us up ahead. Now the most likely place for an ambush would be just where the road passes between those two hills. The forest is thick and the slopes are steep. There's a clear enough field of fire, so archers could be posted at either side." He made certain that each understood the exact area to which he pointed. "I want each of you to take two men and carefully work your way around on foot, coming in behind each hill and searching out the hostiles. If and when you make contact, give a meadowlark call and hold your positions; don't let them see you until we move in on the main trail. We'll spring their trap. Attack from in back while we charge them from the front."

At the count's order, all began donning battle gear: Leathern armor, chain mail, iron helmets with the cheek plates lowered. Bows were strung and arrows checked, while swords were loosened in their scabbards and shields were hung on their mounts' harness, ready for use.

Dismounting, the nobleman checked over each man as Gort and the old sergeant moved out, each with their pair of men, disappearing noiselessly into the forest. Waldmann paused for a moment to watch Tanithia disapprovingly as she stripped off her clothes and carefully folded the garments off to the side. Sensing his eyes on her golden form, she looked up at him and smiled.

"My lady," he said with just a trace of exasperation, "It's likely that we're going to have a pitched battle coming up shortly. Your charms are considerable, but you're going to need something more substantial in protection."

"Of course," she said, strapping on a soft leather jerkin that came to her thighs. "Would you help me get that chain mail over my head? It's heavy and a trifle awkward." She smiled at him. "Have no fear, love. I'm not so fey that I'd not take normal precautions. There. Doesn't the mail shirt cling nicely? If it weren't so heavy I'd wear it more often." She positioned a longbow between a leg and a foot and strung it.

"I do some hunting for small game occasionally." she commented, counting her arrows. "It should be interesting to try hunting some larger beasts." He gave her an iron-strapped helmet and she fitted it to her head with a look of distaste. "It's so heavy," she complained, spreading her hair down her back and shoulders. "No wonder you've got such a thick neck."

They walked to the area where the others were waiting. "You don't want to wear armor on your legs? And no boots? Very well . . . I'll place you where you can give us cover with that bow. Here, let's build a campfire and have a light meal to give Gort and the old sergeant time to move around into position. We're being watched from a distance, I'm certain, and a break for food would give a reasonable excuse for waiting a little."

For a while they sat and talked loudly, laughing from time to time, though no one seemed to have an appetite for more than one or two bites. Eventually came the faint call of a meadowlark.

Count Waldmann looked up at the sun. "All right, one is in position and the other one should be shortly. Let's move out."

They rattled forward, conspicuously talking and laughing, approaching the knolls. "Cover your armor with your cloaks," said Waldmann. "We don't want to make it too obvious that we suspect."

Another field lark call, this one from not too far ahead. The count loosened his sword in its sheath, as did the others.

"Tanithia," he said quietly, "Dismount here behind these last bushes and take cover off to the side. Get ready to cover us when we attack."

"Milord, I'd rather be with you . . ."

"Dismount and take cover," he repeated, interrupting her. You're excellent at magic, but we're trained for this!" He looked at her briefly with some concern in his eyes. "Also, they might be out especially to get you, no matter what the cost. Aim well, but stay concealed." She nodded, swung a golden leg over the horse to dismount, tethered the steed briefly, and vanished into the bushes on silent bare feet.

Waldmann silently led the others forward, all scanning the silent hillsides as they prepared to move fast. "Remember," he said softly, "As soon as the shooting starts, you three break left," he pointed. "The other two break right with me. Move in fast, but don't take chances. There's too much loose rock on the slope to remain mounted, so let the horses go . . . they can take care of themselves.

Silence. The rattling of horses' hooves on the road. Deceptively quiet.

An arrow whipped into Waldmann's cloak, snapping on his chain mail. Feathered shafts seemed to fill the air as they vaulted from their horses and ran into the brush to either side. A horse screamed and reared as an arrow sank into its hip. Raised shields deflected others that were well aimed for necks and faces.

Swords sang from their sheaths as the men dodged in for the attack. Running low and behind any boulders or trees, they made for the source of the arrows that came so dangerously close. Shouting and yelling came from either side, and the sound of swords clashing. Gort and the sergeant had closed their flanks.

Arrows suddenly snapped wildly upwards, uselessly, then no more were loosed. Waldmann and his men broke cover and charged in, swords at the ready. Brown- and green-clad men ran towards them from cover, swords out.

Count Waldmann parried a blow from a big man who was suddenly before him, then caught another blow on the iron-rimmed edge of his shield as he brought the man down with a hip cut. He moved rapidly on.

"There are more of them than we thought," he muttered, using a shield blow to deflect a thrust that would have hit one of his men. The count's man smiled a brief thanks and dispatched the green-clad assailant.

But the pincer attack had worked, and panic and

disorganization from the surprise rear attack had much lessened the enemy effectiveness. Some of their unarmored ambushers engaged the soldiers in swordplay — but training, armor, and shields made the individual combats very one-sided.

Count Waldmann struck at one of the attackers as several ran past him, and well behind he could here yelling. "Oh my gods," he thought with a start. "Tanithia's back there!" He was about to turn when he was charged by yet another, howling like a demon and whirling a rusty war-axe. His concern for the witch had to wait for a moment. His men were momentarily out of sight, and this fight was his alone. Up with the shield to take a jarring blow, and then, moving in fast for a glancing, too-weak blow at the man's leather-shielded side. Step back to break the other's stride and take another blow that numbed his arm for a moment. But the axe-fighter had lost the momentum of his attack. Waldmann's first blow was stopped hard by the axe, but his second bit into the man's brisket, and his opponent went down in a spray of blood.

Waldmann stepped into the open and looked around quickly. No one nearby. The sergeant was standing out in the open up the slope, grinning and signalling that the flank was secured. On the other side, though, a clash of swords indicated that Gort and his men were still busy.

Behind, three of the enemy had mounted on the abandoned horses, milled about momentarily, then galloped for the rear.

An arrow suddenly imbedded deep in the side of one and he pitched from the saddle to land beneath the hooves. A second suddenly threw up his arms and fell with a cry as another suddenly dug into his back. The last rider reined up for a moment and looked back with shock at his two fallen comrades. Then the sword fell from his hands as another feathered shaft instantly appeared in his chest.

Count Waldmann hurried back as Tanithia stepped gracefully out of the bush, smiling wolfishly. She had taken off her helmet and her red-gold hair was streaming free, He noted that several dead were scattered in fatal disarray up and down the trail. A surprisingly large number.

"You've been busy, love," he said, looking about. "I daresay you weren't bored."

"That was enjoyable," she said with a disturbingly wide smile. "I can see that one could very easily gain a taste for blood!" A mortally wounded man scrabbled in the dirt before them, an arrow through his throat. He looked up at her with mute, wide eyes, blood flowing freely from his mouth. She gently and softly put her toes at the base of his neck next to the wooden shaft and pulled out the arrow. A sudden gush of blood and the man was choking. A few moments more and it was obvious that all was nearly done. His pain-filled, frightened eyes were on Tanithia alone . . . a desperate, pleading look.

She bent over him and touched his scarred and bloody face. In a moment the fear was gone, and perhaps also the pain. In another moment, peacefully, he was dead.

"He was almost smiling," said Waldmann wonderingly. "To him you were the death-goddess Hulda. He knew that you had killed him, yet at the end you were all in the world to him." The older man leaned on his bloody sword, musing. You brought him death, yet he had a sort of desire and even love for you as he died." He paused for a long moment, regarding the now serene face. "Perhaps the male spider feels thus when his mate destroys him . . ."

She wiped the arrow on the dead man's breeks. "It was merciful, really," she said. "He would have died in slow agony otherwise."

"I know."

Tanithia looked at the bodies scattered about, all

the result of her own hand. "There's a savage joy to battle and to killing . . . it's like working dark magic," she said. "I like it."

Waldmann winced. "As a professional soldier, I must say that sometimes you hit uncomfortably close to the things we never like to say." His eyes met hers. "But remember also . . . battle and killing, like Hulda's dark and baneful magic, should only be used when necessary. Otherwise you eventually become less than human."

There was a call and they turned to see that the sergeant and Gort were getting the troop back together, and talking to the handful of prisoners that had been taken.

The prisoners knew very little, it became apparent upon questioning. Their captain had known the reason for the attack, but he was dead. All they knew was that he had been a dour but good-paying man from Drakenstane Province. Tanithia mesmerically blanked their minds, the soldiers stripped the prisoners of their weapons, and released them. All weapons were taken from the dead, lest they be used by random rogues, or by released prisoners who might bear an unwise grudge.

"It's a good thing that I have some ability for healing," she was saying. "the wounded horse will be all right in a day or two. There were no serious wounds among the men, and the minor ones will heal very quickly." She looked at Waldmann. "Help me out of this chain mail, Milord. We've still got a few leagues of travel today!"

HE following days were uneventful, and at length they came to the old and rather shabby inn, maintained primarily for the occasional travellers who happened through from time to time, though much of the innkeeper's support was obviously by farming the rather inhospitable hillsides nearby.

As they approached, the men put their gear into proper military order, if only to be looking and feeling in good trim. And Tanithia, reluctantly, clothed herself decently, for she had shed very much of her clothes . . . as much as she dared without pushing the soldiers too far. And their eyes were on her at all times, she knew, for the cut-off breeks and the remnant of the shirt concealed little and tantalized much. The tight, high-slashed trousers displayed an interesting length of golden thigh and her posterior quite fetchingly as she straddled the barrel of the horse. Her breasts, free and unfettered, and with only the smallest cloth draped partially over them, bounced very divertingly with the slow jogging of her mount.

For now, though, she had clad herself in more conventional men's clothing, with boots, cloak, and hat ... somewhat to the disappointment of those in the troop.

The inn was but little used. As they rode up it seemed that only three or four passing travellers were there at the time. One or two rather seedy individuals were about who might have been city dwellers and possibly avoiding the authorities for some reason or another. Others were perhaps workers or farmers, passing through or on some errand. Whatever it was, Tanithia felt, they were moderately at ease and secure here. She had, however, taken the precaution of picking certain barks and herbs to dye her hair, and had slightly modified her features.

The count folded his leather riding-gloves and dropped them on the rough table before him as the innkeeper came forth. "Good morrow to you, I wish lodgings for my men and for my woman. Food, and stabling and fodder for the horses. I'll need provisions for our journey ahead and ... oh yes ... to have our mounts rubbed down and cared for." The first of the men began coming in, gratefully requesting ale.

"How long will ye be stayin' here," asked the grizzled innkeeper, eyeing the soldiers and especially looking at Tanithia.

"Merely passing through," said the count. "We have an errand elsewhere, and marching orders."

The innkeeper felt mild relief, though his hard features did not show it. If soldiers were not coming to extort taxes they would otherwise spend freely for food, ale, and lodging. Good for business ... which was sparse in these hard times.

All were soon quartered, though mayhap some of the other lodgers were pushed out into the stables for the higher-paying soldiers, for by the time of the evening meal only two of the previous lodgers remained. The innkeeper's wife produced a hearty meal which was much enjoyed by all present, for field rations . . . not particularly inspiring at best . . . were more than a little dreary after days of travel.

Count Waldmann had not given his name, preferring to be incognito on this journey, and while the men were free with words and wine otherwise, they too said nothing of their leader, his lady, or their mission. Waldmann seldom affected the satins and laces of a courtier, preferring instead simple coarse-woven cloth and leathers, and hence appeared as either a country squire of a rough backwoods barony or simply a good and capable, if somewhat greying officer in some noble's army.

Tanithia, as they finished their meal, carefully appraised the two strangers sitting in the far corner of the dim room. Probably they were rogues from the city, she decided. They both seemed that they would, in time, have the mark of the hangman's noose on them, and perhaps even now they were probably in flight to avoid the authorities. Perhaps, she thought, they would eventually come to test the skill of the headsman, if their sins were interesting enough. But country people? Certainly not.

She had more of her magic that she wished to weave, and this was an ideal place with the ideal atmosphere. Well, she felt, the temporary spell would do no harm on a couple of random ne'er-do-wells, and if they became overly desirous, her own men could easily persuade them to mind whatever manners they might have.

She drew forth her harp, and the men's eyes brightened. There were a few scattered calls of approval from them in anticipation of more of her music. She tuned it briefly and then commenced playing.

But not this time the slow and lyrical songs and ballads of an era long past, yet rather the sensuous rhythms of a more southern clime, music that stirred the blood differently. She sang of love and of passion, of lovers divided and lovers reunited. Of beauty, of sensuality.

Those present gave her their full attention, and even the hard-bitten innkeeper and his plain-faced wife, as well as the kitchen drudges, joined the rapt group standing in the far doorways. For music was a thing heard all too rarely in these distant places.

Tanithia calculated her next move for a moment, and looked about. The men were enjoying themselves, though if they drank much more ale she would be uncertain as to their continued control in what she had planned. Thus . . . now was the time.

"Swordsman Gort! Please . . . I've heard you playing idly on this harp several times over the last few days, and I know that you can do well. Play me some music . . . I feel like dancing!" She passed the instrument to him, smiling as their eyes met.

She threw off her cloak to show bared shoulders and a peasant blouse cut very low indeed to show much of the full curves of her breasts. Her hair she shook free so that it tumbled about her shoulders and down her back, then stood and with light dancer's steps swayed to the center of the floor. Her skirt was full, like that of a tsigandi girl, and brightly colored in patches and in squares of light, differing fabrics. She wore golden chains, delicately wrought, about her feet and ankles, and rings on her toes. The chains she wore about her neck, and the bracelets, were of brass . . . seemingly gold . . . and delicately wrought.

She whirled and swayed with eyes bright in the candlelight as Gort thrummed out the rhythms which reflected the passion he felt within himself. His eyes never left her.

Her light feet moved swiftly over the rude floor as she whirled, swayed, sometimes singing, sometimes humming. Arms out or close, her hair rippling and flowing with every silken movement, or sometimes flung about with the wildness of the dance — giving the message of sensuality, of beauty, of passion.

She swayed and trembled, every movement bespeaking love and desire, her skirt oftimes whirling out to show bronzed, perfect limbs. Her breasts bouncing tantalizingly within the very slight confinement of her tin bodice, the red rosy nipples almost bouncing free at one time or another. Her face eager in the joy of the dance, weaving a spell of achingly erotic magic as she glided across the floor, even kneeling to swirl her body and to swing her long hair about like a cascade of spun ebony.

All present clapped, shouted encouragement, and demanded more as she paused to catch her breath. She passed between the benches where the soldiers sat, swaying on light toes, turning sometimes, singing sometimes, so that every man felt the intensity of her dance-spell . . . as though almost inviting more than the raveningly burning eyes and hoarsely shouted encouragement. The dance . . . she loved the dance . . . and she gave freely of it. The passion which she communicated was more than even an excellent dancer could evoke. Her dark beauty, with her

dyed and her skin dusky by a shade due to the days in the sun ... made all feel that they were in the glow of ever-building sexual ecstacy. As if they were touching and caressing the rosy tipped breasts, touching the smooth, well-shaped legs, running hands through that tumbled dark hair, and kissing away the fine film of sweat that gathered on her smooth forehead.

"I have them," she thought, "And I have myself nearly transcendent with the ecstacy of dancing." She smiled and closed her eyes for a moment in the warm, pleasurable glow which swept through her body. "This is going to be a magnificent night!"

The music doubled and redoubled. The clapping, the pounding, the stamping, the rapping of leathern mugs upon the rough wooden tables and benches, ebbed and swelled. The dancing went on, more compellingly, blood-stirringly sensual than before.

None noticed as one of the two random rogues in the back of the large room looked disapprovingly at the coarse fellow near him, who had fallen into the same wild entrancement as the others, who cast as few glances as possible at the whirling and leaping beauty whose dancing so extolled the delights of the flesh.

Trembling and wiping the sweat from his brow, he fumbled for the side door and reeled outside, closing the heavy door behind him as silently as he could.

"Oh my God", he said hoarsely, "Oh God of the skies and the desert, redeemer who shall destroy all as He returns. Give me strength against the sins of the flesh." He stepped into the shadows and fell to his knees, clasping his hands before him.

"I am tempted, Great One. I'm tempted. Let me love thee instead, as I love my pious comrades. I wish not to be ensnared by this trollop. I wish only to serve the mighty, flaming sword of the desert god who will destroy, and cast into the flames, all who are unbelievers." Slowly his breath became steadier and he regained more composure. He walked yet further away, for he could yet still hear the sounds of revelry within. Walking still somewhat unsteadily beyond the stables and further away towards the calm, silent fields, serene in the silvery moonlight.

"Sinful,", he muttered. "Sinful, these passions of the flesh. I love only our desert Lord, and it is only for Him that I must have passion and yearning." He muttered to himself. "I had come into these desolate mountains seeking only a retreat from the worldly ways of the cities and to be alone as He was once alone . . . and hence to become more like Him. And yet the ways of the Dark One follow me even here." He paused for a few minutes more, eyes closed, his hands clasped before him. Then a thought occurred to him, in the midst of his meditations, prayers, and mutterings. He opened his eyes and looked back towards where the distant snatches of song and shouting still could be heard.

"I wonder," he said slowly. "Something was familiar . . . something . . . " He eased back to the inn. "What does she look like? Her face. I've got to look only at her face!" The windows were shuttered closed, yet he found a crack between the boards at one window and watched for a few moments, blinking his eyes and shaking his head as if to dispel some lingering film from over his vision.

"She looks familiar . . . where have I seen her before? That face . . ." His eyes widened. "No! It can't be! Her hair is different, yet her body has the sinful sensuosity of woman, carried to its quintessence as it was with . . . that one. But her face . . . *Magda!*" he exclaimed.

"It must be! No . . . impossible . . . Magda was burned at the stake. I was in the church's holy procession that took her there. I saw her myself, tied to the blackened pillar with the flames licking around her, screaming in agony." He smiled briefly at the memory. "That shameless harlot refused conversion, so we made the flames last longer. From the throne to ashes in only an hour . . ." He peered again for a long moment. "Yet . . . were the hair lighter, this would be the one. Weaving a spell of worldly magic about all within sight of her." He considered.

"Could she have escaped? I don't see how it could be, yet . . ." he rubbed his hands across his eyes, "It *must* be she. It's got to be! Some sort of spells or glamouries, perhaps, but the witch must have somehow escaped, and now she's here." He paused and unsteadily rubbed his face in his trembling hands, as if to wipe away the vision of flashing limbs, of swaying hips and rosy-tipped breasts . . . a vision that brought the sweat to his brow again.

"NO! Get thee behind me, temptation. This can't be . . . I love only the men who serve the One. Her kind are . . . unclean . . . the root of evil. Remember, it's they who have the responsibility for the expulsion from the Garden." Again he looked back. "My eyes are clearer now. My prayers . . . my prayers have helped to clear them." He smiled thinly and looked away, clasping his hands before him as he bowed his head.

"My God of the flaming sword, I thank you. Thou hast smiled on me. I wondered why my faith had to stand the testing, why I had to journey to these misbegotten hills, why I had to retreat from the ways of men to regain

my faith. And now I find you have given me a mission . . .
thou hast delivered into my sight the accursed witch-
queen herself. All think her dead and ashes; all but me.
I the Inquisitor . . . I the Witchfinder-General and Flame
of the Lord in our rebellion . . . I who have burned many
in your name, wrung the truth from lost, screaming
wretches and consigned them to the holy flames . . . I
whom my former comrades and those who now rule the
land have called a fool and a fanatic. I now have my greatest task before me," he laughed softly, though with an
intensity that would have been more than a little dis-
quieting, had any been there to hear.

"I'll bear the flaming sword of the Son again, in
my greatest blow for the One Way of truth, for THE
VENGANCE OF THE LORD IS MINE!" He looked
again, briefly, through the crack, then stole away into the
shadows.

 HE next morning they departed. Perhaps it
was somewhat later than they would sensibly
have wished and later than the count had
planned. But all, it seemed, had heads which
were a bit thick and eyes a bit heavy from
the wine and ale of the previous evening. Yet definitely
none regretted it, for the afterglow of Lady Tanithia's
wild dancing was such that each felt almost as if he had
lain the night in the arms of a lover. And more than one
had dreamed, quite vividly, that the lover clasped in a
long and passionate embrace had indeed been the lovely
Tanithia.

She herself, after the night's exuberant dancing, no
longer felt it necessary to maintain the pretext of being
near-invisible. Quite brazenly, she came out and mounted
her horse, clad in short, high-slit and close fitting breeches

and the peasant shirt which she had much cut, so that only a few strategic bits of cloth remained – to display a maximum of her very obvious charms.

Count Waldmann, rubbing at slightly reddened eyes, stopped for a moment at the sight of her, and smiled, suddenly looking – and feeling – much more alert.

"Tanithia, my dear, you'll have to stop washing that shirt so often. The fabric seems to keep shrinking."

She smiled and took his arm. "I thought you'd never notice," she said with a mock-innocent expression. "I often feel I'm too subtle. Are we ready to go?"

"Aye, we have the supplies packed and everyone looks ready to move out in good form." He chuckled. "That was an evening to remember. Why, even that dour-faced innkeeper seemed to tear his bed apart with his plain-faced wife last night. I daresay they appreciated the music and dancing, in spite of her permanent look of disapproval."

"Hm," Said Tanithia, "She looked far less disapproving this morning. Why, she seemed so pleased she almost smiled. Perhaps a bit more passionate love-making would make her, if not beautiful, then at least a little more pleasing to look at."

"A most successful evening of entertainment, my lovely dancing girl," said the count, snapping his reins as they moved further on down the trail.

"Perhaps . . . but not perfect," said Tanithia slowly. She frowned slightly. "I felt that not quite everyone there was woven into my spell. There was resistance, somehow."

"Hm. It must have been that sour-faced rogue who left early in the evening."

"Ah yes," she said. "There were two originally. One of them stayed the full night, and even had to be reminded of his manners once or twice when he got a bit too eager. The other, maybe, may have been more sympathetic to that puritanical new cult." She frowned again. "He left early this morning, before were were up, didn't he?"

"Yes, Tanithia, though I didn't think it was important enough to ask further." He grinned sidelong at her. "Perhaps even you can't manage to please everyone with your dancing!"

"Perhaps," she said, her expression slightly shadowed.

The column jogged slowly down the little-used road with the tall evergreens close on either side, the soft mountain breeze murmuring softly in the treetops. Eventually they passed from sight. A vulture wheeled overhead, distant in the sky, then turned and flapped leisurely across the forested mountain pass in the direction of the mountain province known as "Drakenstane".

The howling began shortly after sunset.

"Damme, what a sound," muttered the old sergeant to the man next to him. "It's enough to turn yer blood to snow . . ." He sipped absently at his hot drink, his eyes on the deepening shadows beyond the fire.

Gort stroked the forelock of his horse, and spoke gently to the animal. Trembling, eyes wide, his mount glanced uneasily to one direction and the other, then pressed against him more closely . . . seeking human comfort against that which it sensed in the darkness. Gort spoke to another man, likewise consoling and calming the horses.

"Tell the count, please. We need to move the horses in near the fire and tether them closely. If those beasts get any closer our mounts are going to panic and bolt."

Count Waldmann peered off into the gloom and listened to the deep, strange, shifting chords of the howling. "Last night they were off in the distance," he commented to Tanithia. "Now they're close and getting closer. There is one thing that bothers me: they're following us, it seems."

She looked up from her sewing and decided the light was getting too faint for any more close work. Tanithia folded the garment and placed it back in her saddlepack, then smoothed her hair back with both hands and listened attentively for a few moments.

"Wolves . . . how beautiful," she said. "Their singing is the very soul of night."

"Sergeant," said Waldmann with a worried frown. "Have the men gather a lot of firewood. As much as they can without going too far." He listened to the eerie howling as it raised to a cresendo. "And have them be careful. I'll want the bonfire all night long if we need it. The horses have got to be close in. As soon as we have the wood, we'll form into a defensive perimeter with bows strung and ready for use."

As soon as the darkness became deep the first eyes appeared in the blackness, and the firelight limned grey shapes moving far out beyond the perimeter where the men, sweating in spite of the coolness of the night, stood with bows at the ready and arrows nocked.

Waldmann had seen to the horses. They were frightened, but he was certain that fright would not turn to terror. "The howling, and that yapping," he muttered. "It's like the wailing of spectres and not like any living thing." Then, mindful of the responsibility of command, he put his own unease out of his mind and with solid, smiling confidence (or so it seemed) spoke to each of the men to soothe their own tense apprehension.

He saw Tanithia standing still at the edge of the perimeter, her cloak wrapped about her, staring outwards to where the howling ebbed and flowed. He called to her as he came up, and put a hand on her arm to comfort her.

She turned to him, smiling, her eyes bright. "The night side of nature is fascinating, isn't it, milord?"

He was somewhat taken aback. "You're not frightened?"

"No. I've been listening to that magnificent, big pack. They say a lot with that howling and that barking."

"Do they plan to attack? Wolves don't normally do that, except in the coldest winters when all their natural food is gone." Waldmann pulled his cloak about himself and watched the restless, loping grey shadows. And the eyes. "This is unusual," he said. "Distinctly unusual . . ."

Tanithia watched intently. "Listen to them, they're frightened," she said softly. "They don't want to be here, but something's pushing them."

"And whatever is pushing them will probably also make them try to take us," muttered Waldmann.

"Yes," said Tanithia. "There's something wrong. The wolves are being pushed at us, even unwilling." The howling and yapping reached yet another crescendo, and from behind them, in response, came the moaning whinnies of frightened horses.

"Our animals are terrified," Waldmann observed. "I'd better see to them and make a final check of everything. It looks like we're going to have a fight on our hands."

"No," she said shortly, taking his arm to restrain him. "Wait a bit and let me see if I can talk to them." •

He looked at her, surprised. "You can do that?"

"Yes. Have the men hold their bolts while I go out there and see what I can find out."

"Girl, they'll tear you to shreds. Some of those beasts weigh ten or twelve stone. Or more. I'd wager that any one of them could pull down a bull. Look at those teeth . . . they're savage!"

She rose on her toes and kissed him on his cheek. "I doubt that," she said. "They're beautiful creatures . . . I don't want to see them killed or wounded." She walked to the fartherest edge of the perimeter in the light of the crackling bondfire. Waldmann hesitated for a moment and followed her. She watched for a few moments and then pointed.

"There's their leader. And the slightly smaller one next to him must be his mate." Unexpectedly she called out in short, abrupt words that were obviously some other language, but which seemed somehow familiar.

The wolves suddenly stopped, falling silent, some moving in a bit closer to get a view of the human who had called to them, surprisingly, in words they understood. The soldiers as well turned to stare at this interruption of what they fully expected to be a bloody fight.

Tanithia undid the clasp at the front of her cloak and lifted the garment from her shoulders, placing it in Waldmann's arms. The firelight glistened on the red-gold of her hair as she looked down to unlace the front of her long gown. She pulled the heavy cloth off her shoulders and tugged on it, then shrugged it down and peeled out of the gown to stand naked in the silent crackling of the firelight. She drew in a deep breath and fluffed her hair back, pleased to see that for the moment she was completely in control of both humans and wolves, with the complete attention of all. She smiled at Waldmann.

"Clothes might flap and startle them," she explained, perhaps unnecessarily.

He shook his head and sighed resignedly. "All right, pretty one. But I'd feel better if you could carry some sort of weapon, at least."

She touched a finger to his lips briefly. "That's the general idea of being skyclad," she explained, as if to a youngster. "They have to know that I can't hurt them in any way."

So saying, she turned and walked slowly out beyond the perimeter towards the leader of the pack and, indeed, most of the wolves where they stood together, tongues lolling over sharp teeth. Watching intently. The firelight shone on the flowing hair that fell almost to her hips, and on the smooth curves of her naked body as she walked, slowly and with apparent casual light steps.

She paused a bit before the leader of the pack, dropping to her hands and knees, and turning a bit away from facing him directly. He lifted his head and raised his ears in ritual response. She knelt and spoke to him in a language that men would not understand, as the other wolves moved closer on either side.

The talk was different, in basic concept and pattern, from any that humankind would know. A whining, a snuffling, a meeting of eyes and a moving of bodies, a transfer of thoughts. Of conveying meanings rather than words.

Tanithia looked at the leader and then averted her eyes briefly, speaking their tongue. (I give you greetings, and friendship. I am our pack's Lady and a magic-worker, as you've gathered by now. I apologize that our leader can't be here to negotiate, but he doesn't know the Old Ways.) She paused a moment and looked into the leader's gray eyes. (To pledge my honor and friendship I ask you to name me.).

He smiled broadly, showing perfect teeth and seeming even more the essence of dignity as he drew his head back slightly into his silver mane. (You work the art we call "seid." Were you a wolf I would call you Seid Lady. I am called Longrunner, and this is my consort, Grey Lady.)

Their eyes met, formally. While Tanithia sensed a warmth from Longrunner she felt only a cool cautiousness from Grey Lady. "She's a jealous one," thought Tanithia, "And her position means much. I'll have to be extremely careful not to be thought of as a rival. Hm, very human indeed."

Longrunner eyed her appraisingly. (You know our language and our customs. Our legends tell of the ancient art of shape-changing. Can you work that seid as well?)

(Perhaps. But for now I'm here to ask why you've been preparing to attack us. We've done you no harm, and there's enough food about for anyone.)

He rubbed his muzzle somewhat self-consciously. (We don't want to be here, but we're being forced. By the Dark Beings.).

Tanithia's intentness showed her obvious interest. (Tell me about it.)

He glanced nervously toward the high peaks. (There's a place for humans perhaps an hour's run from here. They fashioned it only a few seasons ago, but then all left. It was as if they had a conflict of some sort. Perhaps a moon ago another man came, and fashioned it into a Power place. Then it became a ritual den; the Dark Things came.)

She looked at the moon for a moment. (I think we

can chase it out of the mountains. Would you be able to tell or show where this place is?)

Longrunner sniffed the air and looked off in the direction of the dark outpost. (It's not far for us, though you'd take much longer being in human-form. You seem to know much magic, so I ask again . . . can you shape-change?)

Tanithia looked a bit away from him and scratched at the ground uncertainly. (I . . . don't know. I'm good at changing my face, but my entire body . . .)

Grey Lady snapped a brusque interruption. (If you can change your face, it's simple. Merely an extension of the same method. Come, let's go into the darkness and we can show you.)

With a slight trace of uncertainty Tanithia cast one last glance at the bright warmness of the fire and her watching comrades, then walked into the brush with the wolves flanking her. The trees grew denser and the rocks higher, so that not far from the camp all was in near-total darkness. The stones and roots were hard and sharp against her feet, but she knew it would be improper to show any sign of discomfort or even of cautious stepping.

Grey Lady stopped and looked at her. (This is good enough. Crouch here while we gather around you.) Tanithia eased down onto the center of a dim clearing as the dark grey shadows of the wolves formed into a circle about her, eyes glinting in the starlight and tongues lolling over sharp teeth. Grey Lady spoke again through the darkness. (Look at me, and at Longrunner. Watch us change.)

The forms were dim and indistinct to her, and almost immediately they became even more so, seemingly wrapped in a grayish-green mist. Longrunner and Grey Lady sat at ease perhaps five paces from her, and Tanithia watched them intently. After a few long moments she spoke. (I can't make out your faces any more. You're changing them.)

(Good. So far we're doing your own magic. Now watch our bodies.)

They were facing her, and their bodies were now hard to discern in the misty dimness. Then Tanithia smiled, lowering herself close to the ground in an unconscious lupine mannerism. (It looks like your bodies are . . . are . . . almost human now, though it's hard to make out from the way you're sitting.)

Grey Lady's answer seemed almost amused. (Very well . . . now watch.)

Tanithia gasped. For the two figures slowly stood erect.

On two legs.

The mist and the indistinctness faded from them. The wolves of the pack shifted and growled in wonder and in satisfaction round about the two, and Tanithia stood, understanding the magic and yet still in enchanted surprise of it.

"Why . . . what a beautiful couple you are!"

Grey Lady smiled at her, waves of silver-light hair tumbling unbound over her bare shoulders and over her perfect breasts, her body full and silver-seeming in the dimness. Longrunner was massive and tall, with a mane of thick black hair and muscles that rippled as he moved. Tanithia noted that even in human form his chest, arms, and legs were thick with body hair. He was, she decided, good to look at, and robustly male.

"You're most gracious, Seid Lady," he said in a rich accent that bore much resemblence to his wolf voice. "I trust that with what we've shown, you can infer the rest." He looked at her, and then long and intently at his companion, smiling. "You look strange, pretty love. But you translate well into human form."

Grey Lady pressed her breasts against him and nuzzled at his ear. "There's a certain grace to the human form, but I prefer our own. You're nice, though." She put her arms about Longrunner and gazed at Tanithia with a look that was possessive, warning, and yet intriging by its essential non-humaness. Even in human form they were undeniably lupine. After a long moment she spoke.

"I'd recommend, Seid Lady, that you fetch your man and both make ready for shape-change. You have a lot to do tonight."

Tanithia walked slowly back into the semicircle of armed men, golden and statuesque in the firelight. Count Waldmann held her cloak out for her and put it over her shoulders. She had been wrapped in thought, and now for the first time she looked at him directly, drawing the cloak close under her breasts.

"It's an outpost of some sort, with the darkness from Drakenstane that's making them attack." She absently ran her toe through the loosened soil, tracing a pattern. "I need to go and find the place . . . they tell me that it's no more than over the next mountain. I could be there by midnight." Her expression was grim. "To exorcise and to destroy it."

She smiled and looked at him, breaking the mood. "But the wolves have a very strong custom. I have to go with a male . . . my own, or it could cause dissension in

their pack, and destroy the fragile trust I've built up."
She glanced out towards the wolves where they sat and
waited.

"Longrunner has some interest in me, I think. But
Grey Lady is in a strong position, and definitely not one
to be crossed."

Waldmann stroked his grey moustache reflectively.
"A chaperone in wolf form, eh? I gather that you wouldn't
be going as a human."

She looked at him, smiling, as she absently ran a
finger around her bare nipple. "Yes," she said.

Her meaning dawned on him. "No! I'm getting
much too old for this sort of thing. We need someone
else. What about your Swordsman Gort? Perhaps you'd
like to have your cavalier with you." He looked around
at all the troop, straightening, to call in his best voice of
command.

"I need one volunteer. Swordsman Gort, front and
center!"

Gort made his way from the horses towards the
count, muttering to himself. ("The military never seems
to change . . . "). In a few sentences Waldmann explained
the situation, and by degrees Gort's mood lightened, and
he looked at Tanithia who was regarding him in the firelight, her eyes perhaps telling a bit more of her feelings
than she intended.

She smiled and looked away with feigned casualness,
putting her hands behind her head and unconsciously
striking a pose. The cloak fell away from her form, a
display that both men appreciated. After a long moment
Waldmann smiled, glancing at the two.

"I think I've made an excellent choice," he said.
"You two have a certain spark with each other." He
looked at Tanithia. "Go now, and do a good job
of it!"

With some embarrassment, Gort did as she instructed and stripped off his clothes. She outfitted both with talisman neckpieces from her saddlebag and chose similar earrings for herself. Then, with a kiss to ease his apprehension, they walked out towards the wolves as she told him what she could of the language and customs of the mountain-dwellers, and of what she planned.

The wolf pack closed in on either side and they walked off away from the camp into the darkness. Waldmann followed for a ways, watching. On out to a meadow in the dim moonlight and then into the trees beyond. Tanithia and Gort separated and walked some distance from one another, then both crouched in the grass, turning to watch each other.

It was hard for him to tell what happened next, for their bodies were indistinct blurs that seemed hard to define, for they seemed to take many changes.

But, very definitely, it was two large wolves that ran from the trees to join the pack. Then all were gone.

Tirelessly they ran through the dim moonlight, all following the lead of Longrunner, who was running with the were-creature that was Tanithia next to him. Grey Lady loped beside Gort.

(That was a very interesting change of form, Claw Fighter.). She looked at him with a smile. (And I must say, you make a very impressive wolf.)

He thought for a moment. "Claw Fighter" was a passable translation of "Swordsman," all things considered. And it was interesting just how rapidly the wolves had become friendly once he was named. By Grey Lady, as custom dictated. He glanced at her. (It's exhilarating, the power that comes with this change!)

She trotted just a bit closer, so that her thigh brushed his. (We could always head off to the deep trees for a short while . . .). Her suggestion was obvious, with her smile directed rather obviously upon him.

(Grey Lady, I don't do this sort of thing. You're nice, but . . .)

Her eyes flashed momentarily. (You're a wolf now. One of the Noble Ones. Let's not have any of that supposed human superiority!)

He avoided her eyes as they proceeded. (I'll have to admit, you're quite a lovely sight yourself. But . . . but I'd rather not get Longrunner angry with me. He's too smart and massive.)

(Don't be fooled by him. He's just a pup at heart.)

(A pup? He's strong enough to snap a bull's neck!)

Her smile was proud. (Oh yes . . . he's done that as well.)

(Er, let's change the subject, shall we?)

Longrunner glanced briefly behind. (Seid Lady, it looks as though my consort is trying to get your friend off to herself. He probably won't agree, though.)

Tanithia looked at Longrunner. It was interesting how a change in shape also affected the mind, making her think and feel far more like a wolf, and to see events from their own not-entirely-alien viewpoint. Longrunner, for example, was solidly muscular and extremely handsome now, with a commanding presence that explained his position as pack leader.

(And what are your feelings toward me, milord?)

Longrunner looked at her with a smile. (You were graceful in human form, and you're even better in wolf-shape, Seid Lady. I like you. But I have my responsibility to the pack, and custom dictates that only Grey Lady can be my mate. It's reality, pretty one. Were things different, though . . .)

Tanithia looked ahead, her sharp wolf senses viewing much more than could her human ones. (What's that glow ahead? I sense something unpleasant there.)

(It's the den of the Dark Ones, as we told you. A little closer and the pack will have to leave you . . . it wouldn't be good for the Dark Ones to know we've brought you here.)

"It's a chapel!" exclaimed Gort. "Of all things, it's a chapel!" They were in human form again, with the high mountain night air cool on their bare skin. For the time being they were concealed while they began the building of Forces prior to attacking, using the jewels from the tower rite a week before.

The talisman that had hung around her neck as a wolf now dangled between her breasts, glowing of its own light, though most of its large stones, removed, lay in a pattern before her. She was engrossed in using a breathing exercise to build Power within the talisman, then transferring much of it to the stones, so that they glowed like brightening coals before her.

Their eyes were well acclimatized to the dim moonlight, so the scene before them looked clear and bright. The dark ruins of a small village, once the home of hunters or miners, but now tumbled and decayed. The only structure which was totally intact was the nest of the evil they had come to destroy. Ironically, it was housed in a place of worship for the new cult of the One true God, its Unbalanced Cross mounted atop it.

She had removed one large pulsing diamond from its mounting and after charging it still more had proceeded to affix it in her navel. Immediately its glow brightened and its swirling sparkles of power linked with the handful of glistening and pulsing jewels she held, making their glow yet more intense, flaring in accordance with her will. She saw that he had flint and tinder waiting. "I think we're ready," she said. She stood, a smoothly rounded sculpture of silver in the moonlight, and held her arms out to him.

"Embrace me, dear Gort. The feel of our naked bodies together will give us both extra strength and power when we attack that pesthole." He swept her into his arms, luxuriating in the feel of her warm body against his. They kissed, long and passionate, with mouths open and tongues seeking. He felt of her breasts, caressing her erect nipples and pressing himself against her more and more excitedly. Her hips pressed hard against his loins.

With an effort she pulled herself back from him. "That's good . . . so very good," she said thickly, the passion sweeping her deeply. We've got work to do, love. Think power. Think magic."

The effort was hard for him as well, though he did as she said. To his surprise, their talismans, the handful of power jewels, and the nexus-diamond at her navel sparkled in even brighter light, a numbus of power about them.

They struck a fire and lit several torches. In the brilliant flaring light they slowly advanced on the dark chapel, the stones and grass cold beneath their feet. She carried softly glowing stones, and each also a crude stone knife.

"Did you feel it when we lit the fire?" he asked softly. "It was as though suddenly something realized that we were here."

"You're right," she answered. "Be ready with that flint dagger you've fashioned. There's mist coming out of that open door."

He had time to look at her briefly and to admire her perfect, unclad form, with her long hair swirling about her. Wary, alert, confident.

Icy cold . . . a sudden, bone-chilling iciness. Something was sliding out from the darkened doorway, half-hidden in the mist.

The fat, looping tentacle suddenly lashed towards them, its sucker pads undulating.

He slashed at it, sidestepping, and feeling the rubbery flesh part. Tanithia hurled a flaring torch unerringly in through the doorway, then immediately threw one of the flame-stones she had been charging.

The tentacle pulled back, and something snapped through the air for her throat . . . to splatter against another of the jewels she held up as a shield. He transfixed the squirming thing with the slightly glowing blade of the flint knife, and a wordless shriek rent the cold, moonlit air.

A Presence, mordant and evil, thickened in the air about them, until their hackles stood erect. The first torch seemed to have gone out or to be put out. Holding her own flint knife at the ready, she threw another torch into the building.

A scream, high and unhuman. And sobs, breaking into insane laughter . . . and back into sobs again.

Gort felt a breeze start, and began flaming the grass windward of the chapel as Tanithia cautiously stepped around towards the back of the building, searching for another entrance.

Like the snap of a thick whip, a tentacle darted out to snap about her naked waist . . . to break away as it hit the glowing power nexus flaring at her navel!

Tanithia swung furiously, glowing stone in one hand and flint knife in the other, beating and slashing at the thing as pieces of the looping horror sloughed away.

Gort rushed in, slashing. Constant, agonized shrieks, and waves of horror and revulsion emanated from the now flaming interior of the chapel as old, dry wood flared like tinder.

A gaunt, ravaged figure ran screaming from the building, robes burning, to fall scrabbling at the ground. Gort and Tanithia ran close, then halted as one, remembering that though this was a human it was also a very evil human. In short, quick movements Gort rolled the screaming figure on the ground, to put out the flames. A pain-controlled face glared up at them.

"I served the Dark Ones, I did their biddings. You ruined it . . . you ruined it . . ." The robe had flared again, and the man's skin blackened as the fire licked over it. Agony twisted the gaunt frame as suddenly it convulsed violently and then, as suddenly, stilled.

"His heart," commented Tanithia. "The agony drove it to stop." She looked up, and around, smoothing back her hair over her shoulders as, crouched, she looked about. "The evil feel in the air. It's gone."

"As are those repulsive . . . things," Gort observed.

"They were his emanations, with no existence other than his own," she said. They stood and watched as the flames wrapped about the building, and as it fell in. They were still there, sitting with their arms about one another, as the wolves quietly came up alongside them.

Longrunner nuzzled Tanithia. (Thank you, Seid Lady. We felt the change immediately.) She rubbed him behind his ears, and for a few moments he allowed her to place his head in her lap as she stroked him.

Gort looked at Tanithia, smiling as she enjoyed the feel of Longrunner's fur on her skin. "Dawn will be soon, Tanithia. Do you think we should be returning?" Grey Lady nudged close, and rubbed her shoulders softly.

"By all means," she said. "We couldn't hold wolf form in the daylight. I'll put the remaining power jewels in the ruins . . . just to make certain they don't use it again . . . and we'll change back."

Dawn was breaking as they walked back into camp.

HE shadows of the evening were deepening. The hymns had been sung and the minister was well into his sermon for the night's prayer meeting. The parishoners were intent, and his voice had been thundering forth on the wages of sin and the utter damnation of the wicked, in this world and the next.

As he paused for a moment of dramatic effect, the sound of a horse could be heard, galloping rapidly nearer. The minister frowned. In the darkness such speed on a horse would be reckless; there must be a reason for such unseemly haste.

The rider reined up outside the hall, the horse snorted and stamped, the sound of its heavy breathing loud and obvious as those in the meeting hall paused and turned towards the rough-hewn door.

Abruptly the door flew open, and a cloaked figure, haggard from hard travelling, strode in. He took off his riding gloves and slapped them against his hand.

"Forgive my interruption, brother," he said, looking around.

"Brother Elijus!" exclaimed the minister. "The Inquisitor and Witchfinder-General! This, to say the least, is a surprise." There was an astonished muttering and exclaiming from the congregation as they turned with renewed interest to gaze on the newcomer. Many of the men stood, for this was someone of whom they all had heard. Perhaps a few of the women shrank back slightly, and perhaps one or two of the girls flushed, bit their lips, and hoped that none noticed that they averted their eyes, hoping that this pious man, so noted for his uncanny finding of witch-women, would not look at them, for the Old Ways still lived – a bit here and a bit there, within them. And there were others, adherents of the new cult of the god of fire and sword, who felt on the surface that they were devout . . . yet something deep within them felt a pull otherwise. And they hoped they would not be seen, for the guilt within them, though they might not have recognized it, showed their true inclinations.

For the Witch-finder was known for his merciless and icily brutal approach to wringing confessions from women and even, occasionally, from men.

He looked around. "I ask your leave, Reader. Send the women home: there's men's work to be done. A holy, terrible work." He smiled. "As it was in the old days, so it shall be again."

The women, obeying the commands of their husbands and fathers, hastened out and hurried home. A few that lived nearby listened to the raised voices of the intense discussion that followed for the next hour, catching snatches of words and conversation.

"She's there, I tell you," said Elijus finally. "I know she's there; I've seen her."

"But," said the minister, "She died at Valerium almost three years ago. Some of us here saw it."

"I know, brother," said Elijus. "As did I. But yet the Power given to me by the Great One and the Son of the Sword is unerring: I recognized her. You know that I can see through the glamourie that witches and the other servants of the Dark One can put up, to cloud the minds of men. I'd know her features anywhere. And her dance . . ." He took the minister's arm and shuddered. "Her dance was sin itself!"

"Perhaps," said another. "But even if we believe you, there are others in the Protectorate at Valerium, even the head of our church in the Great Conference, who view you as being too extreme."

"Ridiculous," snapped Elijus. "They've lost the true meaning of our faith: THAT THE WORD OF OUR GOD MUST BE SENT FORTH BY FIRE AND BY SWORD, as it says in the Book of Goodness. If they think that I am part and parcel of some fanatical little cult, then it is they whose minds are fogged by the Dark." He paused for a few moments, getting his bitter emotions back under control. Then he returned to the original purpose of his journey.

"But don't you see . . . she must be brought back to face the divine justice of the Church. And, brothers, this time we'll see that she doesn't escape the stake! She won't serve the Dark One again. And when we've delivered her to the high council bound and chained . . . then they'll realize that our ways are the true ways. They'll stop this soft weakness and return to our divine mission of rooting out those servants of Darkness who still survive in the back hills and the valleys . . . even in the cities themselves. Remember . . . the Old Ways die hard, no matter how many sinful women, using their beauty to spin evil, are sent screaming to the torturers or die writhing in the flames. For it is our god's way!" He smiled triumphantly and most in the congregation heartfully murmured "Amen."

"But", interjected one of the other men, "You say there are soldiers with her."

"Yes," said Elijus, rubbing his chin thoughtfully. "I couldn't tell where they were from. Their officer had the look of a nobleman about him, but though they talked and drank a lot, none of them quite said exactly who they were or from whence they came." He chuckled grimly. "Though I daresay that once we've got her, a few hours of persuasion with the tongs, the boot, the rack, and such implements of godly inquisition . . . we'll know all of her confederates. Don't worry on that account. The Church will dispose of them as the scriptures dictate."

"Hm . . . that might be," said the first. "But if there are soldiers and as sturdy as you say, they won't be merely random rabble that we could simply chase away with a fast attack and some threats. To me they sound like professional men-at-arms. And if they're devoted to the witch it would probably take a small army to overcome them."

"Aye," said Elijus. "That's the reason we'll have to ride close and silent . . . follow them like shadows. We'll have to make it a point not to be seen while we bide our time . . . until we can snatch her from under their proverbial noses! Yet we'd best be careful, since she might have other confederates in her service . . . "

The rusty iron door of the dungeon grated open and shambling steps echoed down the dripping stairs. Rats scurried out of the way into the dark corners, and peered out with fear-reddened eyes. A serpent hissed and slithered

into a crumbled pile of stone, knowing terror in its own alien way.

Steps echoed across the damp flagstones. The mouldering phosphorescence on the walls cast an eerie glow. Faint . . . but sufficient for some eyes. Any who would have the necessity of seeing in so forbidding a place might prefer to see as little as possible.

"Water . . . water . . . "came a tortured voice from the back of a cell. "Please . . . " Then the prisoner, starved and ill though he might be, suddenly drew in his breath at the sight of that which passed his cell. And turned, sobbing in terror, hiding his face against the slime-dripping wall, as if seeking solace. And, above all, to hide his eyes from that which he saw.

The steps paused before another cell. The door grated open, hard and slow. No key was needed, for none dared escape. The walls and ceiling luminesced in a grayish-green. A rat scurried from the floor into its den, squeaking in terror.

The girl crouched in the far corner screamed . . . then stifled yet a second scream. Somehow she was still comely and well-shaped, despite her inprisonment. Neither illness nor starvation were consuming her just as yet, though her sanity was becoming more and more doubtful . . . especially to herself. Her face was beautiful, if strained and dirty. Her dark hair, knotted and tangled, hung down over her bare shoulders as she clutched the single ragged garment about her breasts.

"No," she pleaded. "No! You can't be coming for me again!"

"Quiet, whore," came the rasping . . . almost hissing . . . reply, from a voice which sounded fundamentally different from anything human.

"What do you want of me this time?" She spoke tensely, trying to keep her terror from sweeping all away. She pressed her nearly unclad body back against the cold stone wall.

"Ahhh . . . " hissed the mocking, nonhuman voice. "So the great Sorceress of Evil begs again." A horny clawed hand reached out and seized her by the shoulder, hurling her onto the filthy flags of the floor. "You let your evil get out of control," taunted the voice again as she averted her eyes and tried not to whimper where she lay. "You did many things to destroy many others, but you never felt . . . never realized . . . that you lacked the strength and the courage within yourself to control Ultimate Evil when at last you summoned it forth."

She said nothing, but gazed downward blankly in the near-darkness. A tear dropped into the foul dirt of the floor.

"Come, whore. Queen of Evil you styled yourself, and yet you lacked the strength of character to control . . . US!" A clawed thing something like a hand seized her long hair and cruelly yanked her head back so that she gazed into the hideous face that jeered at her. A stifled scream, then a sob, broke from her lips as she was forced to look at the monstrous visage.

"Stand, O Daughter of Evil You called us forth, but now the puppet has become the puppeteer." Resignedly, her head down, she slowly stood, bare feet flat upon the

filth-encrusted stones, arms down at her side, her hair tumbled and tangled over her bare shoulders and around her face. The clawed "hand" with its strange fingers reached out and ran along her cheek, bringing forth a trickle of blood from the deep scratch. She trembled and kept her eyes downcast. The hand played over her throat, pinching and bringing forth yet another trickle. She gasped slightly at the pain that trailed over her well-shaped shoulder and then down to her full breasts, exposed as they were over the scanty rags she had wrapped about her.

"You are still beautiful," said the rasping voice. Your Art gave you much that we have still not taken in spite of the pacts we have forced you to concede." The low, evil chuckle made her glance upward fearfully for a moment, her hackles rising at the tone.

"No matter how you styled yourself as evil, no matter how many unspeakable crimes you committed against your own kind, there is still the spark of something within you which has not yet been totally perverted." There was a pause. Then the claw shot out, grasped her garment and tore it from her.

"But no matter, sow. You are ours. Come to me!"

"No," she whispered. "No . . . please!" The hand reached out, seized her, and the creature dragged her, screaming, onto the floor. She averted her eyes as much as she could from the hideous being which now mounted her until, with pain, even a perverted sort of ecstacy flowed from her loins, into her very soul . . . being more agony and terror with just a taunting bit of the pleasure she had once revelled in during years past.

"You respond, O Whore of Darkness . . . even though you do not wish to. Look on me, and know who I am!" She turned her face painfully, unwillingly, to the blasphemous visage before her as her hips rose and fell beneath those of the scaled thing which surmounted her.

She screamed. A scream partly of shame at herself, but mostly of sheer, insane horror. She faded towards merciful unconsciousness, the feel of talons cruelly gripping her yet-tender body.

"Oh no," came the voice as the darkness flooded in. "We have a task for you. Else we wouldn't have kept you alive!" The chilling laughter and its possible implications finally drove her into oblivion.

Tanithia's eyes were stern as she stood regally in the flickering firelight before her twelve soldiers. They were drawn to near-attention, clad as if for battle, the firelight glistening from their armor and their weapons. Their attention was completely on the vision of beauty which stood before them.

The firelight glistened on the jewels which hung in her golden-red hair, spread out in a nimbus about her head and sweeping wing-like over her shoulders and down to her hips. Jewels and an ancient five-pointed symbol were clasped about her throat. Fire glistened on her bare limbs, for she wore only a very slight, almost transparent white tunic laced to the curves of her body with cords of silver. A garter of wrought silver and gold was buckled about her well-shaped thigh and anklets of silver and gold jingled slightly as she shifted position. Likewise the jewels of the rings she wore on her fingers and toes glistened like living fire.

The firelight glowed on her full breasts, and off her rounded shoulders, emphasizing the richness of her bosom as she inhaled further. The red areolas pushed upwards above the gossamer white cloth which scarcely concealed anything of her fullness.

She affixed the men with an eye of command. The teasing, erotic playfulness which she had worn like a cloak had fallen away, and all felt that *this* was the true woman of magic who had accompanied them. Perhaps they had suspected it in the past, but now, as the flame seemed to lend a nimbus of fire and power about her . . . they knew.

"Tomorrow," she said in a voice soft, yet calculated in strength and modulated in power, "Tomorrow we assault the Castle Drakenstane. The forces we'll be meeting aren't of human origin by any means: They're the demonic perversion which men have made of great cthonic powers brought forth and shaped in evil and spite. They're strong, and anyone unprepared could die . . . hideously. But you'll be prepared, and you're going to win." She smiled. "You've known, good friends, that I was preparing you during this journey. I've been building a Power within you, and a strength that no demonic evil can overcome; it's the strength . . . the force . . . of that which creates rather than destroys. It's the power of love and desire, rather than that of hatred and repulsion. It is that which ultimately is good for all living things. So now hold forth your blades and cross them all before me, so that you may swear fealty to me . . . and that I may vest your weapons, and your bodies and souls, with Power."

Swords sang from their sheaths and rang crossed before her. From a jewelled scabbard which she wore, strapped about her shapely hips, she drew forth a sword of archaic design on which runes seemed to glisten and glow with a light all of their own. She held it aloft, the firelight glistening more and more brightly on the soft curves of her body, on and through the thin garment which she wore, on the jewels that adorned her, and on the nimbus of red-gold hair which framed her head and shoulders in a more-than-human glow.

And especially the light glistened and sparkled off the sword which she raised.

"I stand here on this night," she began softly, "Acting as vicaress of the Great Goddess. It is She whose power flows though me, though I magnify Her and work Her magics, by what I know, by what beauty and what magnetism I may gain. Thus must I become one with Her . . . to draw forth," her voice became louder now, "The Power which flows from the stars themselves. The Power of the universe. The Power of all which sparks life itself . . . all which gives sentience and strength and the triumph of that which lives everywhere. I call upon thee, O great Witch-Goddess, known by a million names in a million, million universes, to grant for us the Power which we shall invoke on the morrow to destroy the base perversions which the twisted minds of twisted men have spawned. Come upon us NOW, I do ask!"

The glow grew brighter, and ever yet brighter. Her sword was now unmistakably gleaming brilliantly of its own light. She lowered it, raising one hand on high, and it seemed that lightning leaped from the sky to the flaring jewels of her upreached hand . . . that vast Power now suddenly coursed through her.

Her body stiffened, and her hair stirred and flowed out from her . . . almost impossibly far, seemingly, as flame itself leaped from her blade to theirs. They all felt the shock of Power flowing into their weapons and into themselves . . . with a strength as if Light itself were

flooding into their very beings, making their own blades glow and sparkle in the bright firelight, as Power streamed forth seemingly from every star that glowed in the sky above them.

Vast energies flowed through the body of this suddenly awesome witch-woman before them — whose eyes seemed no longer to be human, but something far more, for a short while. Power flooded from her slender but now iron-strong arms into the like steel of her blade, charging them and filling them with the Power and the strength that seemed as one with the mountains, with the forests, with the waters, with the stars themselves.

The almost unbearable glow grew and swelled about them, as though the living light of the heavens were opened upon them all.

Then she lowered her hand, and it began to diminish . . . to fade . . . And was gone.

There was a unified indrawing of breath from all, and a few astonished words . . . for they had felt a beauty and a light which few had known, save in a somewhat similar way: in the arms of those whom they loved.

Tanithia looked at each of them, her arms tired and lowered to her sides, her sword dragging its point in the dust at her toes. The firelight glistened on her, but the supernatural power was there no more, merely a very tired but smiling and comely woman who looked at them with a sleepy warmth in her eyes.

"I thank you," she said softly. "Now, let's get some rest. We're going to have need of this Power tomorrow." She sheathed her weapon. "This rite is ended, and you are dismissed."

They stepped back, as if released from an enchantment . . . unwillingly so. With the grace of a dancer she picked up her cloak and drew it about her shoulders. Briefly she struck a pose before them, breasts swelling against the thin cloth of her tunic, legs well displayed as she spread her delicately shaped feet apart and put her hands on her hips, smiling. "Rest apart tonight. Tomorrow, if all goes well . . . we'll see."

She briefly ran her finger across a nipple, caressing it for a moment, smiled, pulled the cloak about her, and departed.

 HE following day dawn broke gray and gloomy, and as they proceeded the skies grew darker and ever yet more threatening. Rain lashed the hillsides, yet hardly more than sprinkling where the horsemen rode. The horses, sensing what was in the air and about them, were uneasy . . . and their restiveness increased as the day continued.

The soldiers were apprehensive, but like men going into battle who are well prepared, the apprehension only sharpened their complete confidence in themselves and in the witch-woman who rode beside their commander.

Thunders rumbled through the mountain canyons, and once an avalanche seemed imminent. The horses were near panic, and had to be controlled forcibly.

"Dark . . . it's uncommonly dark," growled Waldmann.

"I don't believe I've ever seen it quite like this." He looked around uneasily.

"You're fortunate, my love," said Tanithia. "The Dark Forces are waiting and they know we're coming. They'll try again and again to ward us off, yet if we fled in fear I'm certain that no one would escape these valleys alive." She peered off into the dimness ahead. "How far yet to Castle Drakenstane?"

"Only perhaps two hours' ride, my lady. Though it looks like a long two hours." He wrapped his cloak about him in the gusting wind and looked at Tanithia, who was clad as lightly as ever, her amber hair blowing long and free in the wind. "Aren't you chilly, my lady? Would you care for a cloak? Certainly those breeches which display your legs and your . . . ah . . . hinter areas so well, and that cut-up shirt you're almost wearing can't be very warm. There's quite a bit more of your exquisite skin showing than there is concealed!"

She smiled at him, and for a moment crossed her arms under her breasts, to emphasize the cleavage. Though her nipples stood out clearly under the thin cloth, she didn't seem to have the monumental chill-bumps he would have expected on her fully rounded bosom.

"No, my dear one . . . there are other things that keep me warm," She reached out and touched his guantleted hand. "For once it's not desire or affection for those whom I know and love. There are . . . deeper powers, and when they begin glowing . . . the ordinary world doesn't matter any more." She raised herself even more erect in the saddle and looked to and fro into the storm-torn landscape. It was, he felt, as if she were eagerly sensing much more than ordinary eyes could perceive. The wind swirled her hair about her once more, and she laughed.

"My love," she exulted, "When the powers are like

this . . . I could walk naked through a blizzard, lie in the snows . . . and never care!"

Somehow he couldn't think of anything appropriate to say, as he bundled his cloak closer about his stocky frame.

She dug her bare heels into the flanks of her mount to urge him along, reached forward to rub his ears and reassure him, for the beast was frightened. But the horse drew immediate reassurance from her touch and her words. Lightning split the sky, shattering a tree nearby. The horses started for a moment and then were brought back under control almost immediately by their riders.

Tanithia's rich, challenging laughter filled the momentary silence. Somehow her exultant joy gave strength and reassurance to both men and horses alike.

Elijus reined in his horse briefly on the high promontory and gazed across the valley towards the rugged mountains beyond.

"By the Son," he exclaimed. "Darkness . . . darkness like the Pit is beyond those mountains! Zephanaias, what's on the other side of that mountain range?" His lieutenant rode up behind him, the twoscore men behind him apprehensively peering ahead into the darkening sky. Some openly clutched at their own earth-crosses for comfort.

Zephanaias squinted and looked about. "Drakenstane . . . definitely it's Drakenstane. And the castle should be right over in that direction . . . where it's the darkest."

"Drakenstane," said Elijus slowly. "what do you know about it?"

"Not much," said the other. "It's an old place, built on a site that was there long before the histories. Yet it's remote and most people from other provinces have long thought that it's fallen to ruin. It isn't, though."

"Hm. And yet she goes this way."

"Aye, and all of her men. The signs are clear on the trail."

"I see. Then she must be going there, or to some place near, on some sort of a rendezvous." His eyes narrowed. "I dread to think what congress she'll be having with others of the Dark One. If so, then our mission is all the more important. Follow me!" He laid his rowelled spurs to the flank of his horse, and with a creak of harness and the rattling of shod hooves upon the stones, led the way down into the valley, riding into the gathering darkness as heavy rain began to spatter on the rocks about them, and on them.

Lightning crackled above the crags, crashes filling the darkness and thunder boomed incessantly.

"We're nearly there. But . . . by the Old ones . . . it's so dark!" exclaimed Waldmann, struggling to control his frightened horse. "There ought to be two hours of sunlight left, yet it looks almost like night!"

"So it won't be very long," called Tanithia. "Whatever's taken root here, it's certainly strong!" She stood in the stirrups and looked ahead intently, then pointed eagerly: "There! Isn't that the castle?" A bone-white expanse of stone wall could be seen in the flickering lightning.

"Indeed, that's the place." He glanced about as lightning strokes briefly limned the crags around them. "It's as though all the forces of Darkness are gathered about to protect their own. I hadn't thought they would be so strong!"

She smiled grimly. "The Forces of Darkness do well . . . particularly when they can draw on the evil from the darkest corners of men's souls to give them strength and sustenence," she said. "Let's turn off the trail and prepare ourselves. We'll have to ride directly into a battle, I think."

Shortly they dismounted. The horses were terrified and only the skill of the riders kept them from pitching and rearing. Tanithia walked from one to another, talking into the horses' ears softly, and caressing them. Each in turn calmed with her presence, as she in her own way communicated to them some of her own confidence and strength.

A short while later and all were in mail and helmets, fully girded for battle. Helms glistened in the rain which at long last began to sweep over them from time to time.

Tanithia had prepared herself for the conflict in a different way. Shedding her shirt and wearing only the breeks, which she slit even higher to completely bare her thighs, she adorned her neck with the jewels she had worn the night before. Her fingers and toes were bejewelled likewise, with rings of gold and silver set with precious stones. She slipped anklets of intricately wrought precious metals over her bare feet. Strands of sparkling jewels were strung in her hair and draped about her full breasts, even using perfumed gum to fasten them about her nipples. A single large diamond hung in her wild hair directly over her forehead. She girded her loins with the ornate sword belt and unlaced the breeches for comfort so that only the sword belt remained, low across her hips, to barely hold the breeches in place.

"You look ravishing, my lovely one," said the count as they mounted again. "And I'm sure that every man here would like to do so if the circumstances were, shall we say, a bit more hospitable." The wind rose to a howl behind them, and lightning split the rain-sheeted sky.

"Indeed, my lord," she smiled back, though with an undertone fully as grim as his own. "Yet you know the reason as I do. Even more than the need to inspire and draw strength through the men, I've got to make my body free to send forth as much of that Power as might be needed." She peered into the dimness ahead. "And I think we'll be needing a lot to overcome this."

The walls, gray and wet, loomed over them, with the flashing of the lightning becoming incessant now, limning the great castle in unnatural brightness. Yet it seemed to each of the twelve men that they themselves were bathed in a different, better sort of nimbus. And each felt more than just his own courage within him. Each felt the rampant, inexorable flux of the power they had felt the night before, in the rite with the supernally gifted witch-queen.

Something dark abruptly flew over the castle wall, fell towards them. A shriek of unhuman madness seemed to come from it. Tanithia snapped her sword aloft, and it seemed as though blue flame licked along it . . . to solidly blast that which fell through the damp air. There seemed a scream that faded abruptly, and something ragged and flat hit the rocks near them and shattered.

"A corpse," muttered Gort. "Merely a rotten, dried corpse."

"And now as harmless as any useless clay would be." said Tanithia.

There was a rumble of the portcullis being raised. The moat, if one ever existed there, was long gone, so the path into the castle was clear. A moment of silence, and the air grew thicker and heavier.

Then a horde of white, gibbering creatures charged from the great doorway, swinging rusty blades as they ran towards the troop. The men spurred their horses into a defensive line and met the unholy beings with their own swords, which flashed and glowed in the darkness. The creatures shrieked and died, dissolving into slime and to bone as soon as they were sliced. The remainder, gibbering and falling back, eyed the soldiers' glowing swords with terror.

Tanithia led the troop yet closer to the main gate.

Lightning flashed, outlining her features and limning her upturned breasts. She gestured for them to halt before the castle gate and shouted an invocation, while swinging her blade such that glittering sparks flew from it . . . as if she were weaving a glowing star before her.

Suddenly the gate disgorged vast quantities of bulbous things that half-flowed, half-lurched toward them. Tanithia flexed her hands together and drew them apart, and a globe of sliver light grew, shining brightly, flared between her palms. Abruptly, she hurled the ball at the first of the creatures. The ball shattered in a soundless explosion of brilliant light as a shriek of unearthly agony came from the creature, and it dissolved back on itself, to be swallowed up by another, which made its way dumbly towards her. Again her fingers flexed gracefully. Her bracelets and her jewelry glittered, and yet another even brighter ball of pure light built in brilliant intensity between her palms. This again she hurled at the next creature attempting to come from the gate.

Her lips moved, smiling in silent concentration as yet again and again they came. Some she destroyed and others ran to be annihilated by the troopers until the great portal stood empty.

Tanithia laughed and threw back her hair, calling to Waldmann and to the others. "First you've got to get the pus out of a boil. Then you've got to go in and heal it!"

Again she evoked, sword flashing, the sparkling pentagram before her. A few small monstrosities ran forth, to be quickly dispatched by the troopers. Then . . . nothing. The storm itself seemed to have eased, and the sky seemed a bit brighter.

Digging her naked heels into her mount's flank, she urged her horse under the massive gate of the portcullis. Waldmann caught his breath. If that huge gate fell she would almost certainly be smashed instantly.

Instead she drew her sword and cast a powder from a pouch on her saddle all about the portal, and even up into the crevasses overhead. Stretching forth her blade, she seemingly extended herself, sitting tall and compelling in the saddle. The sword grew brighter, and brighter yet as she allowed the radiance to build around her stronger and stronger. Then she aimed it above into the crevasse from which the portcullis would fall, and flame leaped from the edges of her weapon.

Shrieks of nonhuman agony split the night, and a smell of brimstone was strong in the smoke which wafted from around the huge gate and its openings. Her horse reared briefly and she reined him tightly as she called back to the men. "The gate is secure. Follow me!" She galloped into the courtyard.

For a few moments, she was ahead of the troopers who followed her. And in those moments, yet another attack.

Repellent scaled beings, larger than a man, rushed upon her from various portals about the central courtyard. She swung her blade, cleaving one in twain. One, coming swiftly from the other side, suddenly grasped for her bare foot, as if to yank her from the saddle. Yet not quite did the creature touch her, for a brilliant flame leaped from her jewelry . . . the anklets and toe rings . . . and seared the creature's arm, so that it howled with agony for a moment as the flame consumed it. A sudden backstroke by her blade sent a flaming, hideous head rolling across the paves.

Others ran for her, and yet found themselves even unable to touch her horse before the flame leaped to their shambling forms and began consuming their unwholesome bodies.

The soldiers galloped in rapidly, swinging their weapons with deadly efficiency, and sounding war-cries.

More of the creatures swarmed out, to die immediately, falling in noisome heaps that began almost immediately to rot away.

The unearthly din and demonic shrieking raised to its crescendo as others came forth. The swords of the soldiers swung viciously, and Tanithia's blade darted back and forth . . . all of them weaving flame and light, to litter the great courtyard with dead and dying demon-creatures.

Something was hurled from a balcony. Gort caught it on his sharp blade, and it dissolved even before he could make out the form of the repulsive thing. Tanithia saw his action and again producing one of the balls of light, hurled it to the balcony, where its dazzling, soundless flare destroyed the unseen things huddled there.

In fast order she created and flicked several other glistening white spheres which hit and flashed dazzingly . . . leaving balconies and parapets empty, save for shadows and dust.

"Look . . . up there!" cried one of the men, pointing with his sword. "One of the creatures. It seems to have a woman struggling with it!"

Tanithia looked up sharply. Indeed, there were several of the creatures on the high parapet, as if preparing for a last stand. Tauntingly, the largest lifted, between its two clawed hands, the body of a young woman who writhed piteously in its cruel grip. Her black dress did not conceal the full roundness of her white breasts. The beast pulled up the hem of her dress and lay her roughly on the balcony.

"By the Gods . . . that blasphemous thing is raping her!" cried Gort.

Tanithia vaulted from her saddle, for she was the closest to the balcony. Up she ran, with the soldiers only a few paces behind her. The first of the creatures came at her with an ear-splitting screech which keened even higher as with a single slash she disemboweled it. Then yet others swarmed towards her, swinging blades which could not meet the nimbus of Power about her body, and which were beaten aside by her blade, or by the swords of the soldiers, who were now at her very heels.

Ahead she could see the largest of the demon-creatures, its body rising and falling over the girl, who writhed as if in a paroxysm of either ecstasy or of screaming agony. Then the last of the creatures were falling.

The large demon-beast glared at Tanithia, its scarlet eyes glaring balefully, stepped away from the moaning girl, and hurled her at Tanithia. The girl's body hit Tanithia full and hard, for the witch-woman would not sidestep to sacrifice the other. The two women's bodies slammed into the stone wall, knocking the breath from Tanithia, then went down in a jumble of bare limbs and full skirts.

The troopers lost stride for a moment, then swarmed past, though Gort was immediately beside them, shaking Tanithia back to alertness and seeing to the other.

"Take care of her," the witch-woman gasped, then sprang to her toes and ran towards the doorway where the thing was momentarily fending off the blows of three soldiers. It saw her and its resolve seemed to melt. The thing turned and ran in a single serpentine motion. She sprang past the men after the demon-creature, which had rounded a corner. As she leaped to a guard position just beyond the corner, she saw that rather than waiting to ambush her, the bestial thing was vanishing down a dim corridor. For all its huge size it was very fast indeed.

Soon, though she ran swiftly after it, the creature had disappeared in a maze of darkened passageways. She paused and spoke an unkind word as she stubbed a toe into a decorative but badly placed piece of stonework lost in the gloom, and realized that she had no light save for that which glowed from her sword. And even that glow had dimmed much.

Perhaps, she thought, she and the others could track the demon-thing down later. She retraced her steps, now conscious of the coldness of the floor beneath her feet. The light was brighter now from the occasional high windows and she realized that not only had the storm broken, but the darkness of the sky was fading as full daylight was returning.

By the time she reached the parapet, the sun was breaking through the incredibly dark clouds, which were in turn dissolving rapidly away.

Waldmann had deployed the soldiers to search the castle, starting with the courtyard, to kill whatever they saw.

"In pairs," he was saying. "Remain in pairs, and each of you keep the other covered at all times. Search the place carefully and don't miss anything. Anything at all!"

He looked at her. "Did you get the last big one?" he asked as she limped up.

"No, it eluded me in the darkness. I think it may have made for the cellars or the catacombs. If you can get free let's go looking for it."

Swordsman Gort was attending to the bruises of the girl who otherwise seemed not too badly hurt either physically or, rather surprisingly, emotionally.

Her gown fit her closely, laced closely over her slender arms, and ending in dagged hems, clinging closely to her shapely body, to display rather than to conceal her full bosom and emphasizing the cleavage between her breasts. Her hair was jet-black and combed straight; it was remarkably well in order, considering the mistreatment she had undergone in the last few minutes, Tanithia thought.

And indeed, her manner was extraordinarily well composed. She smoothed the black dress over her long thighs and eased her white feet into the sandals which lay nearby.

"I give you greetings," she said. "And thanks. It's been an incredibly terrifying time for me." She looked at each of them and then at Tanithia. Her eyes seemed darker and even more intense as they rested on the witch. She drew in her breath.

As did Tanithia . . . for this woman was beautiful and magnetic as well. "How are you feeling?" asked Tanithia, touching the other's shoulder near a bruise that marred the fair skin. "You must be hurting all over."

"Nay, not any more, thank you. In the time I've spent in this haunted place . . . an eternity, it seems . . . I've learned to ignore pain as much as possible. Forgive me . . . I am called 'Lyia'. Welcome to . . . this place." She smiled ruefully and gestured at the massive walls about them. "Whether I wanted it or not, this place seems to have been my home for a while."

"For a while?" queried Count Waldmann. "What of the nobleman who administered this province? He dwelt here until these . . . monstrosities . . . took over."

"I don't know," she said, looking deeply at the count. "There was no sign of him when I came, two or more months ago."

Gort stiffened almost imperceptibly beside them, but said nothing.

"I am, by calling, a sorceress," she said. "And I was drawn to this spot. Things went out of my control badly . . . very badly indeed. I found myself imprisoned in the dungeons by these . . . creatures of the night."

"Yes," said Tanithia, her eyes still on the face and form of this strange woman. "I sense the flow of Power about you, and it's obvious that something has gotten very much out of control. Yet . . . you're not harmed by the attentions of that nightmare thing?"

"A bit sore, yes," answered Lyia, but my own Art is healing me rapidly." She smiled, but the smile seemed to be only on her lips and not in her eyes.

Perhaps, thought Waldmann, she was still too shocked from the hideous experience and the indignities to really be herself. Instead it seemed that she was being almost icily calm, considering what had happened. And, implicitly, considering what she must have undergone in the days and weeks before they had come to her rescue.

They looked about. The soldiers had all disappeared into the chambers and halls of the castle, and from here and there could be heard their voices calling to one another, as occasional skirmishes were joined, and shouts of victory as inevitably the men-at-arms triumphed.

Lyia looked up and squinted. "Oh, the sun's coming out . . . and it's too bright for my eyes. Let's go inside."

The two women led the way, their hips swaying almost in unison as Waldmann and Gort followed. Gort considered. One with golden-red hair, almost like the sun, scarcely clad in anything but the slashed trousers about her shapely hips and striding on silent bare feet as jewels swayed and sparkled about her. The other clothed in clinging black, with black hair that hung straight to fall in a swaying mass down past her hips. Both voluptrous, and both should have been achingly desirable. Yet he felt himself as distrusting of Lyia as he was drawn, with fervent passion, to Tanithia.

They walked on into the great hall, where a soldier was busily lighting the cresseted tapers in the walls about them. Lyia stopped for a moment before the great table and touched a finger to her white throat.

"Count Waldmann and Swordsman Gort I've met, but your name, lovely Lady, I didn't get." Lyia turned towards her, and their eyes again locked.

"Tanithia," said the witch-woman. "It's Tanithia."

I'm a sorceress myself, though if you'll pardon me for saying so, it looks like I'm a better one than you."

"I can't deny that," chuckled Lyia without humor. "Yet sorcery, witchery or whatever, and the company of many handsome men does well by you." She stepped back to gaze openly at Tanithia, from her jewelled toes to her tumbled golden hair. The intensity and boldness of the other's eyes was such that Tanithia found herself blushing.

"Yes, you're lovely," she said. "And these jewels." She touched gently at the chains and precious stones on the witch's breasts. "They're of an ancient design. And magical, aren't they?"

"Yes they are indeed. And quite useful in a magical battle such as this. Though over the natural power centers of one's body especially they can draw and send forth a vast amount of Power when it's really needed."

"Yes, I see," murmured Lyia, her eyes again meeting those of Tanithia.

Ridiculous, thought Tanithia to herself. Why should I feel like this? In spite of herself she felt fascinated by this dark-tressed woman. Her nipples had come to stand erect, and she wished briefly that she had a cloak or a shawl . . . unusual for one who normally was almost arrogantly proud of the perfection of her body, and never shamed by its erotic signals.

Lyia almost casually eyed her breasts as well, not missing Tanithia's erect nipples. She smiled slightly at the obvious sign of arousal that the witch-woman could not hide.

"I think, Count Waldmann," said Lyia, "that nearly all of your men have returned. It looks like they're finished scouting the castle and the grounds."

Each checked in with the count, describing the areas scouted and reporting them clear. Waldmann mentally double-checked to be certain that all portions of the great structure had been covered.

Tanithia felt an almost crackling touch as the tip of Lyia's thinly-covered breast brushed gently across her arm. She looked back sharply to find her eyes caught again by Lyia's dark and compelling gaze, and by the slight smile which curled her red lips while the raven-tressed sorceress gently ran a finger around her own nipple . . . clearly visible in outline as it pushed against the thin cloth of her gown.

"Tanithia," said Count Waldmann, and she started in surprise. "My dear, the men have all reported in. They've done their work and I think that it remains for you and I to commence with the final cleansing of this place."

"Of course," she said. "You're correct, as usual."

"Swords Sergeant," he said to the grizzled old trooper, "Take Swordsman Gort and set up quarters. Get the horses stabled and check the outside of the castle while we still have a little daylight left. You may see the Lady Lyia to her chambers if she desires.

"No," interjected Lyia. "Forgive me, but after all that's transpired, I'd much rather go with you, and with Lady Tanithia." Her eyes flickered from one to another like a frightened wild thing.

Ah, so she can actually show some emotion, thought Waldmann to himself. Perhaps there's still some soul left in her after all.

Together the three descended the broad stairs leading downwards, Lyia between the two of them. Count Waldmann deigned not to notice, though in truth he was somewhat amused, by the fact that Lyia always seemed to be a little closer to the Lady Tanithia, always seemed to be touching her arm, or being sure that her skirts brushed against Tanithia's legs.

As they went, Tanithia scattered a fine crystalline dust, sealing the castle bit by bit as she went. Occasionally she paused in some darkened chamber to hold a torch within, and then to slowly traverse the apparently empty space within, with the point of her luminescent sword. And from time to time there seemed to be distant screams of agony . . . though it could merely have been one's own imagination.

Yet on and on they went, methodically going through each level of the castle. Then, down into the cellars and into the lowest dungeons.

Tanithia went first down the narrow stairs, with Lyia behind her and Waldmann following to bring up the rear. Yet of all the places they had searched and purified, there seemed less of the evil presence here.

The witch-woman was very aware of the other's presence behind her. Always it seemed a soft, cool hand touched her shoulder or brushed her hair. Once as she paused the Lady Lyia was a bit slow and, by happenstance, bumped into her . . . then turned away in such a manner that her breast rubbed slowly across Tanithia's bare back, and her hair swept softly over Tanithia's arm.

"The cells seem empty except for bones," observed the count, thrusting his flaring torch into yet another of the fetid cells.

"Yes," said Lyia. "The creatures detested all things which live, and any whom they brought here considered themselves fortunate when finally death came."

"There's something up ahead," whispered Tanithia, peering into the dimness. "I hear a sound!" On her guard, she led them closer, and stared into a cell, shuddering as the tips of her breasts brushed against the cold, rusty iron.

The gibbering, starved, wild-eyed remnant of a man stared back at them with eyes that held no sanity. "Creatures . . . creatures of madness . . ." he muttered.

"The creatures of madness and evil . . . Beware . . ."

"Easy now . . . Easy now, poor fellow," said the count. "You're with friends." A whimpering came from within.

"They hide. They're everywhere. My God, they're hideous!" He lapsed into a terrified gibbering, his eyes on them.

"The only one who still barely lives. I could hear him from my cell," said Lyia.

A slight shading of sanity seemed to come back to the blank eyes as they focused on Lyia's frame. He laughed, though he did not smile. "Beware!" he said. "The Harlot of Darkness . . ." He laughed again even more. "The Harlot of Darkness . . . the opener of the Dark Portals!" His laughter broke into sobbing, then he paused to speak again. Lyia's hand moved slightly, unseen, and he lapsed merely into more insane laughter.

"Do I gather," asked the count drily, "That he has a low opinion of your magics, Demoiselle Lyia?"

"True, I failed disastrously," she said, casting her eyes downwards. "I ruined things, and it was only you who saved everything . . . including me. I would have had a fate as terrible as his, or any of the others whose bones are scattered in these stinking, empty cells."

Count Waldmann pushed hard on the rusty iron grating and it creaked open on corroded hinges. "Let me see the poor wretch," he said, picking his way distastefully through the filthy cell, then reached down to pick up the now unconscious prisoner. "My gods, he's light," muttered the count. "Though he should be. There's nothing to him but bones and a little skin. Perhaps only his madness kept him alive in all this starvation and torture."

Tanithia came close to the old, white-haired madman and touched his wild hair softly, murmuring small words of reassurance. For a moment, and a moment only, he stirred and looked up at her with eyes that were not totally insane. He smiled slightly, then lapsed again into unconsciousness.

"Count Waldmann," she said. "Stay here with him for a short time more. There can't be much more of these wretched dungeons. Lyia and I will check them out together. I for one am going to be happy to go back to the upper levels." She looked down distastefully at the floor, and smiled crookedly. "For once I wish I had worn your cavalry boots. The look and smell of these filthy floors is nothing to the slimy feel on my feet. I'll be very grateful to wash this scum from between my toes."

"There's no problem, milady," said he. "Thanks to your spells I'm certainly perfectly safe here. As is, for once, this sad creature." He looked down at the sleeping form of the old man.

"He may die soon," observed Lyia.

"True," said Tanithia. "But we'll care for him . . . he's one of us, poor thing. Not one of . . . them."

The two walked on together, Tanithia scanning each cell with her sword, and casting a bit of the consecrated dust from her now nearly empty pouch into each empty room. They rounded the last turn and found their way to the very last short corridor of cells.

She felt Lyia's hand, soft and cool, on her arm, gently restraining her. She stopped and turned, to meet again, almost unwillingly, the dark eyes which burned into hers.

"Tanithia," said Lyia softly. "It's a lovely name."

"As is 'Lyia'", Tanithia responded, feeling very much the near nakedness of her body before this beautiful, intense woman. Lyia put the torch that she had been holding into a rusty cresset on the stone wall and regarded the one before her.

"Your hair is very beautiful," she murmured, caressing Tanithia's tresses softly, then gently running a hand over the witch's bare shoulder. Tanithia noticed again how the black gown of her friend clung so very close to every curve of her body, and was cut low, very low to show the white shoulders and the deep cleft between her full breasts.

Then, as Lyia touched her cheek, Tanithia clasped the other's hand and held it softly to her lips and their eyes melted together. With her other hand Lyia caressed Tanithia's arm and ran her hand gently over the curves of her breasts, to touch finally Tanithia's erect nipples.

"You have very shapely breasts, and your nipples stand erect so fetchingly," she said with a hint of a smile. "Mine do also, if you'll notice." She drew her hands back, breathing in fully to show her own magnificent structure, and running her hands over her full breasts. Her dark eyes devoured Tanithia's for a long moment, and then she melted her body against Tanithia's.

Her voice was low with passion. "Oh, you came . . . someone came . . . and of all people it was you, dear one." She clasped her body against Tanithia's, the warmth of her barely covered breasts pressing and mingling with the warmth of the witch's own.

"Your men were brave, and you, Lady Tanithia, were most magnificent and most magical." Their lips brushed. "I was fortunate," she said, leaning back with her warm hips pressed firmly against Tanithia's. "Very fortunate."

Hips against hips, loins against loins, they stood for a long moment. Lyia again brushed her lips across those of the other . . . very softly. Tanithia responded with a long, open-mouthed kiss, almost unconsciously grinding her hips against those of her friend, for passion was pulsing through her. Lyia's red lips softly found her breasts, and she moaned softly. Lyia reluctantly pulled herself away, her eyes filled with desire.

"There. That must do for now, my beautiful one. They'll be waiting for us in the main hall," she murmured. "Oh!" she gasped in surprise and pain, stepping back.

"What's the matter?" said Tanithia, her voice thick with desire.

"I cut myself, just lightly, on your jewelry. See?" She stepped into the full light of the torch, cradling her breasts. Just above the cloth, indeed, was a slight cut where the jewelry that Tanithia had placed about her own firm breasts had somehow injured her friend.

"No problem, dear one," she whispered. She bent down to kiss it and to touch it, long and lingering, with her tongue. "It will heal, and heal faster. And next time I won't wear this jewelry."

Their hands clasped, and their eyes filled, each with the other. Their lips touched just briefly,then they turned and, hand in hand with Lyia removing the torch from the cresset, they walked back to where Count Waldmann awaited them.

The soldiers were awaiting them in the great hall, where a roaring fire had been built. One of them was saying that he had found some good food in the buttery and good drink in the wine cellars, and that there would be some good feasting on this night.

Leaving the still unconscious old madman to be

scrubbed clean, Count Waldmann, Tanithia, and Lyia, followed by many of the troop, walked around the outside of the castle in the fading twilight as Tanithia cast the last of her glittering powder about the castle in a final rite of exorcism.

Tanithia dared not bring her eyes to meet with those of her new-found friend, nor apparently did Lyia look directly at Tanithia as together they completed the circling. As the stars came forth, all settled down within the great hall to celebrate their victory.

Lyia showed them other stocks of good food and of wine. Also she mentioned that, over the great fireplace in which so hearty a flame was blazing, there was a reservoir of water which soon would be warm enough to use for bathing . . . a custom which had fallen into disfavor since the recent government and their puritanical ways had taken power.

Soon the smell of cooking food wafted through the great hall. The castle was alight everywhere with torches and burning tapers, though for common protection all determined that they would sleep within the central hall. The exorcism seemed to have been completely successful, yet it was considered prudent not to take chances. Still, the mood was festive.

Tanithia took the privilege of testing the warm waters first. Gratefully she removed her sword and her jewelry, wrapping them neatly in her pouch. Then she proceeded to lay out her garments for the evening.

"A pity that there seem to be no mirrors here," she said to herself. "I'd really like to see my reflection. But then it's really just my vanity again." She chuckled. "And I do enjoy being vain." Shrugging herself to and fro, she peeled herself out of the breeches and struck a statuesque pose as she tested the water with one toe. It was perfection, just as she'd wanted. She paused and brushed her tumbled hair into some semblance of smoothness, then bound it up with silken bands of cloth. She eased into the water, luxuriating in the sensuous warmth as it crept up over her entire body. She closed her eyes in contented bliss at the soft touch of the water, and the warmth that so relaxed her every muscle.

"You look lovely in the water, my friend," said Lyia softly. "Like an undine, you're so natural there."

Tanithia opened her eyes and smiled at her friend, who knelt at the edge of the pool, clad only in a scanty shift.

"Lyia, dear. Are you here to join me?"

"If my lady so desires," smiled Lyia, and swung herself to a sitting position, her legs long, white, and shapely, her feet slender and graceful. She smoothed back her raven hair and shook it luxuriantly for a moment before looking back.

"I do indeed desire. I desire much," replied Tanithia.

Lyia dipped a delicate toe into the water, then stood in a lithe movement. With her eyes on Tanithia she stood proudly, jutting out her breasts and reached to the neck of her shift, undoing the drawstring. She pulled it down over her breasts, the thin cloth catching for a moment on her erect nipples, then down over her curved hips to well display her flat belly, then the dark cleft beneath.

Her eyes still on Tanithia, she eased first one foot and then the other into the warm water. The witch-woman swept towards her, and the two embraced closely, their lips seeking each the other, their arms about each others' smooth shoulders and caressing each others' bodies . . . feeling every curve, every softness in a passion which knew no bounds.

Tanithia responded, rubbing her breasts against those of her friend, touching and being touched. She spread her thighs apart, and Lyia caressed her gently and firmly until she cried out in pleasure. Then the two of them joined . . . limbs interlocked, hips quivering, so that each gasped in ecstasy as, without thought, each one's hands fondled and caressed the other's warm breasts and felt the cleft and arch, touching, caressing, penetrating with delicate fingers. And gasping in a paroxysm of ecstasy.

Finally they crawled from the water onto the soft cloths laid out at the pools edge. They touched more, feeling each other's loins, each other's breasts, each other's lips . . . again and again. At length, spent for a while, they relaxed in each other's arms.

"Tanithia?"

"Hm."

"Which do you prefer more, men or women?"

"Sometimes one, sometimes the other. Usually men, but if a woman is very . . . very special, very magnetic . . . then I find I can love her as well."

"Do you love me?"

"I lust for you. There's a strong pull between the two of us. Love? I don't know for sure. Yet perhaps it is . . . time will tell."

"Do you love Count Waldmann?"

"Very much. He and I have spent some very magical nights together. And young Swordsman Gort, though I don't think he realizes it. The two of us have something in common . . . he wants to possess me, but he doesn't know that I want him very much indeed."

"And the others?"

Tanithia laughed, deep and throaty. "I've built a bond of magic with all of them . . . they realize it and so do I. It's a bond that can be broken only by such close-ness as you and I have been sharing." She gently kissed the other's eyes.

Lyia drew her breath in amazement, her wet breasts pressing against Tanithia's naked flank. "You mean . . . all of them?"

"Of course," purred Tanithia, leaning back luxuriously and raising her arms to unbind her hair and raise the points of her breasts even higher. "Maybe I'm more than a little scandalous, but some magics must be closed off in one way and some," she ran her hands significantly over the curves of her breasts, "Some must be closed off in other ways. I prefer dealing with the magics that have their base of power in the raw passion that resides between the loins . . . that must be drawn forth with lust and must be finally grounded with lust, once the need is done and the magick worked."

Tanithia rolled over onto her belly and cupped her chin in her hands for a moment. "I should feel, perhaps, a little ashamed of my actions." She laughed and turned over lightly, grasping her friend about her slender waist and putting her head on Lyia's soft breasts. "But I love it. And I love them. And tonight . . . they'll know it. Even more than they do now. After all, like any other art, magic works two ways . . . and I can be unaffected no more than they."

"But," worried Lyia, wrinkling her brow. "But . . . you do this sort of thing all the time?"

"No," said Tanithia, taking a brush and running it through her friend's raven hair. "Only when the need is really great . . . as it was in this case. A lot of Power was needed, I'm sure you'll agree. And now that the castle is cleansed the remaining Power must be released."

"And tonight . . . " she stood, golden and beautiful over her friend. "Tonight seems a manificent night to do so."

Lyia ushered Tanithia to her chambers, and gave the witch-woman free choice of her own wardrobe in addition to the light garb that Tanithia had brought and had laid out. A while was spent devising the dancing dress she would wear for this evening, and in setting the atmosphere with candles, with incense, with perfumes, in her own luxurious and private chamber adjacent to Lyia's.

When Tanithia complained that she could not find a mirror in which she could see the effect of her dress, Lyia showed her a room off to one side in which an old intricately framed mirror was the sole furnishing. With delight she sorted through Lyia's cache of jewelry; all was antique and all was valuable. She selected the items that appealed to her, and tried them one after the other. Finally satisfied with the effect, she surveyed herself with considerable pride.

A full-circle skirt of gossamer silk, spangled in gold, was fastened about her hips and fell to her toes. Over this a surcoat, showing the silk skirt in front, but laced closely along the arms and under her breasts . . . the better to show off her slender waist and to stress the fullness of her rounded bosom. The lacings were undone just enough to partially conceal, yet mostly display, her breasts down to their rosy tips. Her hair was brushed and full, with jewels fastened within . . . sparkling diamonds that caught the light in a myriad of rainbows. Rings of gold set with diamonds adorned her fingers and her toes, complemented by intricately wrought anklets and bracelets. With gentle fingers, Lyia brushed a scarlet enamel onto her fingernails and toenails. To complete the effect, a wide cloth-of-gold band, fastened closely about her neck and set with gold and jewels.

She examined herself closely in the mirror, running a finger in between the breasts, over the lacings that went down below her navel. The effect, she decided, was excellent. She spun quickly in a light dancer's step and her skirt stood almost straight out from her shapely legs, with a garter of red silk attached above one knee. And aught else beneath.

Tanithia considered the overall effect. It was this sort of costume which had made her so notorious when she was in the palace . . . definitely not the sort of thing to wear when visiting a maiden aunt, mayhap. But yes, this would indeed be the right thing for such a night of pleasure as she planned. Displayed as she was tonight, she could bring a stone statue to life, and with very interesting results, she was certain. A thin silken cape clasped about her neck and tucked over her bare shoulders, and she was ready.

Lyia also had dressed, in a long, close-fitting black glown that clung to every curve of her own voluptous body. The collar was high on the sides but slashed down between her breasts and well below her midriff, with close-fitting sleeves and a belt of wrought gold about her hips.

Strands of jewels draped through her black hair, which hung smooth and straight down her back and to her hips. Black leather footstraps, set with diamonds, adorned her white feet. Like Tanithia, she wore rings and diamonds on her bare toes as well as on her fingers, and a pendant of a single bloodstone which hung between her breasts.

Lyia looked at Tanithia and took her hand. "You look ravishing tonight, my pretty one, and I'm sure that every one of them will want to."

Tanithia eyed her friend's own comparatively simple garb. "And I see that you're not so flamboyant as I. You'll be allowing me to be on center stage tonight."

Lyia smiled and brushed her lips gently. "I wouldn't dream of trying to compete with one so lovely. And I wouldn't want to be in the way when you enchant and love your faithful men tonight."

Lyia touched Tanithia's hair, and then her lips, with her slender fingers. "Tonight, my dear, I'll be your musician, and sit demurely on the dias to play the music that will set men afire while you sway and dance so beautifully." She smiled as her eyes looked deep into Tanithia's. "Tonight they shall enjoy you. A night or two hence *I* shall enjoy you."

The great hall was brightly lit by scores of bright candles, and by the roaring fire in the huge fireplace. The men had been relaxing, and most had availed themselves of the bath vacated somewhat before by the women. They too had dressed in fine silks and velvets as were available. Silken breeches, doublets replete with embroidery and fine laces, and shirts of fine damask linens.

A dozen voices shouted greeting and huzzahs, and called words of admiration as the two women proceeded gracefully into the hall. Count Waldmann bowed before Tanithia and in return she curtseyed low, that he and the others could enjoy the full effect of her costume.

"Milady, you are the very quintessence of loveliness tonight, as is your very charming friend." The Count smiled likewise at Lyia, admiring her as well. "Have you quite recovered from the day's ordeals?"

"Yes, Count Waldmann, and I thank you for your consideration," said Lyia, removing a stringed instrument of antique design from its case nearby.

The Count proferred a goblet of wine to each. "Here my Ladies . . . the men and I have perhaps been getting a little ahead of you with this excellent vintage. To the most exquisite beauties, may I present the most excellent wine which the cellars possess."

Tanithia took her jewelled goblet and stepped lightly, with a dancer's swaying stride, to stand before the center of the great fireplace. Striking a statuesque pose and pausing for effect, she smiled as she looked each of her men in the eyes and called to them all.

"My good friends, faithful and loving companions, I propose a toast . . . to the scouring of Castle Drakenstane!"

A dozen voices shouted assent, and they all drank deeply. She looked at them with a certain smile and looking, perhaps, more like a fox than a woman. Her eyes sparkled, and it was obvious that she near bit her lip to avoid saying much of what she would have liked to say. "May I propose yet another toast," she declared. "Let's drink now to celebration, to revelry," She looked around at all of them, and drew in her breath, running a finger gently down in the deep cleft between her breasts. "And to love!"

Again the shouted calls of assent . . . more animal this time. She drained her goblet and, whether she really needed to or not, wiped a perhaps imaginary droplet of spilled wine from one round breast. She smiled as Lyia settled gracefully into a carven ebony chair and began to play.

The music surged and faded, ebbed and flowed, and Tanithia swirled and swayed, whirled and stepped gracefully, sometimes slowly, sometimes rapidly. Often leaping on graceful bare feet, other times standing alone with her long hair swaying like some magical cloak, swaying to the sensuous throb that swelled and ebbed and flowed so seductively.

All were woven into a spell as she danced faster and ever yet faster, throwing her head back in wild abandon, golden tresses flying free, jewels sparkling on her forehead and on her breasts . . . which bobbed and bounced, often free of her low-cut bodice, to give flashes of rosy aureolas and pointed nipples.

Then the dance slowed and . . . as if by chance . . . she was before Count Waldmann, draping herself lithely into his arms as the music faded. He paused for a moment with his face reddening somewhat, then gave her a warm, and then passionate kiss, his hands running through her hair and revelling in the soft feel of it.

"I desire you, my lady," he whispered hoarsely into her ear. "I desire you greatly!"

She gave him a long, open-mouthed kiss, her tongue darting like a serpent against his. "Then come," she murmured. "Why should we stay, my lover?"

"Lyia," she then said loudly in a voice which feigned casualness, "Would you kindly play something for the men for just a little while? I'll have to regain my breath. And the Count and I must partake of some . . . pleasant conversation." They walked out, she draping her body against Count Waldmann, and blushing at the encouragement and rather obvious innuendoes that some of the men called to their leader. Her words, obviously, had fooled no one as to their intentions.

They passed into the corridor and he seized her, enfolding her in his arms and smothering her with kisses . . . pressing his firm body against her and pinning her momentarily against the wall.

"My love . . . I want you, my love," she murmured softly and urgently as his hands reached up to fondle and to caress the breasts which were so well displayed.

"Where is your chamber, Tanithia?" he whispered, undoing the lacings of her bodice. "I shall have you, and I shall have you now!" Again he kissed her eager mouth and swept her from her feet to carry her into the candle-lit bedroom. He looked around to take in the effect. "Ah, a very pleasing place for lovemaking," he said, and laid her down upon the couch. The resumed quickly and sometimes clumsily pulling her clothes from her as she writhed in anticipation of ecstacy, and likewise pulled eagerly at the fastenings of his clothes, and touching him as she helped remove his own garb.

Then she was naked before him, stretching luxuriously

with feline grace upon the velvet covers. "Am I not love-ly?" she purred. "Do you not desire me?"

"My gods!" he growled like some feral animal, "I do!" And he was upon her again, feeling every part of her body, touching her breasts, her thighs, the cleft of the arch between her legs, kneading her buttocks, kissing her throat, burying his face in her perfumed hair. She returned his caresses with little animal sounds, seeking long passion-ate kisses again and again.

Then he penetrated her as she eagerly arched her hips upwards towards his, and she gasped and shuddered as a first wave of ecstacy swept through her. Then she again arched herself against him, panting and moaning, and then crying out as they both reached the height of pleasure together.

A time of passion, a time of joy. From the great hall could be heard her cry, just once, as he took her. The men smiled into their cups, each knowing that there would be many such cries on this night of sensual magic.

Mayhap it was an hour, mayhap less. They returned from the bedchamber, the Count more casual-seeming than his men had ever seen, his doublet unlaced, holding a lovely and slightly dishevelled Tanithia next to him. Tanithia, for her part, was touseled and not nearly so perfectly coiffured as before. And with her gown now somewhat . . . wrinkled. She had not bothered to lace the bodice again, and it was open well below her navel, show-ing a large expanse between her breasts, which swelled invitingly outwards.

Yet her eyes held the eagerness and fire and passion that bespoke a power and a craving within her that her . . . conversation . . . with the Count had scarcely lessened.

She smiled at Lyia, who nodded her head and com-menced another throbbing and passionate melody from her lyre-like instrument.

Again the dance of wild abandon, wantonly magnificent as once again she became the primal, elemental female — evoking much of the primal male from those who so eagerly watched her whirling and swaying.

In her dance she looked about for Gort, but could find no sign of him. She danced slowly, shimmying enticingly as, unknown to them, she counted her audience. Nine, ten, eleven . . . he was gone! Perhaps to take care of the old man? Perhaps jealousy? Probably with shock at her brazeness. No matter, she threw her head back and swirled her hair like some living thing. She stepped up the pace and bared her full breasts to an appreciative audience.

Tonight is for pleasure . . . and for release of the Power. Though I'd like to have him now, she thought, I shall have him in due time.

And she swung into a wild and frenzied finale before selecting another of the soldiers, to depart again, his hands passionately upon her. One hand caressed the fullness of her breasts, the other fondling her posterior as again she was escorted to her chamber.

And again a cry of ecstacy echoed through the hall.

The night passed, a blur of dancing, of whirling, of wine. Of eager lovers and frenzied lovemaking. The vast Power which she had so carefully built over the last week and more she now returned to each and every man in the best way she knew.

Before long she had divested herself of all but her scarlet-spangled skirt of gossamer silk, and danced wildly with breasts bobbing invitingly. The skirt had been laced so low that it showed the cleft between her shapely buttocks as well as the beginning of the dark curls in front. She drew the men out to dance with her . . . one or two or three at a time. The caressed her, they loved her . . . some in her bedchamber, some as she swayed and slowly rotated her hips while on the darkness of the balcony outside.

She remembered making love in the warm water of the pool while one of her cavaliers fondled her breasts, another kissed her and fed her sweet fruit, and yet another rubbed her bare feet.

The night was glorious. Perhaps the only small shadow was that Gort, whom she wanted so much, was nowhere to be found.

Tanithia sleepily pulled herself up on her elbows and brushed the hair back from her eyes. She was naked in her bed and with . . . she counted them . . . five of her troopers, all in various degrees of undress, sleeping about her. All looking definitely satiated and all perhaps a bit heavy with wine.

She untangled herself from the various arms that lay across her body, smiling. For they loved her, wanton though she might be, and she returned the emotion. Strange, she thought, easing herself out of the bed and enjoying the cool feel of the stone floor beneath her feet, how it would be possible to love not just one, but many.

Tanithia stood unsteadily and realized that she was very tired still, and a bit sore in many places. More rest would definitely be in order.

One could definitely love many others, she thought,

but seldom ever with so many as on the past night's festivities, even though it had been as exciting as a carnival! This night had been particularly special, of course, since the magical power which she had built for the cleansing of the castle had needed to be grounded out.

She went into the chamber with the mirror, and admired the perfection of her body. Her hair was thoroughly touseled, most of the jewels gone . . . taken off for comfort as had been the case with the jewels on her fingers and toes. She ran her hands over her full, rounded breasts and down her sleek thighs. It's good to admire oneself, she thought, for unless you love yourself, how can you love others?

Yet not quite all of the Power had been released, she realized . . . for Swordsman Gort had disappeared as she was off with the Count, and had not come back for the rest of the evening.

Ah . . . jealousy! A sweet lad, but her wild ways were too much for him to understand. Certainly by now he was heartbroken . . . calling her a harlot and worse for her behavior. Yet could he not understand that when Power is called forth, it must also be returned? She dealt with magics that were strong, always.

She leaned against a granite column, feeling the coolness of the stone against her breasts and her belly. The sensations felt so good . . . every sensation felt so good . . . because she was so alive on this morning. Had she done this without the Force that lay within her, it would have been far more exhausting . . . perhaps impossible at the level of last nights "carnival!" And if repeated too often it would do no good for her body or her soul.

But every now and then . . . she smiled . . . and swayed on graceful toes. Every now and then . . .

It occurred to her to try the pool, and indeed it was fresh and warm. The water seemed to flow in from a hidden mineral spring some place, constantly replenishing itself, warmed by the stone of the great fireplace. She settled down upon the cool stone and splashed her feet back and forth in the pleasingly warm water. Tanithia smiled meditatively, watching the ripples.

Well, she mused, the night is done, and before long my lovers must all go their way. It was an evening well worth remembering. Quite diverting.

She eased into the pool and enjoyed the sensation of feeling the water rising up her legs, warming and soothing, for she realized that she was a bit bruised from the attentions of so many. The warm water rose up over the smoothness of her body as she knelt, and then covered her breasts, which had bobbed free and seemingly impossibly full and round in the water.

She dipped her long hair in the water, found soap to the side, and began scrubbing herself down. She finished and was toweling off her body as Lyia appeared at the door, a steaming mug of hot drink in hand.

"Well, Lady Tanithia. I daresay you had an enjoyable time last night! Judging by your expression and by all of those with whom you had, say . . . 'pleasant conversation' . . . you seem to have the ability to throw some quite entertaining parties!" She smiled.

Lyia herself looked as though she had been resting. She wore only a single, very thin and sheer garment that swept around her slender ankles, hanging loose from her shoulders. Tanithia took the cup and drank thankfully of it, under the amused gaze of her friend.

"Delicious," she said. "One sip of this mystical potion and I magically return to being a human being once more. It returns my will to live."

"Your will to live, I think, is very strong indeed, from what I've been able to make out. The night was a spectacular one, and there were quite a few times when I almost joined you in your . . . entertainment," Lyia said. "Yet last night was really yours, with all of your handsome cavaliers."

"Mine perhaps no longer," said Tanithia, rubbing the moisture from her hair. "As of last night my bargain with them is complete. They'll always be close to me. And I'll probably never turn down the chance to couch with any of them." She chuckled. "Even the grizzled old swords-sergeant. But he's a dear." For a long moment she was silent, wrapping the towel about her hair. "We all have a common bond now . . . one that goes well beyond the best of sensuality. It was built in the cleansing of the castle, and probably will always be with us."

"There's much love, much life, and much power in you," Lyia said. "I like that and I must say . . . I envy you." She reached up to the clasp on her shoulder, and the diaphanous garment dropped from her. The two embraced one another, reveling in the warmth of each other's naked body.

"Tanithia, you'll have to stay with me for a while until we can get the castle and the province in order once again." She touched Tanithia's breast. "Hm, milady, I believe these lovely things are a bit swollen from too much admiring attention. And also," her leg moved in close between Tanithia's, pressing against the witchwoman's softness, "I'll wager that you're sore in other areas as well. Come with me, pretty one . . . I've some salves and ungents that should restore you completely within a few hours."

Arm in arm they left the chamber, and then only the sound of water dripping into the pool could be heard.

"Then it's settled," said the Count. "We leave in the morning for my estates. Our work here is complete."

The Count, his men, Tanithia and Lyia were seated around the great oaken table, still slightly dusty, in the castle's council chamber. Night had fallen again and the nearly full moon was casting its brightening glow over the quiet landscape. All had rested much, and showed no signs of the wild revelry from the previous night. Yet there was a closeness among all, so that discussion needed only to be at a minimum.

Tanithia, by common, unspoken assent, sat at the head of the table. With these who were close friends in magic, and also her lovers, she felt no need for formality. Nor, since she had loved each and every one of them, did she feel any great need for propriety. She wore a lounging gown open at the neck and scarce fastened at even her loins, showing her full-rounded breasts, themselves no longer displaying bruises or marks from the night before. Her hair, brushed and lusterous, fell over her shoulders and her breasts.

Lyia, a bit more formal and not one of the 'circle of passion' wore one of the close-fitting black gowns that she seemed to prefer, cut as low as ever. And while Tanithia was unshod as usual, Lyia wore delicately embroidered black slippers.

The men were dressed casually, yet again seeming more formal and military than they had been.

"We'll leave at dawn," Waldmann continued. "Swordsman Gort, I'm told, has already departed. I understand he was concerned about the old madman and was seeing to the old fellow's care among his own relatives hereabout. Lady Tanithia," he smiled at her, "will remain here with the Demoiselle Lyia to see that all is fully cleansed in the castle and in the province. I'm told that this will require one full turning of the phases of the moon. Is that right?"

"Indeed, milord," She assented.

"Very well, then let's get some rest. The adventure is over and, dear one, we'll be looking forward to having you return among us in a month's time. Tomorrow is going to come all too soon, and those of us who will be riding out are going to need a good night of sleep." The meeting over, they all stood and went their own separate ways.

FROM the highest battlement Tanithia watched the soldiers as they rode out of sight. She raised her hand for yet a threescore time in farewell, yet knew that they could no longer see her. The sun was bright and the day was fine, yet she felt a coldness and a loneliness.

Eyes downcast, her arms clasped across her chest under her breasts, she walked slowly into the very empty-seeming corridor. And slowly, each step seeming to take so very long, walked on down to the great hall where Lyia awaited her.

She looked around like a child who realizes that she is alone, then came to sit next to Lyia, who watched her with dark eyes. She buried her face in Lyia's dark hair and Lyia stroked her head softly.

"Oh Lyia . . . It's so lonely with them gone. I hadn't

thought this great place could seem so empty . . ."

"There, there, my lovely one," said Lyia softly. "Let me console you. For after all, haven't we wanted this time alone together?"

Yes, you're right of course," Tanithia said, wiping her eyes and giving something of a smile.

Lyia, gently holding Tanithia's face, kissed the tears from her cheeks and then kissed her eyes shut briefly. "Come, sweet one. Let's go to my chambers and try on some of the fine garments there. It'll rouse you from your sadness."

They walked down the echoing hallways. "Then afterwards perhaps we can go to the kitchen and prepare a few delicacies. In a week or two we must see about getting servants . . . but that will have to wait until all is completely secure, don't you think, Tanithia?"

Their soft steps faded down the dim hallway, and their voices likewise with the closing of the door. And all that remained in the darkening hall were echoes.

True to her word Lyia soon roused Tanithia from her sadness. They tried various gowns and improvised different scanty garb which each modeled and both applauded. Jewelry they both tried, picking the pieces that they liked the best, and chattering gaily over the choices and the probable histories of the pieces that they selected.

Trying on a particularly flounced and insubstantial little garment, Tanithia announced that she wanted to dance. And the two of them ran to the great hall and whirled about the floor on graceful feet, beating rhythms on small percussion instruments which had lain at hand since the revel.

Their dancing was frenzied and joyous, and finally they collapsed across a couch, catching their breath and laughing.

"Ah, that's good," said Tanithia breathlessly. "You dance so well, my friend. And so freely. It occurrs to me this is the first that I've seen you do it.

Lyia smiled softly. "I haven't danced in a very long, long time. It feels good, and I'd like to do it more. Now come! There's time to prepare a small bit to eat. Then perhaps we can visit the wine cellar for a really good vintage." She was off, running fleetly across the stone floor, with her thin skirt swirling about her white legs. And Tanithia was after her. One nymph of gold and one nymph of ivory, running careless through the echoing stone halls of the great castle.

As evening fell the two, clad simply in light chitons, short and sheer, walked leisurely through the gardens, enjoying the cool feel of the soft grass and the soft breeze, as well as the delicate scent of the flowers as they passed.

"The garden is wild and untended," commented Lyia. "For quite some time it's been without decent care. Yet in a few weeks, perhaps we can have gardeners on the grounds to care for it and to return this wild place to its former beauty. It was quite lovely, you know."

Tanithia plucked a rose and slipped it into her hair, observing the effect in a clear pool. Then plucked another and put it into her friend's hair. She looked at it for a moment and decided to try it another way. Lyia smiled.

"You change so much, Tanithia. When first I saw you, I thought I beheld a demi-goddess of iron and fire. For a while you were a regal noblewoman, managing a military operation. Yet another you were a wild wanton . . . teasing and tempting, and revelling in the joys of lovemaking. Now . . . this afternoon . . . this entire day . . . you've been merely a girl enjoying life."

Tanithia sat on the side of the pool and dipped her toes into the water, feeling the coolness and watching the ripples. "One should drink deeply of life in all ways, I feel.

There's magic, there's mystery. And yet there is much which is solid and real. There's darkness and storm in the world, and yet also there's brightness and sunshine. Too much of any and you lose some of your essential humanity."

"Are you not a witch as well?" asked Lyia.

Tanithia smiled and touched the flower softly. "I'm a seeker of the ancient mysteries. There are a lot of words for it, and perhaps only a few are worth applying. There are realities far beyond what we know, and we must ever explore them or lose some of our true essence." She ran her hand through the water, stood and waded into the pool.

"But always we come back to the beauties of the world about us, for our roots are here in this good earth and under these good starry skies, no matter how far our minds may range or our souls may wander."

Lyia was quiet for a long time. She picked a flower, smelled it, and dropped it. "I envy you, Tanithia. You taste much of life and you enjoy it. While I . . . I have sipped far too much of Darkness, and I fear that in doing so perhaps I've destroyed my soul."

Tanithia looked at her questioningly, but no answer was forthcoming.

"Pretty one," said Lyia, "Let's leave the castle walls and, before it gets too dark, explore the forest and the meadows nearby. They're very lovely."

"And perhaps we can stay longer if the mood so suits us," said Tanithia. "The moon is full tonight." On soft, silent feet they walked again through the great hallways, lighting tapers where they went, and even putting some wood into the great fireplace so that the banked coals would have a fire going when they returned. Then they walked hand in hand to the main courtyard.

"Such a huge place," commented Tanithia, looking

about her.

"Many of the walls have wooden frames, nonetheless," said Lyia. "Otherwise they wouldn't be quite so high. Now . . . off to the main gate. Try to catch me!" and she ran ahead, the short chiton flowing about her full form as she ran, and Tanithia at her heels.

The meadows were almost elfin in magic, and twice they found wild deer regarding them from across the glades. They reveled in the soft touch of the cool dew, and garlanded each other with night flowers as they paused beside a small stream in the moonlight.

The moon rose higher, and still they pressed on until they were not far from the few scattered lights of the small village.

"Soft now!" said Tanithia suddenly. "I hear something ahead." They crept quietly ahead, as silently as sylphs through the moon-dappled darkness, and peered carefully and cautiously through the low bushes at the hilltop.

"There seem to be a group of men down there. Perhaps . . . let's see . . . about twoscore of them in that camp. I wonder what they're doing in these parts? They have the look of strangers," whispered Tanithia.

"Hm. They've got the look of arrant rogues about them, I'd say. When we get back to the castle the two of us will have to see if we can't get the portcullis closed,"

commented Lyia. "Their horses are staked out over there
. . . perhaps they're just passing through."

"Come," said Tanithia in a low voice. "Let's go.
We'll go back to the bald hillock. That should be a safe
distance away from this doubtful band. It should be
better than a league away. I feel like dancing, and I'd
rather do it where there's no chance of being discovered."
They silently made their way back. "I'd hate to be set
upon and raped."

"You?" exclaimed Lyia in a voice of mock surprise.
"After all of your cavorting on these previous nights,
you're afraid of being violated?"

"Shall we say I prefer to control when and where,
and be entirely the mistress of the situation. Come . . .
let's be gone!"

Silently they disappeared, running through the night
on silent, light feet, back in the direction of the castle.
Time passed and they meandered idly through the brightly
moonlit night, listening to the call of night birds and the
occassional rustling of small animals here and there.

"The forest was well cared for, until recently," Lyia
observed, "We can move easily through the darkness and
the shadows even now."

"There!" said Tanithia softly. "What a lovely place.
A stream, grass, and bright moonlight. I feel like dancing!"
she laughed, and ran to the center of the circular meadow,
and began springing, whirling, and leaping about with the
grace of a born dancer. Shrugging out of the top of the
chiton, she revelled in the feel of the cool air and the soft
touch of evening dew against her bare breasts as she whirled
and swayed, joined by her friend as they wove patterns of
delight and abandon beneath the moon.

Tanithia hummed a song, and the two of them circled
and bowed, singing and chanting through the low-lying
mist with moon-halos about their dancing shadows. Night

birds called hither and yon, and dewy sparkles glistened in the mists about them.

Then suddenly she paused. "Ah," she laughed. "I've been overdoing things a bit." She swept her wild hair away from her face and shook it back over her smooth shoulders. "Look! There are times when I can't get away from witch-hood."

She stood, legs spread and arms akimbo, standing tall and alert and smiling as she watched the forms that began to take shape in the mist.

"What . . . who are they?" asked Lyia with a trace of apprehension.

"The elvish folk," said the witch. "Or the manifestations of them, which we can summon forth, sometimes. Good people, in their own strange way. Another, earlier race of beings who were here long berore humankind arose. Now they've long since gone into another land . . . another world beyond. One of the 'rainbow lands', the traditions say. I've done a lot of study and magical research about them."

One shape swirled and took the form of a woman, impossibly slender and graceful, with slanted eyes and pointed ears. Strange silver eyes that had little of humanity in them, yet which bespoke a strong intelligence and even a certain warmth. The elvish woman was clad in soft and filmy rainment which swirled about her ankles as she, too, danced and circled in the mist and fog which had been rising from the wet grass.

"Isn't she lovely," exclaimed Tanithia, a note of enchantment in her voice.

"Are there others of her kind about?" asked Lyia, looking around.

"Mayhap . . . but perhaps just out of eyeshot. They seldom see us, nor do we usually see them. Yet I'm afraid, pretty dear thing, that our dancing and certain patterns in

my mind have opened a small . . . portal. Here and now."

Tanithia sprang forward, and whirled and danced with the elfin visitor . . . not quite touching, smiling, and being smiled upon. sometimes the elf-woman seemed as solid as Tanithia, other times a delicate and insubstantial, gracefully swirling composition of transparent light and shadow. The flowing light hair of the witch-woman seemed at times to merge and flow through the even lighter and far more fine tresses of the other as the two weaved and undulated. Human and unhuman eyes locked, and material hands almost caressed the willowy, immaterial body while immaterial hands delicately drew sparkles of light over very firm and real shoulders, chin, hips and breasts. Then away again in a swirl of mist and barely-seen sparkles.

"Come join us!" she called at length. "Hurry, Lyia . . . it's beautiful . . . it's magical!"

"I . . . I can't," came Lyia's plaintive answer. "I'd like to, but . . ."

The elvish woman seemed to hear Lyia's voice, and her strange, nonhuman eyes turned in Lyia's direction, perhaps following Tanithia's laughing gaze.

The smile and hint of laughter faded from her high cheeks and slender face, and her strange eyes grew wider and yet wider. A look of perhaps anger and even distaste suddenly crossed her face. For the first time came the silvery tones of her voice.

"Begone!" came the soft cry, "Begone!" And then she vanished.

Tanithia stood flatfooted . . . suddenly perplexed and puzzled . . . alone in the mist and moonlight of the glade. She was amazed and shocked by what had happened; shocked and disturbed.

The magic was gone, and it was just she and Lyia . . . standing in a misty meadow under the full moon.

"Why . . . what happened?" she asked. Lyia came

forward and put her arms out to Tanithia.

"I'm sorry. I'm so sorry. Remember, I've been a sorceress, and I've made some ... some very serious blunders. Not the least of which has been in my dealings with the elemental kingdoms. I ... I have fewer friends than I should. Especially in nearby dimensions."

Tanithia looked around, still with disquiet in her eyes and amazement in her voice. "But I know of the elvish folk. They're wise! Not much like us, perhaps, but their words carry importance. A lot of importance."

"Now, now," said Lyia, pulling Tanithia into an embrace, and pulling down her own chiton so that their bare breasts pressed together with a feel that sent a thrill through Tanithia. "Come, my love. I'm sorry that my past ... my own failed experiments ... have ruined part of the evening for you." Her lips softly touched Tanithia's. "Come on. Let's return to the castle," she whispered softly into the other's ear as she stroked Tanithia's hair softly. "We'll dance more after we've bathed and supped. And ... perhaps ... our enjoyment will return again."

She stroked the sides of the witch's head and put her arms about the other's shivering shoulders. They touched lips again and Tanithia responded as her body reacted to the closeness, the warmth, and the softness of her friend. She felt Lyia's toes on her own as Lyia ran her fingers very softly up and down the other's back.

"Yes . . . let's go," she murmured.

They walked off through the wood. As they passed from sight the mist whirled and almost took shape. Seeming for a few moments to be an impossibly slender woman, gazing about with anger and revulsion in her strange eyes.

Their walk back to the castle was a long one, and they proceeded almost wordlessly. The two paused to enjoy the sweetness of an occasional brushing of lips, and touches and caresses in the moonlight. To touch and to be touched. To speak softly from time to time, and mostly to merely know the presence, each of the other.

She's beautiful, thought Tanithia to herself as they walked together in the moonlight, arm in arm. The moonlight on her smooth, dark hair, the full, pointed profiles of her rounded breasts. The perfect slenderness of her belly and her loins . . . only slightly, very slightly covered by the thin whisp of pale cloth. Smooth, well-shaped legs, slender ankles and delicate feet. And arms which were graceful and light.

Tanithia prided herself on her own voluptrous beauty. Yet here was someone slightly more slender, slightly more fine-featured.

Someone who attracted her, and fascinated her greatly.

B EFORE long the castle loomed before them, dark save for the torches they had affixed in the courtyard. The great structure was somber and massive in the night, and Tanithia had to remind herself that it was a refuge and, for now, a home also.

"Here . . . let's go up into the gate tower and lower the portcullis," said Lyia. They lightly ran up the winding stone steps of the tower. The two of them together strained to pull the heavy capstan about, and it slowly lowered the massive iron gate solidly and heavily into place. Firm and impenetrable . . . and for now also immovable.

They paused and leaned against the great, heavy wheels to rest for a moment. Tanithia wiped her forehead and tapped her friend on the leg with her own shapely foot.

"You're quite strong, Lyia. Though I don't think either one of us could have managed it alone. We can do a lot together, can't we?"

Lyia smiled at her and looked away. Perhaps there was a trace of wistfulness in her voice. "Yes we could. We could . . ."

"But now," she said, breaking the mood, "To the pool! Let's bathe . . . then we can dress and find ourselves something to sup on."

Laughing, they ran down the stairs and raced through the torchlit corridors, breasts bouncing and long hair swirling in their light-footed flight. Though torches and tapers were much burned from before, the light was soft and yet quite sufficient.

Throwing off their whispy garments, they happily leaped into the warm pool and soon were splashing about joyously. From time to time their limbs would touch, a hand would brush a breast, or a toe across a thigh, and each felt the need growing, yet said nothing . . . merely enjoying the pleasure of increasing the temptation and the enchantment, one upon the other.

Then they were out of the pool. Lyia and Tanithia rubbed each other down with heavy towels, rubbing each other's breasts, thighs, arms, legs. Rubbing one another's feet and brushing one another's lustrous mane of hair.

The touches grew to be caresses, and the caresses into passionate fondling. Tanithia gasped in pleasure as Lyia touched her lips delicately across her friend's nipples, caressing her shoulders softly.

Her hand softly brushed over Lyia's face, and the other grasped it, closing her eyes and holding the soft hand against her cheek. She looked into Tanithia's eyes with just a hint of . . . regret, perhaps, . . . in her own. "I'll want to always remember you this way, my love," she murmured.

Tanithia kissed her gently, and felt her response more eagerly to her own touch. "Let's dress," said Lyia, a bit thickly. "We'll dine on a few delicacies. Then I too would like to dance."

With few words they walked to their chambers to dress . . . if such could be said to be the case, for each attired in thin rainment which concealed very little and which displayed nearly all.

Tanithia donned a full dancing gown with long, light skirt and full sleeves, but which left her golden breasts bare. She put on jewelry rings, bracelets, anklets, straps studded with glistening jewels about her bare feet, and a pendant which hung below her full breasts, down in the deep cleft between them.

She found, with a small cry, that Lyia had happened to dress almost exactly the same, though in black rather than gold. Lyia looked at her appraisingly, smiling.

"We make quite a picture together," she said. "If your soldiers could but see us now I'm sure we'd have another orgy on our hands. Come . . . let's go! I've prepared something for us." And they were off to the hall.

They nibbled at sweetmeats, sweet red wine, and cakes. Then as Tanithia sipped a bit more, Lyia picked up the stringed instrument that she had played before, and began to strum a soft and plaintive, yet very insistent tune.

Tanithia looked up to find that the other's eyes were on her, with the unmistakable glint of passion as she intently watched Tanithia's body.

"My love . . . you're beautiful." Tanithia blushed and threw her hair back, thrusting her breasts outwards and upwards, gazing with similar boldness at her friend's form.

"Like attracts like, lovely one," she said, and touched her friend's nipple gently so that Lyia gasped and smiled. "Tonight we shall love," she murmured. "Yes, tonight we shall love." Their fingers touched, and their lips brushed softly.

"More gentle. Softer, and more sensitive than the men. They mean well, but we puzzle them oftimes, it seems," Tanithia mused.

"Come," said Lyia, springing lithely to her toes, breasts bobbing and her ebony hair swirling about her. "Let's dance!"

"But there's no music!"

"We don't need any. Look into my eyes, and we'll feel the rhythm within ourselves. Let's dance as though the throbbing of passion were the throbbing of drums!" They swung about the broad floor, bodies weaving, black and red-gold hair rippling and swirling, lithe limbs flashing. Faster and faster the two whirled about the floor, holding each other's hands, each one's eyes locked on the other, totally and completely engrossed in the dance and in their desire. Weaving and swaying, Tanithia smiled . . . seeming dazed, entranced, yet captivated by her friend's amorous beauty.

On and on they danced, white feet and gold feet in perfect time together, across the polished floor, their gowns swirling, breasts bobbing, jewelry glittering and flashing. Coming together to touch briefly, to kiss briefly . . . so that the fire built higher and higher within them. More and more intense, and yet ever faster.

Then Tanithia dropped to her knees in a daze and a trance, looking up at Lyia . . . her golden head weaving round and round as if trying to throw her hair about. Yet enwrapped in a trance, arms out as if in entreaty.

"Come to me, love," she said, as though losing her senses. "Come to me. Please."

"I shall," said Lyia. She came and stroked Tanithia's wild hair, her eyes always deep within Tanithia's . . . drawing her in, overwhelming her, taking her will. Lyia stroked the dazed one's shoulders and gently felt of her breasts as Tanithia shuddered . . . yet always kept her eyes, eyes that now were blank and devoid of consciousness, on Lyia.

Lyia eased Tanithia to the fur-strewn couch, keeping their eyes locked, and laid her gently in the softness. Then touched her toes delicately, kissed them, touched her ankles, her calves as Tanithia looked at her blankly, the light of reason almost gone.

Lyia's hands touched gently even higher, in the arch and the cleft, and Tanithia gasped in ecstasy as she explored deeper. Eyes closed in unconscious, tranced pleasure. Lyia, touching and caressing, leaned close over the other beautiful woman, her knee now pressing, and finally their legs entwining with each other, her full breasts pressing their warmth against the firm warmth of the other. Lyia crooned softly to Tanithia as she ran her hands through the red-gold mane of soft hair.

Then she smiled, and sank her long fangs into Tanithia's neck.

Tanithia, in a mindless ecstasy, writhed and moaned, swinging her hips back to and fro as pain became pleasure in her mazed senses. Consciousness faded as wave after wave of exquisite pleasure swept through her shuddering body.

Lyia passionately drew more and more from the arched neck of the senseless Tanithia, her own sleek body responding to a pleasure that was sensual and more. Drawing sustenance and great, full Power from the other.

Until a horned claw grasped her soft shoulder and threw her back roughly to sprawl on the stone floor, dishevelled and surprised. She rubbed her breasts as if in memory of the pulsing sensuousness, touching her nipples, and pressing over her womb where the waves of throbbing

pleasure were subsiding.

"Back, whore of darkness," rasped the strange voice of the large demon creature. "Away! You mustn't drink too much of her. Not yet. The life-power you've drained from her would already have killed a score of your kind!"

"Why? Why not?" Lyia's voice came low and intense. "She's in my power. I have her!"

"You have not, O whore," said the creature. "Go back to your coffin-room and sleep there. You have enough sustenance for now, and you may not realize the depth of the defenses for which she was trained. Even unconscious, she's dangerous!"

"But I must be with her!"

"Why?" rasped the demon-thing. "That you may draw more of her Power and try to rival us again?" He kicked Tanithia's unconscious body with his clawed foot, and she rolled from the dais onto the stone floor, bleeding. Lyia gasped.

"So. You have mixed emotions. She has gotten to you, hasn't she?" came the mocking voice.

"No!" hissed Lyia, flame appearing in her eyes. "I want the sustenance which she can give me!"

"Take not too much, slut! You've taken too much as it is!" snarled the creature. "Deep down in her mind she'll know that something is wrong, and her defenses are very strong indeed. We must destroy her, but it cannot be done so simply or so crassly as you seem to think, vampire harlot!"

"What . . . what will you do with her?" asked Lyia, wiping the blood from her lips as she eyed Tanithia's still and silent beauty.

"The bitch shall be taken to her chamber," said the creature, grasping Tanithia by her neck and between her legs, lifting her effortlessly. "And tomorrow you shall do the same. Enchant her more, and draw more from her.

And the day after, and the day after that. Soon her will as well as all her magical and physical strength will be totally gone, and we can dispose of her. Perhaps in a rather amusing way."

The creature looked scornfully at Lyia, and she cringed slightly. "But do not, " it said, "Do not underestimate the Power that resides in this witch. She's very strong, even now." So saying, he unceremoneously carried the unconscious Tanithia from the hall to deposit her on her own couch.

For a long moment Lyia gazed at the empty doorway, her face, aquiline and perfect though it was, contorted in hatred. In fury she pounded her fists on the stone flags of the floor as dark hair fell over he white shoulders and the roundness of her breasts.

Then, at leangth, she rose slowly to her feet and stalked from the great room.

Tanithia awoke blearily on the following morn. Her throat was raspingly sore and her head thick. Her limbs were heavy, as if illness pervaded every fiber of her frame. And her head . . . her head hurt as well.

Oddly, she had no recollection of the night before. At least not the end of it. Of dancing, of whirling . . . she smiled in memory of an ill-defined ecstasy. Yes, she must have had far too much to drink. Far too much indeed, she mused.

She roused herself from the bed. She was naked: her gown of the previous night lay in a pile beside the bed. She frowned and walked further, on into the next room. Finding an ewer of water she drank of it . . . then tipped it up and drained it. Her hands shook, and the coolness of the water was gratifying as some ran down her chin, between her breasts, over her stomach, into the softness below and down her legs to puddle around her feet.

"So weak . . . so tired. I feel completely drained . . ." For one so used to the peak of vitality and perfection of health the feeling was distressing in the extreme.

She fumbled about, and found herself at the shuttered window. She threw it open for a moment . . . then found that the light was excruciatingly painful to her eyes, and she closed it again. She found a long skirt and pulled it over her hips. She added a sleeved shoulder-cloak which barely covered her breasts, and . . . uncharacteristically . . . a wide-brimmed hat. She was unused to disliking the sun, but this was indeed the case.

She walked slowly through the emptily echoing, dim halls of the castle, unsteady, the stone floor seeming hard and cold beneath her feet, and her body seeming tired and heavy. The tapers had all burned down to nubs of gray wax, and the fire in the great hall was out. She seached, but could find no sign of Lyia. She called, though her voice had little strength.

Finally the stone flags were making her bare feet very cold and sore indeed, and she limped out into an unkempt garden, squinting against the brilliance of the sun. She sat for a long while in the sun, drinking in the warmth, yet trying not to let it hurt her eyes too greatly.

She pulled up her skirt and examined her legs. They seemed a bit more pale than before, though still satisfyingly shapely. She examined her bare midriff, and lifted the shoulder of the cloak to examine her breasts. Yes, there was a definite unhealthy pallor, and the skin seemed pulled more taunt. As though her body was beginning to age.

This was ridiculous! With a sigh she roused herself to her feet and, staggering slightly, wandered on into the buttery to find . . . something . . . anything . . . edible. She eventually found something that looked like leather and which tasted about the same. But she could at least chew and swallow it, then washed the doubtfully palatable food down with some good strong wine. Feeling somewhat more alive, Tanithia plodded back through the dim, silent halls to her own chamber and fell heavily across her bed.

A dull stupor of fatigue merged by slow degrees into an uneasy sleep, with dreams of undefined menace.

She awoke and dragged herself up from her bed. Outside night was falling, and the last colors of the sunset were fading. She rolled over on the bed, feeling somewhat better than before, and saw that someone had thoughtfully placed a small oil lamp there. The small flame cast a bright, reassuring light in the chamber.

"Lyia!" she smiled, and rose to her feet, still not entirely steady, though feeling considerably better than before. A few flickering tapers lit the long hallways as she walked, steadying herself every now and then, through the semi-darkness towards the great hall.

There was a glow of light ahead, and she relievedly hastened towards it.

"Lyia . . . Lyia?" She came uncertainly in through the great carven doorway, to see the other sitting, musing, in the archaic rich chair that she seemed to fancy.

The hall was dark, save for a single candelabrum near her. It seemed as though Lyia had been awaiting, as she looked at Tanithia with a wide smile, her teeth glistening white in the candle light.

"How beautiful you look tonight, Lyia," said Tanithia. And indeed she did. Her long black gown, jaggedly dagged, fell to the floor and was gathered at the sleeves to fall free about her wrists. The jagged neckline also displayed her full breasts, down to their rosy tips, most temptingly. Her hair fell over her bared shoulders like black wings.

Lyia eyed the other appraisingly for a long moment. "You look both vulnerable and fetchingly lovely tonight,

Tanithia," she murmured, as the other sank wearily onto the cushions strewn over the dais at her feet. There was silence for a while.

"You look rather wan this evening," said Lyia at length. "Are you feeling badly?"

"Yes, one could say so," said Tanithia, looking about with dark-rimmed eyes. "I don't feel so well. It's almost that time of the moon, yet normally I don't feel this badly even at my worst times."

"Hm . . . perhaps too much revelry," suggested the other with a slight smile. "Too much too soon and not enough time to rest."

"Perhaps," said Tanithia uncertainly. "And perhaps also some effect of the magic lashing back in a way which I had not anticipated." She absently rubbed at her throat . . . then touched at it more cautiously. "I seem to have some sore spots on my neck, Lyia. This castle has few mirrors in it, and I definitely don't have the strength to go and find one of them. Tell me, do I have anything like insect bites here?"

Lyia looked at the two angry red sores spreading about the wide punctures on Tanithia's arched white throat. She smiled and ran her tongue delicately along the edges of her white teeth. "No," she said. "Perhaps a slight scratch from your fingernail . . . but barely noticeable, pretty one."

Tanithia leaned her head wearily against Lyia's leg. "We ought to examine the entire castle very carefully," she rambled, barely listening to her own voice. "To see if there are any places we might have missed during the exorcism . . . any places where the Dark Forces may perhaps be seeping through. But later. Later . . . when I'm feeling a bit better . . ."

Lyia touched her hair and stroked it. Tanithia leaned against her knees with a sigh. "Lyia, you're a comfort as well as a friend," she murmured.

Lyia's brows knitted briefly, as if in a momentary pain, and then she smiled softly. "There . . . rest, pretty one. Rest and relax. You won't be feeling this bad much longer." Her hands caressed Tanithia's temples and rubbed her neck and shoulders, as Tanithia sighed in tired contentment.

Then, settling down on her knees beside the other, Lyia rubbed her back and shoulders, underneath the shoulder cape. Then came around before Tanithia, who was drowsy and pleasant-faced. Lyia's lips brushed her hair and her cheeks, while her hands kneaded the witch-woman's shoulders and arms further, then reached under the cloak to caress the warmth of her breasts.

"You wear a high collar tonight," she commented. "It's not like you.

"Hm . . . the cape is for you to feel and to touch beneath, my lover. Let me feel more of your magic touch." Her hands reached drowsily to touch the cheeks and bare shoulders of the one who knelt intently before her.

"Tanithia?"

"Hm?"

"Let me see your eyes, dear. Perhaps I can get a better idea of what's wrong." Lyia continued caressing Tanithia's breasts, and Tanithia jutted them foreward pleasurably as the other fondled her nipples.

"Let me take a close look at your eyes," insisted Lyia. Slowly and sleepily Tanithia opened her eyes and found herself gazing into the dark, intent eyes that, quite unexpectedly, were transfixing her.

"Look at me and look deeply. Look at me and look deeply." She continued caressing and speaking softly as Tanithia looked, staring forward, more and more engrossed in the other. Fumbling occasionally to touch Lyia's hair and to clumsily caress her breasts. Then finally sitting and staring blankly.

Lyia pushed her down onto the silken cusions, and luxuriously stretched her body out over Tanithia's. She touched her sharp teeth to Tanithia's throat, but the witch-woman stirred uncomfortably, almost waking. Something deep within Tanithia seemed to know . . . Lyia drew back for a moment and, caressing and fondling the other's body so that more asleep than in a trance Tanithia smiled, moved her hips, and jutted out her breasts.

"Lyia . . ." she whispered softly. Lyia felt beneath the other's high-slit skirt, fondled and pressed up on the cleft. Tanithia gasped and smiled more. Another touch at the throat. But this again drew the deep unease which would break the trance if continued. Biting her lip in impatience, Lyia again caressed Tanithia to pleasure her and to relax her again. But it was slow, and difficult.

Lyia's face by degrees became more and more animalistic with the nagging frustration and her desire to consummate her blood-desire, for Tanithia was, on a deep level, resisting her; a deep part of her mind seemed to understand, though her conscious mind was mazed. Lyia's eyes were more and more feral . . . she was so close to the life-blood of the other, and yet could not go futher for fear of awakening her.

She caressed the soft breasts of the unconscious woman and leaned forward to kiss the rosy nipples that stood at their tips, to stroke them with her soft tongue.

Then, on sudden impulse, she buried her fangs in Tanithia's naked bosom, and Tanithia writhed and moaned in an agony that had become ecstacy. Her body arched and shuddered in waves of orgasmic pleasure.

Lyia spread her own body over her victim's, drawing in much blood, and much of that indefinable yet vastly potent Power which itself is the essence not only of life but of magic—of the prime matter of the universe.

Lyia drew deeply on the sustenance from Tanithia's breast, filling and expanding herself, and feeling arousal within her own cool body. Knowing that she was taking, and taking brutally, the helpless one beneath her. Waves of ebony black hair intermingled with tumbled curls of red-gold tresses, and their bodies moved and swayed rhythmically. Tanithia gasped and whimpered in her unconsciousness, though the one arching over her continued to draw and to drain ever yet more.

"Get up, slut!" came a rasping voice. "You've nearly awakened her . . . and why drain from her breast, you fool! She might see it all to easily."

"She nearly awakened every time I came near her neck . . . I couldn't get close without her stirring and nearly breaking the trance. She may be beginning to understand what's going on." Lyia's eyes remained hungrily on Tanithia. "Yet mayhap this will have taken more strength from her. Please . . . let me have more of her," said Lyia.

"No! Any more and she will be certain to notice. You may already have gone too far, sow."

"Just a bit more of her," pleaded Lyia, her hands clasped tightly beneath her breasts, pulling upwards until the dark rose tips lifted from the top of her gown.

"Ah, always you try to regain the power you lost to us. It shall not be, slut!" And the creature swung at Lyia, its blow sending the vampire girl sprawling. Her hair strewn in disarray, her legs bare, clutching at her bosom, she fixed her near-mad gaze on the demon-creature.

"Please . . . let me have more!"

"Begone sorceress. Begone! You're our slave now, remember?" The creature picked up Tanithia by her neck, as one might pick up a discarded doll, and regarded her for a moment. A travesty of a leering smile spread over its face. "This one I shall take back. I'll put her into her bed again, and leave the place dark so she won't be able to see your fumbling handiwork. Tomorrow you must repeat this tawdy scene once again." It began shambling towards the nearby door, dragging Tanithia's limp body. "In the meantime I have my hellspawn to raise, so that we may continue as we had before ... as soon as her worthless carcass is hung to rot on the upper battlements."

Throwing the unconscious Tanithia over his horny shoulder, the creature shambled off into the darkness.

Lyia looked after with fiery eyes, and a snarl that slowly faded from her scarlet lips. Then suddenly, she buried her head in her hands, dark hair tumbling over her clenched fists as her body heaved in silent sobs.

HE following day was well-nigh spent before Tanithia weakly struggled to sit up in her rumpled bed. She rubbed at her eyes and clasped her aching head as she rocked back and forth to try and soothe the fevered throbbing.

"Terrible . . . I feel terrible," she said, rubbing her temples, her hair falling in tangles about her shoulders and over her bosom. She pushed aside the coverlet and swung her feet over the side of the bed onto the cold floor. Her garb of the night before lay in an untidy pile next to the bundled dancing gown she had worn an eternity ago, it seemed. Was it only two evenings? No . . . an eternity, an eternity of pain, darkness and nightmares ago. Even the jewels she had worn were scattered about, she noticed as she kicked one with her toe. Only this time, she groggily observed, Lyia had put her into a soft sleeping gown, and a rather nice one, as nearly as she could tell in the twilight dimness. Though certainly her friend could have done a neater job of fitting her into it, she thought.

Was it another night of pleasure that once more was too much for her? No, bad dreams and a feeling of unease were never the aftermath of her usual erotic carousing. Perhaps an illness? An unfortunate after-effect of having revelled far too much with her men, some evenings ago? She wistfully thought of them, and wished that even one of them were here now, to care for her, and to console her.

"This castle is so dark . . . and so cold . . ." she said. The fabric of her gown was soft and comfortable, and warmed her legs a little, as well as her breasts. Her throat seemed less sore. Perhaps if she rested a bit longer . . . just a bit longer. No, she should see Lyia again, and perhaps have her friend prepare some food, and call a healing-woman from the village below.

Ridiculous! She thought to herself. I'm a healing-woman myself! Healer, heal yourself! Easily said, yet difficult to do.

Painfully and slowly she eased herself out of the bed. "I'm weaker than before . . . how strange." she muttered. "Yet I don't think it's quite that time of the month just yet. And I've never felt like this before on any month."

She staggered forward and settled at a low carven bureau. A hairbrush was before her. Absently she picked it up and began working the tangles out of her long tresses. They came hard and difficult, yet she was somewhat soothed to do this very ordinary task.

One particular tangle in front gave more trouble than the others. She pulled hard on it and the tangle gave suddenly. The brush hit her breast and she cried out at the sudden pain.

"What . . . can it be?" she muttered to herself. She

pulled down on the neckline; oddly, it had been drawn tightly to be quite high about her neck. The drawstring would not readily loosen, but she tugged at the silken cord until it was undone, and pulled the front of the nightgown down to bare her breast.

She drew her breath suddenly in with shock. Two angry, large sores with what seemed to be ugly, wide puncture holes in the center marred the perfection of her left breast. She touched them gingerly. They looked terrible, she thought, noisome and festering. Perhaps they would heal after a while, given care. Or so she desperately hoped.

Unconsciously she touched a finger to her throat. Yes . . . it felt like the same thing there . . . not noticeably closer to being healed, and still raw and painful. Lyia had said there was nothing to be seen, though . . .

Quickly . . . or as quickly as she could in her weakened condition, Tanithia staggered to her feet and reeled into the other room, hitting her toe painfully against the heavy wooden door.

"The mirror . . . I must look at the mirror!"

The light was out, but flint and tinder were at hand. She struck a glow quickly to light a taper. Yes, her throat looked fully as bad as the raw wounds over her nipple. She considered. Why had Lyia spoken false, when obviously she could see the ugly, infected punctures?

Tanithia gazed at the angry, ulcerated sores in the mirror. Both sets were the same . . . and she was weak . . . she looked so pale . . .

"Damn!" she snapped. "How blind have I been! When will I ever, ever learn? I was so mazed by wanting her that I never saw it, even though the signs were all there, and the evidence was right before my eyes!"

She stood for a moment, then sat down again with a

sudden weakness.

"Of course . . . she's never eaten much, and always shunned the sun." Tanithia snapped her fingers. "And she never let me quite finish exorcising the last few of those deepest dungeons. What may have been there? Whatever it was, I think it's come forth since then, and it's here in the castle with me!"

She staggered down the hallway. "No . . . not the great hall. If I go there again she'll do the same once more. What was that the old madman had raved . . . something about, 'the Harlot of Evil'. I should have known . . . I should have seen!" In frustration she beat her fist against the stone wall.

"My jewelry! It's been charged magically. I can use it to get out of here!" She stumbled back to her chamber, searched and searched more, with increasing desperation. It was not where she had put the leathern pouch, and try through she might, she could no find it.

"Oh, have I ever been a fool," she muttered to herself. "A fool! I've got to get Count Waldmann and his troop back here again, and I've got to escape this place while I still have the strength. Neither will be easy, I'm afraid," she said grimly to herself. "And I may have a lot more pain and suffering to undergo before I can escape from the consequences of my blindness!"

Absently she laced up the neckline of her gown, winced briefly as the cloth, soft though it was, rasped her wounded breast, then unlaced again so that the soft cloth all but merely hung from the tips of her nipples.

"Yet I'm not without resources." Incense, yes, there was a lot of it still left from the revels. The perfumed casques were still where they had been left. She gathered up a handful of incense and some tapers, carrying them into the mirror chamber.

Far down the dark, stone hallways were faint echoes.

She studiously ignored them, and even made it a point to push the awareness from her conscious mind. Particularly, she did not want to think of what, in the far darkness, might be making those echoes.

In the chamber she lit the tapers, so that there were five placed about her. She lit the incense so that the smoke rose thickly before the mirror. Wearily, she sank down to her knees, put her hands on the floor to brace herself. Then with a deep breath, with hands on her knees, she sat upright in a formal meditation position. She tossed her hair back over her bare shoulders and smoothed it to hang gracefully. Breasts thrust out proudly, she eyed her image in the mirror with approval.

"I might be haggard . . . I might be battered . . . but I still have beauty, and strength. I still have power." She took another deep breath, carefully channeling her mind. "I still have magic, and no one can equal me. No one!" She smiled to herself at the brave, vain-glorious words— trapped here in a great, ominous tomb, in a desperate situation that was bound to get worse.

Yet the preliminary words had their effect. The edge of confidence was hers again for a while; the confidence needed for magic.

She spoke words and performed smooth conjurations with her arms. Her weakness actually even helped, for she dropped into a totally focused trance far easier than she would elsewhere. Her image in the mirror gradually faded and dissolved into blackness.

"Count Waldmann . . . Gort," she droned. "Count Waldmann . . . Swordsman Gort. Dear ones, hear my call . . ." A part of her mind pushed out into the blackness of the mirror, searching, and willing, seeking in a dim space that lay beyond the edge of existence. If only she weren't so terribly weak . . .

The images began to slowly take shape in the mirror.

Her words that followed were unspoken, yet she knew that they were sensed and the meanings understood. Help . . . desperately, help! Danger and horror all about. Deception . . . betrayal. I need your help, and badly . . .

It seemed as though two faces looked at her for a moment in the mirror. Then, before she could say more, she toppled forward into unconsciousness. A small part of her mind gave an unheard shriek of anger and frustration at the weakness . . . the damnable weakness that crippled her just at the time when she needed all her wits.

Then all was insensate darkness.

Tanithia awoke, the coldness of the stone upon her cheek, and against her bosom and her feet. The thin cloth of her nightgown protected her but little from the chill of the stone. Shivering, she pulled herself up.

"But I reached them," she said to herself. "I reached them."

The tapers had gone out, knocked over by her fall perhaps. She stood, and staggered from the room . . . and froze.

She sensed a presence. An evil, unsettling presence.

The darkness was almost total, yet the eyes glowed red. With a gasp she shuddered back, easing away in some vague hope of escape. Backing away, until she was stopped by the feel of the hard stone against her bare heels.

"Ssso," hissed a harsh, unhuman voice from the darkest of the darkness. "You want to call to your friends." Then an evil chuckle which had no sanity to it. "You are not leaving here alive, witch-woman. You have been weakened, and your body and soul are ready to die. TO DIE!"

From out of the darkness a clawed semblance of a fist struck, hard. battering her half senseless against the opposite wall. She tried to raise herself with an involuntary

sob at the pain, only to be hurled back again into the cold stone. Near senseless, yet conscious enough to wish she could somehow escape the red, awful agony . . . and the horror of the thing that loomed, mordantly horrific, in the shadows before her.

"You die, witch! I draw the rest of the Power from you now. Take your strength." Again the laughter that made her turn her face away as her hackles rose, regardless of the numbing pain. "Then tear your heart out." Insane, mocking laughter.

Cruel claws raked down between her breasts, ripping away the front of the gown in one sudden motion. A clawed "hand" seized her shoulder and crushed her down onto the cold stone yet again. She looked up with tear-rimmed eyes, only to know the horror grow worse.

A faint glow now came from the creature. An obscene, odiferous caricature of both human and reptile, stood over her. Leering, it roughly pulled her legs open and yanked her body up against its insanely ugly maleness. Seeing now its intent, she steeled herself and pulled into herself whatever Power she could muster out of her terrified weakness.

"You shall be raped into submission and then die, witch woman. Slowly and agonizingly, you will die."

Something obscenely cold and sharp touched between her legs. Her inner essence reached for strength.

Then a crackle of blue fire that brilliantly lined the stone hallway. The creature suddenly burst into flames and shrieking in inhuman agony, clawed its way across the floor and fell, gibbering and moaning as large pieces of its repellent body began to break away in the fire, and then finally dissolved into putrescence. And the putrescence into dust in the fading blue light.

Tanithia pulled herself up against the wall. In spite of pain, in spite of the depths of weakness.

"Well, demon creature. You underestimated my strength . . . the deep strength that is a part of my very being." Then she sagged once again to the floor.

"I've got to escape. Now. Even though I can still fight a little, and my body and my soul will fight even when my senses are gone . . . it still weakens me, and I can take only so much." She buried her face in her hands, finding some small comfort in the feel of her hair hiding the faint dimness of the scene from her view. "They'll win. Eventually they'll win."

"How to escape . . ." She steadied herself, and pressed her head against the coolness of the wall. Her strength was desperately low, and ebbing rapidly. How to get out. The main gate? Even were she whole it was doubtful that she could turn the massive capstan to raise the portcullis.

And now she doubted that she could even crawl up the stairs.

Shakily she rubbed her head. "Think . . . think!" she muttered in a strained voice. No, the walls were too high. They couldn't kill her just yet, but they could wear her down, throw her into the dungeons, and gradually bleed away her sanity as well as her life forces. Caught, mayhap, like a rat.

She reeled back to the mirror room, struck a flame, and lit the remaining incense. If nothing physically could be done to effect an escape, then the only thing left would be whatever magic she could call forth in her present weakened condition.

Her image in the mirror was not a good one. Hair streaming over her face and shoulders, only the tatters of the thin gown hanging to her naked body by the torn sleeves and nothing else. Ugly sores and cruel, scarlet claw marks that marred the fullness of her bare breasts, and an angry bruise swelling the side of her face. Eyes that reflected pain and apprehension.

Slowly, deliberately, she cleared her mind of her fears and even of the battered and haunted-eyed image in the mirror.

The mind must be prepared, and sensitive, for magic. An invocation came unbidden to her lips.

If nothing direct,
Then may it be indirect.
O Great Goddess of my people . . .
I am in my extremity.
Help me, please.

Her intent concentration nearly faded as a sob broke from her throat. She steadied herself and then continued.

I do ask, O Patroness of the Stars,
Bend events, I do entreat,
That I may find my way free
Of these dark walls . . .
No matter how harsh the consequences.
Bend events . . . bend . . . bend . . .
Alter circumstance, and let me
Make amends later.
So mote it be, gracious Lady.
So mote it be . . .

Tears streaming down her face, she threw the last of the incense onto the glowing ember. She faded again into unconsciousness.

Tanithia awoke in her own bed, to the sound of glass being shattered in a room nearby. She listened for a moment, then dropped her head back on the soft cushions. Now her one improvised place of ritual and of magic had been ruined and perhaps desecrated.

Lyia stepped softly into the room on pale feet, her black gown and the winged sleeves seeming to make her all the more a creature of darkness, no matter how appealing were her soft breasts and her sleek form.

"Tanithia, my darling," she smiled, her teeth white and sharp.

"Away, vampiress! I want thee not!" Tanithia turned her face aside.

"But Tanithia . . . pretty one . . ."

"No! Begone, Lyia . . . deceiver. Whore of Darkness."

Her brows knitted, still as if with great effort, Lyia moved forward even more closely. "Please." Her outstretched hand reached to touch Tanithia's bared breast.

A spark of fire leaped from Tanithia's body into the vampire girl who, shrieking in pain, found herself hurled to the opposite wall.

In a moment Lyia regained her composure and stood gracefully, clasping her injured hand. She found her voice. "Tanithia . . . you wouldn't."

"I would." Her voice was weak but firm. "And I shall."

"I know you for what you are, daughter of darkness. Your demon creatures I shall kill. You I shall . . . I shall . . . begone. Begone, you whom I thought to be friend." Her voice was pained.

Lyia paused for a moment, uncertain. Then, with a sob, she ran from the room. Her sobs and the soft sound of her feet echoing, echoing as she ran further and further away. And finally vanishing in the dark distance.

 RESENTLY Tanithia awoke again. Was it still the same night? Was it yet another? She had no way of knowing, and her strength was no more than before.

Tired . . . she was desperately tired. But to lie here abed would be the worst possible course. "I've got to find my way to the parapet," she muttered in a fevered voice. "I've got to find my way out. To escape."

She crawled from the bed and stood, the remnant of the ruined gown falling from her body. She wished that she could see her injured breast in spite of the darkness. To hopefully see if it were healing . . . for she could not stand the thought of having herself so marred.

No. She could not let her mind slip.

Methodically, now, to the wardrobe. Step by painful step. Feeling within . . . There . . . a soft gown of some sort. Now, shrug it on. Too tired to tie the laces of this long garment. Too tired to do more than cinch the waist slightly, leaving it loose for her injured breast.

She staggered down the hallway, step by determined step. Finally to the parapet overlooking one of the outer gardens. The garden was fenced on the outside of the castle . . . but the fence was twice the height of a man. Anxiously she looked about, to and fro.

"How can I possibly . . ."

She froze, and her hackles rose. For something had followed her.

Again the feeling of mordant, gnawing horror as something shambled towards her in the darkness.

"You seek still to escape?" Rasped an eerie voice from the darkness. "You seek still to leave? Kill as many of us as you will, witch-woman, your body shall inevitably rot upon these parapets." An evil chuckle.

"We shall bleed you to death, and your body shall rot upon these walls!" It came closer. "We will kill you slowly, if we cannot rend you quickly."

She began to call Power up within her once again, to defend herself, but the demon-creature sensed it, and stepped in.

With a single cruel blow, the being smashed her down upon the floor, dazed. "Nay, witch-woman. Do not try your tricks upon me." A cruel kick into her ribs and the breath was knocked out of her. She gasped in agony.

"You wish to get out, witch?" came the mocking sneer. She clawed herself weakly up to her elbows and looked up through her streaming hair. She touched the fullness of her breasts and looked up appealingly, the pain rimming her eyes with tears.

"Nay, your human charms will not move me . . . I am of no kin whatsoever to your despicable breed. So looks of pathos or appeal, or the sight of a body which is supposed to be so beautiful to your kind will not move me. You will be meat upon my table. Nothing more." The repellant face came close to hers, grinning like a vision of insane death.

"You wish out?" It's voice raised. "HERE!"

With demonic glee it seized her agonizingly by the neck and between the legs as she screamed, and threw her over the parapet.

The fall seemed to be an infinity, and her long scream permeated the air as her body dropped through the darkness. To land with a shocking, resounding splash in the large and ornate pool below.

The water was not deep, but deep enough to break her fall. And cold enough to make her catch her breath again, quickly, after the shock of the impact. Momentarily to gain her a little more strength.

"There!" came the mocking voice from above. "This is as close to the outside as you will be. Stay there for a few days, for our slut of evil has tainted you with her own blood. The sun will be agony to you, witch girl. Agony. One day in the bright sunlight and you will be screaming to come in and seek refuge in darkness . . . even knowing what we plan to do with you."

"But we shall leave you until you are withered and brown and weak. Until only the smallest spark of life remains in your agonized remnant of a body."

Gasping, she dragged herself painfully to the edge of the pool and pulled herself out, the water running from her hair, her shoulders, and her breasts.

"Stay there, witch-girl. We have you now, and we shall wear you down!" The foul delight of the unhuman creature was obvious as it departed, laughing in demonic glee, back down the halls of the castle. She tried to shut it out of her ears, but then gave up. Then, shivering, dragged herself fully out of the pool to lie on the wide stone rim.

"Well," she thought blearily to herself, "Is this the result of my magic? Have I merely gone from the cook pan into the fire? Out of the cauldron and into the brimstone?" She smiled without mirth.

A movement. Atop the wall . . . the outside wall. A high wall, yet definitely someone or something was there! She held her breath and looked. Yes, it seemed to be a man, though in the dark shadows she could make out no details. He seemed to be lowered down carefully from the wall by a thin rope, to be followed by yet another. Tanithia wiped her eyes with a shaking hand.

"Count Waldmann? Here so soon? Impossible! But who . . . who could these be?" Warily, looking about with great care, the two quickly came over to her. Scarcely able to move from the chill in her limbs and the pain in her body, she merely looked up at them dumbly, as they stood over her.

"Is it she? Is it the witch?"

"I don't know. But she's the only one still in this castle, remember? So it's got to be her!" The other looked up at the empty parapet above.

"The only one? Then who . . . what . . . was that?" The first man took him by the arm.

"Hellspawn, brother, hellspawn. Where you find witches, you find the Hordes of Dark. The Book states it." The second man bent down and looked at Tanithia, rolling her over for a better view. He drew in his breath. "By the Son! What's happened to her?"

"Evil consumes its own minions, friend. Here. Take the wench and gag her. Tie her hands and her feet. Quickly now! Before that . . . that thing comes back. We've got to be over the wall and gone quickly!"

They trussed her, and Tanithia smiled grimly to herself. Indeed . . . out of the cookpan and into the fire . . .

into the stake and the flames. She was too weak to maintain any real consciousness as they hoisted her up and other hands grasped her limp, wet form and lowered her over the edge to the outside.

"It is she?" asked others in low voices.

"I think so. But let's get away from here fast and we'll look her over more carefully."

"Verily, brother," came yet another, deeper voice. "I know my feelings, and I know what I feel here. This is the witch. Quickly now!"

Two men lifted her, trussed and gagged, and hurried her off into the wood, then draped her unceremoniously over the saddle of a horse, lashing her hands and feet to the harness. As quickly and as silently as possible, they moved away.

The jouncing of the horse, her wounds, and her weakness were great. She wanted to moan, even to cry out in pain, but could not.

Soon, mercifully, darkness enveloped her.

A long while later, seemingly, she awakened slowly. She began to open her eyes, then remembered what had happened, and continued feigning unconsciousness. At least she was warm . . . that was good. Warm and tucked between covers.

There was the sound of voices and of men in the room. "You're sure she's the one, Elijus?" The voice was anxious.

"Yes, yes, yes! As I've said so many times, I know what I feel. I've never been wrong in divining a witch yet, and I'm not wrong now. This is Magda!"

"But she was burned . . ."

"She was *not* burned!" snapped Elijus. "I don't know who went to the stake, but it was not she, for she is with us now. And those witch-marks, raw and awful, upon her neck and her bosom. Verily, she has been having congress with the Creatures of the Dark One since she first came here, days ago."

"But if they come for us . . ." said another.

"We're protected by the Book and by our sacred sigil."

Ah, she thought to herself. Their unbalanced Cross of the Elements, itself flawed and uneven. No, they won't be able to keep the demon creatures away for long. Unless I do the keeping. After all, my chances are better here than they are back in the castle. I'll at least be brutalized a bit less here.

She settled back, still apparently unconscious, but weaving in her mind a spell, as strong as she could muster, of protection and of invisibility to the eyes that seek. She planned for these coarse fanatics to be shielded, she and they, for as long as necessary.

She wove the spell, pretending unconsciousness, building matrix upon matrix, and then exhausted, dropped off into a deep sleep.

She woke again, and this time felt that waking for their benefit would be in order.

"Ah, the witch awakens."

"Water?" she asked tentatively. "Water?"

One of the men, a hard-faced, cruel-mouthed rogue, drew a gourd of water and came close. She pulled herself up on the rough cot and looked around. She was in a large hut . . . perhaps a farmstead. He held the dripping cup before her. Her eyes were on the cup, and on the cup alone.

"Please, may I have water?" She was indeed thirsty, of course. And perhaps it would give them the feeling that they were totally in control if she played a bit of an act at this time.

"Your name, wench," he demanded, holding the dipper just out of her reach. "Your name!"

"My . . . name?" she said, looking up at him and feigning hurt innocence. "Why, sir, I don't know what you mean!"

"Your name!" Another man brought his face close to hers, his breath rank and strong. She drew away, repelled.

"What are you called, girl?"

"Why . . . sir, may I not have the water?" She clasped her hands to her breasts.

"Cover yourself, wench, and don't try working the Dark One's wiles on us. Lead us not to temptation!" The first man abruptly thrust his face immediately in front of Tanithia's, with a suddenness that made her flinch, and all but shouted.

"What is thy name?"

"Ma . . Magda," she said, seemingly intimidated. "It's Magda."

"It's she," came a voice triumphantly. They whooped-ed, laughed, and congratulated each other.

"Here . . . drink, witch." She greedily gulped down the water.

"So . . . the once mighty queen, now haggard and run to the ground. And scarce able to move out of bed. You have too much congress with the minions of the Dark One, girl."

Their leader, a gaunt, rangy man with the slightly wild-eyed look of the true believer about him, put his face close to hers, his voice rasping and his breath as foul as any of the others.

"You're going back with us, woman. You're going back to burn at the stake you escaped, and none of your creatures can save you! For the One, True, and Only God shall protect us."

She felt it was appropriate for the time being, and under the circumstances, to feign weakness and resignation, for the weakness was definitely there, though the resignation was not. She sagged back against the straw-filled pillow with a few convincing, deep sobs.

(Look at their faces, Tanithia thought to herself. A woman may not have the brute strength of a man, but men are so easily misled by a woman's tears, genuine or not.)

With tear-rimmed eyes she looked imploringly at their leader . . . as she smiled inwardly . . . "Please sir, food. I'm terribly hungry. And . . . and more water." (Pretty good, she thought. I should have been an actress.)

"Feed the witch," he muttered, turning on his heel. "Feed her and water her. We have to keep her alive until we reach the capital city. After that . . ." He smiled without humor. "After that the Sword of Our God will strike for all to see."

Her shudder at his voice and the glint in his eye was not feigned this time.

It seemed to be day outside. She felt better, having eaten the rude fare they thrust at her. The sores on her throat and on her bosom were likewise better, though she knew that more than a little rest would be needed to cure them. Her strength would be increasing rapidly, and before long she would be able to think of escape.

Settling back into apparent sleep, she prepared the deep part of her mind. Tanithia probed outwards with her senses, and felt that the shallow protection she had woven was still sufficient. Magical means could not, for now, detect her presence here. But she knew full well that the night creatures would be searching far and wide for her, and soon. A few more days . . . that would be all she needed.

She relaxed the tight rein on her mind. Her body had taken a lot of abuse, and both conscious and unconscious magic-working had drained her far more than would ever be safe. She was ill, weak, and injured; only food and rest could restore her. Her mind fogged with oncoming sleep. Those damnable demon-creatures hadn't broken her, but they'd come all too close . . . And Lyia . . . that was the cruelest of all . . .

Elijus regarded the sleeping woman. In fevered sleep she looked weak, vulnerable, and sorely battered. What, he wondered, could have happened? The contrast between the wild, laughing dancer at the inn and this pathetic, wounded creature was very striking indeed. She stirred slightly in her sleep, and her brow creased in some disturbing dream. She made a small, unconscious sound, and a tear ran down her face. Without thinking, Elijus reached out to wipe the tear and mayhap to touch the tumbled hair that covered the pallet about her head. Then he caught himself.

"Get thee behind me," he muttered. "The wages of ungodly evil are death, and the Dark One always takes his due. She'll have her chance to accept the True Way at the trial, and before we burn her." He turned to several of his men, talking across the room.

"The witch looks to be in a fevered condition. We don't want to take the chance of having her die before we reach our destination, so we'll spend perhaps three days here before leaving. Now, check with the sentinels. I don't think it would be wise to have any of the local folk hereabout wandering in on us."

"Prepare the horses," Elijus directed, rousing his men as dawn broke on the third day. "For who knows where the loyalties of these heath-folk might lie. And the farmer who left this stone house empty might just be coming back . . . I've been nervous about staying here this long!" The others departed. Tanithia was pretending to sleep, for she had rapidly learned that if she were obviously awake she was immediately the target of one or more heartfelt diatribes designed to save her soul. She could hear activity in the stables which obviously lay just outside. Elijus was in the process of some final instructions to a last few of his men.

"Leave us now," he said. "I want to talk to the witch one more time to see if she'll return to the Way of the Son before she goes to the stake." As the others left, Elijus walked over to the cot and stood regarding her for a few moments.

"All right, girl. You can open your eyes and sit up. Perhaps you've been fooling my men with your sleeping act, but you haven't been fooling me." She opened her eyes in surprise to find him staring down at her sternly.

"You'd best eat," he said shortly. "We'll be leaving presently."

Tanithia sat up and began helping herself to a bowl of stew which had been sitting on the hard dirt floor by the bed. Perhaps it had originally been someone else's meal, but she didn't really care. Their leader sat on the edge of the rude bed, his eyes almost kind.

"Girl, as you know, I'm Elijus. I'm also known as "The Sword of the Loving Son". His eyes never left her. "Does that mean anything to you?"

"Elijus," she said with a flicker of recognition. "I've heard of you. The witch-hunter."

"Aye," he said with pride. "Scores have gone to the stake or to the headsman because I, and only I, identified them as your kind. I did this in the name of my Lord: I've done His will be shedding their blood." He looked sharply at her. "Your blood too will be shed. Do you recant of your evil ways?"

She deliberately took her time as she finished the last morsels of food and sat the wooden bowl aside. Then she turned to look at him.

"Why should I?" she asked. "What do you know of them, that you think I must change?"

"I follow the ways of the Lord. I know that all other ways are evil."

"Are you certain?"

"Don't speak blasphemy at me, girl," he said sharply.

"Doesn't it bother you," she asked, "that so many human beings have died in agony because of what you call 'the true, one-and-only religion'?"

"That, sinner, was for the good of their immortal souls," he mused, clasping his Book before him. "Will you accept our Book? Do you accept our Cross?"

He held out the book in one hand, and the Unbalanced Cross in the other. Suddenly he moved forward and touched her forehead with the cross. If he expected her to cry out and to fall back in terror, perhaps with a smoking mark on her forehead, he was disappointed. Quite deliberately she reached up and took it, smiling with perhaps just a hint of mockery.

"What a fine piece of pewter work," she said. "It has a good feel to it." And she gently placed it back in his hand.

His face fell slightly, and she saw with repressed amusement that he had indeed expected her to collapse, perhaps burst into flame, or any of the other usual misconceptions.

"May I hold the Book, my lord?" she asked, then paused and looked intently at him. "And please . . . hold my hands and hear my words."

She affixed his gaze with hers. Suddenly, though imperceptibly, she gained command and strength in her voice. "Gaze into my eyes, Elijus, that I may hear you better. Gaze into my eyes!" His slightly startled look faded into a totally neutral stare. His eyes were held by hers as she made passes with graceful hands in the air before him.

"Sleep, and rest . . . rest and sleep . . . Elijus. Rest and sleep, because we're going to talk about the Book."

"The Book," he repeated sonambulistically.

"And we'll talk about other things." She paused. It was so easy to drop him into a trance. For all his self-avowed resistance to things not of his religion, he was terribly, pathetically vulnerable.

"Let's speak truth, Elijus."

"Speak truth . . ."

"Do you really wish to kill people?"

"To kill . . . yes. For only blood will fulfill the sacred laws of the Books of Justice."

"Isn't your God a deity of love?"

His flat voice continued. "My god has a sword. He slashes mercilessly."

"Why bother others if they don't bother you?" she asked.

"Because they are sinful, and only my way is the one way." She was impatient with his singleminded returning to the one point.

"Do you like blood?" she asked.

"Yes!" The voice was venomous.

She was taken aback for a moment. She thought briefly, and determined to try another approach. Pulling herself upright on the bed and pulling the covers away from her feet, she slowly pulled her dress up to display her shapely legs. She undid the drawstring on her rather tattered dress and slowly pulled the neckline down to display more and more of her breasts, lips parted and inviting with her smiling gaze. She fluffed out her long hair and smiled softly at him.

"Look at me, Elijus. do you think I'm beautiful? Am I not desirable?"

"No," he muttered.

She was shocked by his unexpected response. And more than a little piqued, for she had great pride in the effect of her obvious charms.

"No," he repeated, making as if to shield his eyes from her. "You're evil. Women are evil, tempting, unclean!" His face contorted, and for a moment it looked as though the trance might break.

"They haven't got any souls, these agents of Darkness!" A flicker of consciousness began returning to his eyes, and she hastily pulled the covers up over herself. "They are responsible for bringing sin into the world . . ."

"There, there," she soothed, and continued for a while to calm him and re-establish her control. Finally she returned to her questions. "But whom do you love?"

"I love . . . I love my God, and I love the Son. I love the Son because he's so handsome . . . he's so powerful and strong. I must be one with his love and beauty and his deadliness. I want him so much, so much . . ."

Tanithia paused as the words mumbled off into silence. "Oh Horns!" she muttered to herself. "He doesn't like women . . . he likes men. And more, he loves the ideal man." She smiled crookedly. "I can see I'm wasting my time trying to exert my wiles on this one. And now I begin to see why so many women . . . as opposed to so few men . . . have died because of his efforts." She looked at him contemplatively for a few moments, then spoke to him again.

"Elijus, hear me," she said. "Hear me and listen well. When next I speak to you of 'the pure lily' . . . remember, 'the pure lily' . . . I will wish to recant. I will wish to do as you desire. When I say so, unlock me and untie me that I may pray." She looked calculatingly at him for a moment. "And pray beside me yourself. And while you pray you will fall into a deep sleep. You will fall into a deep sleep. Do you understand?"

"I understand . . ."

"Very well, repeat what I've told you." He did, in complete detail, and she was satisfied that her mesmerism had its effect.

"Excellent. Now you will awake, feeling that you've made good progress, and that when next I call you, mayhap I shall recant."

"Mayhap you shall recant . . ."

"All right. Now I must rest. Thank you, Elijus," she said, snuggling down beneath the covers for a few last minutes of rest. "It was a good try. You may awaken."

Elijus sat tranced for a moment more, then sat up with a start and looked around. He smiled at some inner thought, then stood, turned, slapping his Book with joy, and looking triumphantly at his pewter cross. Then, whistling the beginning of a hymn, he strode from the room.

Tanithia closed her eyes and smiled resignedly. "Oh well. It was a good try."

Elijus had decided to move out by first daylight, deciding . . . wisely ehough . . . that the creatures of darkness were more to be feared than the local peasantry. The demon-creatures would be less likely to haunt them and to attack them in broad daylight.

Yet it took a while to get started, and things seemed unaccountably to go wrong. Finally in mid-afternoon they did depart, a rather conspicuous column of twoscore men riding down the one main road that led to the inner provinces and the main city of the land.

Her feet tied to the stirrups and her hands lashed to the horn of the saddle, Tanithia had little choice but to go where she was led. The tiredness was still with her, and it became obvious to them that other means of transport would be needed if the witch were to reach the capital city alive, for she sagged and lost consciousness . . . or so it seemed . . . when they were but three or four hours out.

A litter was rigged, which for her was far more comfortable. She watched carefully as they continued and carefully, as sundown approached, eyed the spring at which they paused to refresh themselves and their horses.

"An old spring," muttered one of the men, wiping his chin of the cold, pure water.

"Aye. Look at the carvings in the stone. They're ancient." He picked a thick stick from the ground and tentatively hit at the stone, snapping off a small piece of it. "The old pagan ways are still strong here. The water is good, but someday we'll have to return and tear down these stones and their heathen carvings." His attention was diverted for a moment. "I see that brother Elijus is giving the order to mount up. Let's go."

They continued for a ways, and sunset drew on. Tanithia had listened carefully though, as usual, feigning unconsciousness, and she knew just where they were. Her escape would have to be now, she considered. Else she would be too far from those who would soon be trying to rescue her.

"Elijus," she called. "Elijus!"

"Yes wench, what is it?" he said, coming up along side of her.

"Elijus, when we camp for the night, I'd like to speak with you of the . . . of the pure lily. Of the pure lily."

He did not speak, but she recognized the look in his eyes that indicated he was responding. She continued.

"The darkness that approaches bespeaks also the darkness in my soul. I've thought it over and . . . and I feel that perhaps I'd best accept your offer."

Tanithia clasped her hands before her. "Milord, let's pitch a tent here that I may pray." Elijus smiled broadly and raised his hand as a signal.

"Ho!" he called. "Hold up the column, men. We pitch camp here tonight. Make concealed shelters and guard your campfires well. We don't want to be seen."

"Why here?" came the query.

"I may be making a convert," he said loftily. Tanithia inconspicuously muffled her smile.

The moon was coming out as the evening meal had been completed and a few tents had been pitched, while bedrolls were scattered under the trees. Campfires were kept carefully shielded. The men kept with them their Books and their Unbalanced crosses, though only Tanithia realized how futile these would be against a true attack by Dark Forces.

Elijus had been watching her since they stopped for the night, and Tanithia had been very careful to properly play the role of one smitten with guilt and desiring redemption. Finally he came over to where she knelt quietly.

"Now are you about to recant, girl?" he asked. She looked at him and raised her manacled wrists, and indicated the chains on her ankles.

"Let's step into the tent, deacon, And . . . and unshackle me that I might pray." She looked about. There were no guards nearby, and the shadows were quite deep.

She entered the tent with him behind her, and he pulled the flap shut. He unlocked the chains from her wrists and ankles, and she smoothed her long hair over one shoulder and knelt, looking steadfastly at him.

"Kneel with me, brother," she said. "Kneel with me." She paused, and clasped her hands before her as she began.

> *I call upon you, O Great One*
> *I call upon you to give sleep, to give peace,*
> *To give quiet.*
> *To give release . . .*

She looked across at Elijus, whose eyes were already closed, and continued on briefly in this vein. It was obvious that the witch hunter was quite obligingly in a deep sleep. She ended her prayer in a way that would have startled him, had he been awake and listening.

> *And gracious Mother*
> *Let me always serve thee better*
> *O beautiful one!*
> *Blessed Be!*

She stood erect again. Elijus was motionless in his sleeping trance, hands still clasped before him. Carefully extinguishing the oil lamp, she quietly pulled the tent flap aside and looked about, at the dark, forested camp. No guards were nearby, and she slipped quickly and silently into the shadows.

On silent, soft feet she eased to the edge of the encampment, cautiously staying low and in the deepest of the shadows. Then onto the road and quickly back in the direction from which they had come. In the darkness she could not always pick her way carefully, and the stones were harsh on her feet, for she could see little of where she was going when out of the moonlight. She continued on, a desperation growing within her as she hastened up the moonlight-dappled roadway. Was it one league? Was it two? Certainly not three. It would be a long walk, and a hard one on this road and in this darkness.

And the weakness . . . the weakness . . . that damnable weakness! She stumbled onward, concentrating more and more on merely keeping one foot ahead of the other, of ignoring the weakness and pressing onward, and not thinking of how much further it might be. Her breath came in gasps, and she slowed a little.

Her breast ached, and her neck hurt. Three days had healed much, but these wounds had been deep, and tainted. She was tired. More, she knew that the creatures of darkness would be finding Elijus and his men shortly, with her protective shielding now gone from them.

She wished to be far away when that happened. Very far.

A seeming eternity of stumbling down the rock road on aching feet, of having her dress, frayed thought it was, catch again and again on the bushes and brambles to the side. Yet moving as fast as her weakened condition would allow.

Suddenly she fetched up. Someone was ahead.

Could it be . . . after all this . . . that she was trapped again like some hunted animal? A gasp, partly of pain and partly of dispair, escaped from her throat. And from the shadows ahead came a questioning, intense voice.

"Tanithia? Tanithia, darling, is that you?"

"Gort!" she cried, and ran for him. "My faithful, wonderful Gort!" She threw herself into his arms, embracing him thankfully and burying her head in his chest. "Oh Gort . . . of anyone I'd wanted to see, it's you that I wanted to see most, right now at this time and this place!"

"My love . . . my sweet one! What's happened to you?" He pressed her against himself, very conscious of her frantic clinging.

"Many things," she said. "All of them bad. But kiss me . . . kiss me now!" His lips met hers, and they kissed, long and lingering. Again he pressed her trembling body to his.

"Oh! Be careful, dear one. My throat and my breast . . . the left one. They've been hurt, and they are still sore."

"My poor, hurt love. Can I carry you?" His eagerness brought joy to her heart.

"No, just merely support and steady me. Up there ahead a ways . . . there's a spring, isn't there?"

"Aye, a few hundred paces from here."

"Good. Let's go there, and go quickly!"

"But why? What's so important about that old spring?"

"The demon creatures are back, and they're about to strike at those misguided fanatics who had me prisoner. You and I have got to be in the security of that spring. It's a safe spot!"

They hastened back along the road, he supporting her when she staggered . . . at times even sweeping her off her feet and carrying her, and she clung to him as to life itself.

"Why the spring?" he panted. "Why is it safer there than other places?"

"Because, Gort, it's ancient. Once a long time ago, and for a very, very long time indeed, it was a spring sacred to the Goddess. And even after all this time She is still the patroness of the place. And She is also my patroness. Her protection and the force about that spring, ancient though it is, will act to perhaps shield us."

"How did you come to know this?"

"The carvings, my love. Meaningless to the others, but very clear to me. They tell the entire story." She peered ahead. "And there it is, just a little ways ahead!"

Hurriedly they rushed to where the gentle sound of trickling water was peaceful in the night. The two settled in on the far side of the spring in the dark shadows.

He spread his cloak about the two of them, and took her in his arms.

"Gort, you can't believe how glad I am to see you." She snuggled her head against his shoulder. "Hold me close, my love. And where I'm not injured, touch me. Touch me please. And while you are being good with me, let me weave a spell of protection and of invisibility about us, so that nothing and no one can see us."

His lips sought hers and his hand, guided by hers, loosened the drawstring at the front of her dress, and pulled it down. He fumbled at her breast as she gasped in pleasure and in joy, clinging closer to him. Soon his caresses turned more and more fervent as he kissed her face and eyes, and each felt the arousal of the other. His hand felt higher and higher up her leg, touching softness as she moaned in delight, while her hands roamed as well. He rolled her over onto the soft, leaf-covered ground and pressed her beneath him. The were joined in passionate lovemaking beneath the dark shadows as, with all her pleasure and strong emotion, Tanithia wove the spell impenetratably thick about them.

She was still weaving when they heard, as in the far distance, the flapping of leathern wings and the shouting and screaming of men in the far distance as they fought and died against something unspeakably hideous.

Gort raised himself from Tanithia's naked body and looked off into the distance. She reached up to him and joined her hands gently behind his neck, her eyes on him.

She continued moving her hips beneath his.

"The poor fools," she said. "They think their Book protects them, but it does very little. The protection that should have its root in their own minds has never been allowed to grow, for they wallow so much in guilt, and guilt opens them wide." She closed her eyes for a long moment, her expression pained. "Please dear one . . . make love to me more. I want to forget what's happening. Please . . ."

He embraced her more closely than ever, and shadows of protective, concealing darkness hid the lvoers.

ON the following day they left via the back trails towards the inn in the mountains, for eventually it would be there that the Count and his men would be returning, or so Tanithia felt. But on foot it would be several days of hard traveling, and they did not dare return to a settlement for horses. Not with the demon-things now roaming free in their search for her.

With Gort by her side Tanithia's spirits were high, and fatigue bothered her less. He paced them slowly, for her benefit. Food was no problem, for he was able to snare small game, and they both knew much of the herbs and edible plants that abounded in these forests.

One day passed, and then another. From time to time they came upon small clusters of huts along the road, and always took circuitous detours through the forest to avoid them.

The day was nearly over. Sunset would be soon, and they would once more nibble at the roots they carried and roll up together in his cloak, to enjoy each other's warmth and perhaps to again make love before drifting off to sleep in each other's arms.

Tanithia brushed a straggling lock of hair from her face, and glanced back. She was quite tired, he knew, but she was bearing up well thus far.

"Gort, do you think we might possibly have been seen when we went past that last cluster of houses?"

"Huts, you mean. They were hardly more than cattle sheds. Only the gods know why some folk are satisfied with such filthy hovels. But perhaps. We made it a point to give that place a wide berth, though their dogs did catch our scent and set up a clamor. But I hadn't noticed anyone behind us."

"So I thought. But I keep having the feeling that someone might be back there a ways," she said with a troubled look.

He glanced back, though only the forest, thick and green, could be seen on either side as far as the last bend in the road, several hundred paces behind. "It seems peaceful enough, but I've learned to pay attention to your feelings and impressions. As soon as we round the next bend, let's ease quietly off to the side and conceal ourselves."

Pretending casualness for perhaps a hundred paces made the short time seem a strained eternity to them, though as soon as the turn was rounded, she bounded up the hillside into the forest with the speed of a deer, though with more silence. He was not far behind her. Secreting themselves behind a fallen log, he spread his cloak and they settled in for a silent period of rest.

She pressed herself against him with a sigh, grateful for some much-needed rest. He put an arm about her and caressed her gently. She nuzzled him and clasped his hands against her body.

A noise on the road made them both stiffen and peer cautiously through the brush.

A half dozen coarse-looking rogues were rounding the bend, peering ahead and about cautiously. Rudely dressed, they carried staffs and wore very sturdy-looking knives. One of them pointed on ahead, and they said something to each other in low voices, then walked faster down the road. Shortly they were no longer to be seen. Tanithia put a hand on Gort's shoulder and spoke low to him.

"They look like locals," she said "Do you think they might be able to track us?"

"Not very precisely. The roadway is soft, it's so little used, though in most places there's a thick layer of leaves and grass that will conceal our footprints. But not everywhere. In some places it's only dirt, and here and there there's moisture from springs. We haven't been too careful about where we step, and after a while they'll see our prints aren't there. But I don't think they can find even generally where we left the road. Within half a league, perhaps, but that's all."

Tanithia leaned back against the log. "Then we'd best stay here until we're certain they'll be gone, then move on by night to be well away from here before dawn." She reached into the pouch slung at her waist and found the wood comb he'd fashioned for her. Shaking her hair loose she began to slowly run the comb through her tresses. "Could I have one of those sweet fruits you're carrying? We might be here for some time."

Perhaps almost an hour had passed. She was reclining

on the cloak while he rubbed her feet, she revelling in the feel of having so relaxing a massage, and he enjoying her pleasured expression, as well as the feel of her.

He froze, listening. "Voices! They're coming back."

Again they peered from their hiding place as the six hurried on past, now no longer bothering to be silent.

"... got to be getting back before dark. That old drab of mine had better have something cooking when I gets back," one was saying. Another looked at him.

"I don't know how ye manage to get on, what with that swill she brews. From the smell of it, her cooking would knock a vulture off a manure wagon..." They continued on down the road, continuing to banter about their home life.

"They've given up?" she whispered.

"Apparently. We'll wait until we're sure they're gone, and then continue. Even if we have to go a league or two in the darkness it would be advisable to be well away from here by dawn, as you suggested."

The voices faded, and Gort cautiously eased down to the road and peered around the turn. Then he signalled for Tanithia, and she joined him. Silently in the deepening twilight they continued onwards.

In perhaps half an hour they came to the open moor.

"Damn!" he muttered. "Half a league at least to the forest and the foothills on the other side. There's no cover anywhere out there in case we're spotted, and it would take at least half a day to try and work our way around the far end of this moorland..."

"And it's already past sunset," she added. Tanithia looked back down the dark shadowed road. "I wish we could be completely certain that they had given up."

"If we stay here they may be back at dawn. We can't cut through the thick wood in the darkness, so it looks as if we have no choice but to try our luck." Not very confident, he led her on out where the road went across the moor.

They moved as rapidly as possible under the circumstances, but her tiredness slowed them.

They were well out onto the moor when Tanithia looked back. He heard her gasp and turned to see her anxious eyes on him.

"Gort," she said. "It's a trap!"

He looked back in the twilight, to see six figures running towards them from the woods. With a sudden, terrible feeling at the pit of his stomach he knew exactly what had happened.

"They knew they'd lost us along the road," he said. "But being locals, they knew the moor was just ahead, and that we'd have to cross it. So they pretended to be giving up, and were talking about it to put us off our guard. Then they probably cut across to the edge of the moor on a forest trail, and simply watched for us." He looked at the swiftly advancing figures, and dispairingly at the far distant edge of the moor.

"Come on, girl. I know you're tired and I know you're still weak, but we've got to run. It's our only possible chance!" Dragging her along, they began running. She clutched up her dress and ran the best she could manage.

They had scarce gone a hundred paces and Tanithia was reeling, her breath coming in gasps as she became more and more unsteady. Gort knew with total, lead-hearted certainty that they had no chance. Perhaps if she had not been so weak . . . Were she healthy, Tanithia could run as fast and as far as a gazelle, he was certain. But now . . .

Her long hair streamed back, tumbled, as she ran her head lolling unsteadily back as she depended on him for steadying and guidance, reeling in her exhaustion. Her pale limbs flashed among her hiked-up, swirling skirts, though she was more and more uncertain. Her breasts bobbed behind the thin, low cloth of the dress.

Her bare foot caught on a vine, and she fell, crying out. He stopped and darted back to her. Their pursuers were close now. He drew his sword.

Tanithia raised herself on unsteady arms, her hair tumbled over her face and shoulders. "Go on, love," she gasped. "It's me they want. Too many for you to fight . . . They'll let me go when they're done . . . or I'll get away!"

He kneeled briefly to touch her hair. "I couldn't desert you, love. No matter what the odds." She took his hand and kissed it, and momentarily pressed it to the low cleft between her breasts.

Gort stood, placing himself between Tanithia and the oncoming ruffians.

"Hold right there!" he called. He could see now that they were grinning as they bore down on their quarry, and spreading to surround them.

"Forget it, boy!" answered one of them. "Stand and deliver! We want that woman of yours and we want anything else ye have!" In the dimming twilight his swarthy face was leering in triumph.

Now completely circling Gort and Tanithia, they began to move slowly in, despite his repeated warnings to stay away.

The leader, a solid, hard-faced man, motioned at the others, then drew his long knife and moved towards Gort. Then another came at him with a cudgel. Gort swung. One feinted under his guard and almost was caught by Gort's blade. Another stepped in, and then back very rapidly as Gort thrust.

Too late he realized their tactic and began to circle back towards Tanithia where she lay, only to hear her cry out. He spun to find that the one ruffian who had not been engaged in drawing him off now had one hand in Tanithia's hair, yanking her head back. His other hand held the sharp edge of his dagger across her throat.

"Drop it, young hero, we've got your woman. Drop that sword or I'll spray you with her blood!"

Uncertainly he paused, and let his blade drop. Immediately something hit him across the side of his head, hard, and he dropped in a red haze of senseless pain, only slightly aware that he was being hit again, and again.

It could not have been long before the pain became bearable and consciousness began to return, in spite of the waves of agony and nausea.

They had dragged Tanithia to her feet and she glared at them sullenly, her head half lowered. Her dress was still hiked up, and her captors were obviously enjoying the sight of her bare limbs.

"We've got ourselves a real choice one tonight, boys. She's a real beauty!"

"Aye. How about comin' with us, lass? Your soljer friend there doesn't do too good a job of takin' care of you. What you need is some real men." He reached to touch her cheek and she drew her face away from him.

"That's right, wench. We'll take good care of ye. All of us will, one after the other." An evil chuckle. One of them ran his hand along her bare flank and she struggled to escape, but to no avail.

"Now, now, girl, don't ye struggle so. Hm, you're about to pop out of the top of that dress, pretty thing." One of them reached out to cup her breast, and she gasped as he slid his hand down inside the low neckline.

Gort looked about. One of them had his sword, and they all had knives and cudgels. If he just waited a little, though, there might be a chance to jump one of them. A small chance. If only his head would quit throbbing . . .

"What about a kiss, girl, eh?" One leaned forward towards her, deliberately placing his hand between her breasts to support himself. She drew back. Even in the deepening twilight Gort could see the distaste on her face. The rogue suddenly struggled and leaped back with an oath, holding his lip.

"She bit me!" he exclaimed. "The wench bit me!" The others laughed, making him angrier.

He reached for the front of Tanithia's dress, grasped it between her breasts, and yanked down hard, tearing away the thin cloth. Her breasts bobbed and Gort heard the sudden intake of their breath, in unison, at the sight of her full, bare bosom. He tensed himself to spring, but held for a moment.

She was cupping one of her breasts with her hand . . . the one with the fang marks, Gort realized. The ruffians all gathered close about her, their hands now roaming freely over her body and under her dress. He could see that her mouth was partly open . . . their attentions were arousing her, in spite of herself. But there was anger in her eyes . . . anger that she had been holding back as it grew.

"I think it's time we laid this little wench down, boys. She's probably still tired and maybe needs us to keep her warm . . . why are you covering that pretty round fruit of yours, girl? Here . . ." He grasped her wrist and forced her hand away by his own overwhelming strength.

"Say . . . what's this? Look at this bosom . . . there's something wrong here!"

There was a moment of uneasy silence. They looked at her. One touched the angry sores on her breast and she made a sound. "Damn . . . what strange wounds. What's bit you, girl?"

For the first time Tanithia lifted her chin high, and

with an enigmatic, unpleasant smile, tossed her long hair back from around her neck and shoulders. She slowly ran her fingers to either side of the marks on her neck.

"What in the name of the Dark One . . . on her neck too!"

Suddenly she spun on her heel and ran, her skirt swirling around her legs. After a frozen moment the ruffians took after her in the darkening twilight. For the first time her voice came clear.

"No . . . No! Stay away! Please!"

The faster ones cut her off and in a moment Tanithia was surrounded again and she paused, trembling, hands over her face, arms covering her bared breasts. Gort silently rose to his feet and began easing up towards the man who had his sword, hoping they would be too pre-occupied to notice him in the dim bush and heath.

One of the men came up behind her to seize her shoulder from in back, throwing her roughly down. She huddled soundless, face down and crouched, with her face hidden in her long hair. One of the men chuckled.

"Look at those legs and that pretty bottom. Lads, she's as round in back as she is in front . . ." He laughed and grasped her arm, beginning to twist her around where she lay. Their blood was up again, and they all moved in towards her in the increasing dimness.

She spun around with unhuman suddeness, crouched like an animal, her tumbled hair streaming over her trembling breasts. They drew back.

Her face was hideous.

Her mouth was open in a low, feline snarl, displaying full rows of long, needle-pointed teeth. And shocking, two-inch fangs.

Her eyes were lit from within, and glowing scarlet. Nothing remotely human was in them.

She gestured with one clawed hand, beckoning. And

smiling as she ran a long, pointed tongue over her needle teeth.

The rogues were frozen in shock and fear. The metamorphosis was sudden, and unexpected. Totally unexpected, and horror rose within them.

Gort too was stunned. Her smile was like that of a night-creature, he realized. In a moment he realized that he did not know who . . . or what . . . was really before him.

Suddenly she sprang at the nearest of the ruffians, slashing at his throat with clawed, taloned fingers. ("That was the one who held the knife to her throat," thought Gort.). Blood spurted from him . . . perhaps not quite a fatal arterial slash, but very close to it. He fell back screaming, grasping at his neck.

Another drew Gort's sword. The thing that had been Tanithia leaped before him and suddenly, unexpectedly, shrieked . . . a host-fettering scream that froze him where he crouched. Perhaps her luminous eyes slowed him, or perhaps she had become preternaturally fast, for suddenly her taloned hand was reaching out and breaking his fingers. The snaps were clear and loud in the evening stillness.

Suddenly finding his wits, Gort sprang forward to scoop up the fallen sword and in one motion to slash another of the assailants across the ribs. The man looked from the Tanithia-thing, to Gort, to his bleeding side, then seeming not to feel the wound, back with increasing horror at . . . her.

One of the men, more courageous than the rest, grabbed at her taloned hand. In one sinuous movement, she whirled before him and sank her needle teeth into his wrist, tearing out flesh and veins.

Another of the ruffians had drawn his long knife and was trying to ease towards her. Gort slashed his arm and the knife fell in a shower of blood.

Suddenly they all were running . . . screaming in terror and agony as they fled in mortal fear through the deep twilight. They ran, stumbling and rising again, their sanity unhinged, heedless of wounds or pouring blood. Their shrieks began fading as they ran, much faster than they had come, across the heath towards the dark forest.

Sword at the ready, Gort turned slowly to that which might possibly be Tanithia. Or might be something of unspeakable evil. Slowly and deliberately he lowered his blade, hoping he had made the correct judgment.

And fearing that he had not.

The scarlet eyes, glowing, turned on him for the first time, and the needle-filled mouth curved into a thoroughly hideous caricature of a smile. Laughter came, strange and maniacal. ("The mouth glows red too," he thought numbly.)

The she-creature laughed, loudly and deeply, lowering her . . . its . . . head into the clawed hands, and pale hair tumbled over to conceal both face and hands. The laughter softened, then all was silent.

Silent. And still.

Tanithia swept her long hair back and looked up at Gort, smiling.

"Gort, my love. You should have seen your face. You were terrified!"

He sagged back. Deeply, deeply relieved. He dropped the sword ("Would it have done any good, anyway?") and ran forward to sweep the laughing woman into his arms. He embraced her long and strong.

"Come lover," she said. "Kiss me. What's the matter?"

He dabbed at her lips with his sleeve, his mouth in a tight smile. "It's just a policy of mine," he stated. "I make it a point never to kiss a girl who has blood on her mouth."

A long, joyous, and increasingly passionate kiss as

he crushed her to him.

She drew away at last, her eyes sparkling in the dimness of the late evening. "I can change my features, remember? And thanks to Lyia, this was a very easy change." She sobered for a moment. "Actually, it was all too easy."

"They would have raped you and then killed us both, I think," he said.

"Yes," she said. "But when those rogues get to the first hut the word will begin spreading. Lyia will soon know our vicinity. And having become vampiric myself . . . if only briefly . . . will make it easy for the night creatures to locate this particular spot on the heath."

"Then we'd best go, and now," he said.

She nestled into his arms, and her open mouth sought his. He held back for a moment, recalling what he had seen, then returned her kiss, his tongue fencing with hers. This wild, deadly creature wanted him, and needed him . . . and he was seized with passion for her. She responded eagerly, for the blood was still aroused in her trembling body.

"We can wait for a short while, can't we?" he murmured.

He removed his cloak and spread it on the ground beneath the stars, and she eased her torn dress down over her white flanks, and stepped out when the garment fell about her slender ankles.

"Take me," she said. "Take me now!"

It was more than an hour before they finally resumed their journey.

HE rushing torrent echoed down the valley on its way to the distant sea. To either side of the young river great evergreens embedded their massive roots into the steep mountain slopes and thrust their tall trunks skyward. In the distance the snowcapped high peaks cut through the thin clouds, though here at the lower levels the heat of summer made the scented air soft and lazy.

At a point in the steep valley the small river burst over the side of a sheer cliff and fell in a veil of white thunder over an ancient fault, to gather its strength once more at the bottom and flow off through the green foothills and into the flat plains beyond.

Beyond the top of the waterfall a small stream angled its own way down into the tumbling waters, its nearly inconspicuous trickle starting at a pure spring not far above the narrow, unused road that wound up the mountainside. In the shade near the end of the small creek two figures reclined, resting.

Gort was worried about Tanithia. She was tired, and weak. The hard physical exertion and the magics of the night before had drained her badly, and she needed rest. They had not gone far on this day, and it was likely that they would spend the night right here. For now, though, she rested, her golden-red head in his lap. The sun had been bothering her, he knew, probably an effect of being so victimized in the castle.

She smiled and snuggled up against him, probing with a toe until she found the small creek. With a sigh she eased her feet into the cool water again. He ran his hand through her tumbled hair, and she looked up at him.

"I'm tired, love. Just bone-tired. Even with those rawhide leatherstockings you made for me, my feet are sore. I'm still weak, and my breasts are sunburned." She closed her eyes again and held his hand briefly.

He touched his hand into the cool water and stroked her breasts gently with the wet coolness. The front of her dress had been too ruined to mend, and the summer sun had not been kind to her bared bosom.

She looked up at him with a tired smile. "I want you again, you know. It's just that I don't think I could manage it. But keep on cooling me down, it feels good."

They were silent for a long time, she dozing and he nodding in the late afternoon warmth. Then they both came awake.

"We're being watched," Gort said quietly.

"I know." With apparent casualness she sat up and reached for her comb, he glancing about as he fumbled in his pouch, using the opportunity to likewise look about.

A large wolf loped out into the clearing and stopped,

smiling.

"Longrunner!" they both exclaimed, springing to their feet (Tanithia in a flurry of bare limbs) and ran to him. Tanithia dropped to her knees next to the wolf and wrapped her arms about him, burying her face in his thick mane as Gort, laughing, rubbed between his ears.

The others of the pack began to move silently out of the concealing brush. Gort turned to find Gray Lady at his side, her coat brushing gently against him. He embraced her and nuzzled her neck.

Longrunner was slightly ill at ease, but he rubbed his head against her and playfully licked her face and breasts. (You're an affectionate pet, Seid Lady, and I'd like to keep you around . . . but human-form makes me uneasy. How about changing into a more civilized shape? There's a good dark den near here.)

She unconsciously eased back on all fours for a moment, smiling. (As soon as it gets dark enough, Longrunner. We're so glad you're here!). Again they were close and playful.

As per custom, and enjoying it greatly, they exchanged joyous greetings with all the rest of the pack, then finally all rested at ease in the long shadows of the early evening. Gort leaned up against Gray Lady, rubbing her ears and shoulder blades. She looked at him with a glint in her eye.

(Why don't you do that when you're in wolf form? And don't imply that you're superior in this shape. You're only a human, and there's nothing special about that!). She nuzzled him with a trace of warmth.

Gort asked her. (This isn't your territory. How is it that you come to be here?).

She scratched casually. (Food is hard to come by in the mountains. Most of the small game is spending more time in hiding. The Dark Forces have been returning, and that makes everything uneasy.)

Longrunner agreed. (We were foraging through these mountains to get what we could, and we caught your scent. Things didn't go well, I gather. Neither of you looks particularly good . . . Seid Lady, you look terrible . . . and you're separated from your human-pack.)

Tanithia sat up, her hands on the ground before her. (You're right, of course. A lot happened, but you could say that we were caught in some bad traps.)

Longrunner smiled. (Traps are bad. But at least you lived, though it's obvious to any wolf that you're still being hunted. We owe you a debt of honor: perhaps we can get you away from the hunters.)

Tanithia rubbed her hand across her face uncertainly. (We'd like that, we really would. But I'm weak, Longrunner . . . I don't think I have the strength to keep up the change for very long, let alone keep up with the pack all the way back to the mountain inn.)

Longrunner rested his head on the ground and looked up at her with amused, sparkling eyes. (Oh come now, little pet. Do you really think that you're the only one here who can work seid? Wait until the moon is up and we can sing up the Power. You'll have all the strength you need.)

A while longer passed, and the shadows lengthened and grew into a rapidly dimming twilight as, somewhere behind the mountains, the sun set. Gray Lady looked about, exchanging a significant glance with Longrunner. Gort was dozing next to her. With a smile she touched her cold nose to the back of his neck, and sat back on her haunches in amusement as, startled, he came suddenly awake.

(It's dark enough, Clawfighter. You'd best waken your Lady and make ready to change.)

He shook her, and Tanithia rose to her feet, stretching. "This rest was just what I needed, love. I'm feeling much better." She looked about at the relaxed, scattered wolves. "And the company definitely helps."

They walked off into the deep shadows of a nearby grove, led by a young wolf who indicated the dark den where they could begin the shape-change. Tanithia paused for a moment before the entrance to the little cave.

Gort began removing his clothing as she watched. Then she undid the remaining laces of her torn dress and was out of it in one easy, fluid movement. Tanithia stretched and pirouetted gracefully as he watched her, approvingly.

"You are exquisite," he said softly, and she smiled at him.

"Thank you, love. There are times I need to be told, though I always like to know that I'm appreciated." She swayed close and melted into his arms. "Of course, you're someone very special too. And your bare body feels so good against mine."

They shared a long kiss. "Ready for the change?" he asked at length.

"Yes . . . wait." she stood for a moment, contemplating their discarded garments. "Let's set a false trail . . . it's dim enough now, and we'll have to leave our clothes anyhow." He looked questioningly at her. "Yes, magic, and I'm feeling better now. Anyhow, I'll show you how we can do it together."

She laid her dress out on the ground, then he helped her as they laid out his cloak, breeches, boots, and shirt next to them.

He looked down at the garments. "It looks almost like two people, lying side by side. In this twilight it's really hard to tell!"

"That's the general idea," she said, and motioned for him to join her in kneeling before the empty clothes. The wolves gathered about to watch as Gort and Tanithia knelt facing each other, hands out and almost touching. She murmured a chant, over and over again. He picked it up and together they continued for some time.

It started from between their hands. White, like pale mist in the dimness. A pale mist that grew and thickened until with a gesture of her slender hand she drew it down towards the clothes. The mist came heavier and yet heavier as he emulated her in making passes over the garments time and again, drawing the mist down into them.

The clothes seemed to stir and to fill. To move.

The wolves growled uneasily and stepped back slightly. They sensed the magic strongly. Though they understood it instinctively, it was nonetheless something alien to them.

Gort and Tanithia stood up, looking down at the two figures lying in their clothes. The figures slowly sat up. Gort caught his breath, for they bore a very strong resemblance to he and his lady. He looked at Tanithia.

"What are they?" he asked.

"Simulacra," she said. "They won't last long. About four hours, I'd guess." She passed her hand near the replica of herself, and the face was now almost exact. But the faces of both remained totally blank of expression. Empty-eyed.

"Are they alive?"

"No, they have no more sentience than a clock, or a statue."

"But they move!"

"So does a clock."

The wolves growled, almost in fear. They moved back, their hackles rising.

Tanithia stood before the pale figures and looked at them. "Stand," she commanded. Soundlessly . . . Gort noticed that there was no sound of breathing . . . the two rose to their feet. "Follow us to the edge of the cliff."

Shortly they were at the edge of the river, not too far from where the water poured over the cliff in the high waterfall. She motioned the two clothed figures to sit, and they did. "You will wait here, holding each other." (The simulacra fumblingly put their arms about one another). "You will watch the river. When the demon-creatures come for you, hold hands and leap into the water. You may dissolve when you reach the base of the falls. Do you understand?" They nodded, and both stared down at the water.

Tanithia held out her arms and stood for a few moments like some perfect marble statue, then lowered her hands to her thighs.

"I've withdrawn protection," she said. "Come . . . let's change into wolf shape and be gone. In an hour it won't be safe here."

The night was perhaps only two or three hours older as the pack attained the top of a high pass that overlooked the surrounding lands for scores of leagues in several directions. The organge disc of the moon was cutting above the far horizon, its gibbous form casting dim light on the windblown crags far above them. The tree line was not far below, and the evening wind that blew through the pass filled the thin air with soft sound . . .

a sound made much more vivid by sharp wolf ears.

The wolves moved with a minimum of noise; communicating readily, but in near silence nonetheless. They were spread far enough to scout for any small game that might be foolish enough to be out, and close enough to be certain that they were keeping up with the rapidly-moving pack. In the lead were two large, muscular males and two particularly sleek and lithe females, one of whom seemed tired and oftimes a bit unsteady.

Gort was concerned for Tanithia, but even so he was enjoying himself. His every sense was totally vivid, with eyes that saw easily in the darkness, ears that could pick out the faintest sounds far, far away, a nose that could respond to seemingly hundreds of scents, from the most gross to the most delicate. And not the least was a nimble, powerful form that seemed to be near tireless.

Longrunner scanned the dispersed pack as he loped easily along. (There's no game hereabouts. The evil ones have frightened it all away; it's been a day or two since most of us have eaten. Perhaps . . .) He looked back at the others, then over their shoulders at the lands they were leaving. (Look!)

They paused and looked back, to see what seemed a column of darkness descending to a point near where the foothills broke from the dark mountains. The others of the pack stopped and looked back for a few brief moments as well. Tanithia watched silently for a moment, and shivered slightly.

(That's where you found us, isn't it?)

Longrunner nuzzled her ear and touched it with his tongue. (Yes. Those creatures move fast, but I think your little seid-trick has worked. They seem to be leaving, and returning to their den already. If they had managed to catch your mist-people they would have stayed longer; as it is they are probably returning to report that you two are dead.) He snuffed in an almost-human chuckle. (It could be that they're even carrying back your cloth pelts as proof!)

Then, quietly, they were trotting forward again, heading down the far side of the pass and into the forest below. For Tanithia the way was hard; she was tired, even in this shape.

Some leagues later the moon was rising over the mountain crests, its light soft but ... for them ... silvery bright. Longrunner brought them to a knob of a mountain slope and called the pack to a halt. They gathered close as he addressed them.

(Pack-mates, the moon is high enough now, and this land has a certain power about it. I ... and my Lady .. feel it would be time for us to sing.) There were yaps and growls of assent. It was obvious to Gort and to Tanithia that a group howl was something they all enjoyed.

Gray Lady stood tall and beauteous beside Longrunner. She looked for a moment at the pack before speaking. (There are two things for which we must sing tonight, friends. One is our friend Seid Lady ... she's done much for us in the past, but now she's been hunted and wounded: we must sing strength and healing for her so that she'll recover rapidly and so she can keep up with us.). She paused for a moment and sniffed at the air.

(And secondly ... we're all hungry. The evil forces have frightened the game away, so we must sing for food.). There were sighs and whines of agreement. It was obvious that she had struck a need common to all.

Gray Lady barked a short introduction to set the rhythm, then raised her strong, pure voice clear and high, rising in tone as Longrunner's deep call joined hers, and the entire pack melded in. Swept along with them, Gort raised his voice as well. A small part in the back of his mind mused on how his voice, normally so hearty in an evening at the tavern, was equally as good here . . . though in a completely and totally different way.

Tanithia joined as well, marvelling at the perfect harmony that they made, and the subtle counterpoint melody that they wove, one against the other. Implicit meanings came through, and images: vistas of the past and of other worlds. Strange and hard to understand, alien and yet exquisitely beautiful and mysterious . . .

The night became crystalline about them as the long, eerie howl ebbed and flowed, seeming to rise to the stars and then to sink to the depths of the earth. The beams of the moon grew stronger and ever yet stronger until it seemed that pure silver light was washing through their very bodies, joining every one of the pack in a bond of pure, vital Power. Strength flowed through them all, washing brilliant and luminescent from the rocks about them and, seemingly, in tiny, piercing spearpoints of light that might have come from the stars themselves.

For a seeming eternity of crystal, moonlit magic, of mists and lights and rich, soaring music they were all linked. It seemed that a Power built higher and yet higher within them all, until their very souls were filled, and the fine pitch and timing began to break in joyous, barking laughter as they eased back in jovial cheer. Gort found himself wondering just how much had been real and how much had been in the mind. And, wondering whether these folk shared the same reality as he knew. Perhaps not, he mused. Perhaps not.

Tanithia pranced up to him and kissed him laughingly. (I feel wonderful, love. Their way is different, but their seid is strong . . . very strong.) He nuzzled her back and she danced over to Longrunner as he called.

Gray Lady stepped before him, obviously pleased with her performance. (How was that, my handsome stranger? Didn't it feel good?)

He rubbed his cheek against her and kissed her as she smiled. (It was excellent, you beautiful thing! I've never experienced anything so strangely mysterious and magical. And you have a magnificent voice.)

She looked at him, smiling. (Too bad you weren't born a wolf, Clawfighter. You and I could rule a pack that would be sung in the legends!) Her kiss was brief but carried the hint of passion. Then they were both swept away in the crowd of laughing, affectionate friends.

Some time later they all were making their way on into the lower mountains. Tanithia, now rejuvenated and feeling quite energetic, trotted alongside Longrunner, enjoying the night and the landscape. She nudged him as they went on their way.

(Longrunner, before the singing began, you said that this land has a certain power about it. What did you mean?"

He looked at her briefly in the moonlight. (This land is old, Seid Lady . . . very old. When we are in a place such as this, our kind can sense and see things that have been a very long time gone.)

(How long?)

(Time is different to us. Let's just say it's in the past. For example, look far up that canyon. And now avert your eyes a little to the side.

She slowed, did as he said, and stopped, astonished. (It's a city! Off there in the distance.)

(Very good, pretty pet. You pick things up rapidly. What can you tell me about it, since you know more about human cities than I?)

She eyed the soaring spires, the moving lights, the strange, unfamiliar architecture. (I don't know. It's old . . . very old. Cities like that haven't been built in ages! What would happen if we went closer?)

(Gray Lady and I have been quite close. Even into

the cities themselves once or twice. There were human-folk there, but it was as though they were in one world and we in another. They couldn't see us, while we could see right through them.) He trotted on down the trail.

She paused for a long moment, wondering what mysteries might be hidden in that place, visible through that strange portal. Then she trotted after him.

Dawn was beginning to light the sky. They had come far in the night, and the pack was tired as well as hungry. Gray Lady nudged Longrunner. (They're tired, milord. And they're hungry. I think it's time we settled down to rest . . . perhaps we can forage for food at daybreak.)

Tanithia nodded in agreement. (Yes. Both Clawfighter and I will have to change back into human form before it starts getting light. We can alter the easiest when it's still dark. And we're not strong enough to be able to hold wolf-shape in the sunlight . . . it probably would be fatal.)

Longrunner scanned the terrain ahead. (We'll fetch up just beyond. There should be a stream and, well, I could certainly use something to eat, as could everyone.)

The tired pack was making itself comfortable as Tanithia came up to Gort and gently rubbed her cheek against his. (I'm tired, love . . . but it's a good tiredness. Before we change back I want to go up and rest on that hilltop for a short while. Watch me, and if I motion to you, join me and bring the others. They're hungry and perhaps I can help.)

A good while passed. Gort rested on his haunches, watching Tanithia where she lay flat at the top of the nearby hill, motionless in the early dawn. Gray Lady sat down beside him and rubbed her body against him. (Longrunner is checking out the terrain nearby and he'll be back shortly. What's your Lady doing up there on the hill?)

He nuzzled her ear. (She said something about finding some food and . . . look, she wants us to come!) They loped to the top of the hill, followed shortly by Longrunner and other curious members of the pack. Tanithia motioned for them to use care and they looked over the hill to the meadow beyond.

Gray Lady drew her breath in astonishment and looked at Longrunner. (Rabbits! There must be several score of them down there!)

Longrunner cautiously peered down through the grass. The small creatures were restless out in the field, fearful but compelled. He turned to Tanithia.

(This is your doing, isn't it Seid Lady?) She nodded and he kissed her with a smile. (Thank you, pretty one. Thank you very much indeed.) He turned and softly called for the pack, dispersing them to ease down under cover and then move in from the flanks to catch as many of the food animals as possible.

Gort was the last one to leave her. He paused for a long while, looking at the doomed, entranced rabbits below and thinking. Then he turned to her.

(You called the rabbits; you called them magically. And that's what you did at the ambush, Tanithia. You called the enemy stragglers to you, just like those rabbits. They hadn't a chance!) He was amazed, and a little shocked.

Tanithia sat up and yawned. (I needed the practice and the experience . . . both with the magic and with my marksmanship. Now please, I'm too tired to chase down those creatures. Since you're about to go down there and hunt, please bring me back one.) There was a growing clamor from below as the wolves broke cover and began running down their food.

Gort looked with a slight expression of distaste. (I'm not really hungry for raw, furry meat, thanks. I'll wait until we're back in human form.)

She rubbed her muzzle briefly and cocked an eye at him. (Then go bring one back for me ... I'm not particular. I'm hungry, and this form is ideal for just such dining.)

He shook his head, then ran down to the meadow to fetch her breakfast.

The day passed in contented rest for all. The wolves were clustered together with each other and with the two naked humans who slept in each others' arms. The comfortable warmth and the closeness of body contact made the day lazy and enjoyable.

Gray lady rested with her body pressed against Gort. For a long while she watched him quietly, thinking. Then with a sigh, closed her eyes and dozed again.

Longrunner was similarly close against Tanithia's comely form. He stirred and softly nuzzled her breasts. She came partly awake with a gentle, wordless query, smiled, and rubbed her head against his before they both fell asleep once more.

At sunset the pack dispersed for a while to catch whatever game might still be in the vicinity, while Tanithia and Gort, still in human form, gathered the berries and wild fruit that were so abundant here. As the darkness settled they went into a grove and crouched, channeling the deep part of their minds into the now-familiar pattern that once again put them into wolf-shape.

(We'll be there soon!) Gort was elated. The night was well along, and they had made excellent progress. The pack had stopped for a rest by a stream, scattering for water and the possiblility of some food-game.

Gray Lady eyed the other. (It's a pity, Clawfighter. With time I think we could make you into a very excellent wolf.)

(No luck, my aristocratic one. I don't really care for raw meat . . . particularly when it comes with lots of hair and bones.)

(Don't worry, love. That sort of a taste just comes naturally.) She lay down before him, resting her head on her paws and looking up at him. (You know, I think you're very handsome.)

He softly touched noses with her and rubbed her cheek gently. (You're a very sweet thing . . . and I thank you.)

She rose to her feet and gracefully walked to and fro before him. She paused, striking a very statuesque pose and looked into his eyes invitingly.

(Look at me, Clawfighter . . . Am I not beautiful? Do you not desire me?) She raised her head and shook her long, wild mane.

Gort was wide-eyed for a moment, then coughed, covering his face, and coughed again until Gray Lady was concerned. (What in the world is wrong? Is it something I said?)

Gort wiped his eyes and stifled a smile. (I think I've been here before. Let's just say, lovely one, that your mannerisms remind me of someone else.) Puzzled, she was about to ask further when he thankfully noticed that Longrunner was forming up the pack to resume the journey. (Look. I think it's time to go.)

The moon was high as they arrived on the hilltop overlooking the inn, and began their farewells with all members of the pack. Longrunner moved off to the side for a few moments with Tanithia. He tenderly kissed her eyes and her throat. (Remember, pet . . . you're always welcome back with our clan. We can always use your seid and . . . and I like your company as well.) They pressed close in a near-human display of affection.

Gray Lady pressed her body against Gort with warmth, and he nuzzled her gently. (There'll always be part of us in you, Clawfighter . . . wolf blood is strong. And always know that if things ever go badly for you in the world of men, we'll always be out in the mountains and the forest.) She stood still and looked at him for a long while. (Remember, dear one . . . when the moon is full, think of me.)

The innkeeper heard the dogs barking, and was staggering down the stairs with an oil lamp when the pounding on the door began. He peered out through the peephole and then, astonished, drew the bolt and threw the door open.

A naked woman and a naked man stood in the doorway, she seeming to be drying her tears as she clung to him. They looked familiar, and suddenly he realized that they'd been here during a previous visit with the soldiers.

"Robbers!" the man exclaimed a bit thickly, as though the words were unfamiliar and hard to say. "We were coming back to meet the troop of our friends and . . . and . . ." The young woman broke into almost theatrical tears and the innkeeper called for his wife to bring blankets and something hot to drink.

As the door closed and latched the call of a wolf could be heard, far off in the hills . . .

HEY were given a room together for the time that would pass until the return of Count Waldmann and the others. Though the Count would doubtless reimburse the innkeeper for their clothing and their stay, Gort would usually be found helping with the necessary mundane work in the fields and on the farmsteads nearby. Tanithia, still requiring some rest to throw off the last effects of her injuries, devoted much of her time to spinning and sewing. Perhaps it was that he wished to maintain toughness and a good sword arm, and perhaps also she wished time for quiet meditation. Whatever, the innkeeper and his family felt that their young guests earned their keep quite satisfactorily.

Still, they found enough time to enjoy each others' company, walking often alone through the woods as she gathered herbs for medicine or for flavoring. They ranged far and wide through nearby hills.

She nestled in his arms as they lay in the grass, watching the declining sun and discussing past events.

". . . And so, when I saw what you intended, Tanithia . . . I couldn't bring myself to be there and see you make love to others. I felt it would be the time to leave."

"Dear Gort, you're so very good," she said, stroking his cheek and kissing him lightly for the thousandth time.

"I took the old man to my home. He raved and ranted and two days later he finally died. I stayed with him all the way. He had a lot to say, and for a while before the end he was lucid. He died with his full senses and grateful to be among men again." Gort plucked a stem of grass and chewed reflectively on its tender end.

"He told me of Lyia. Of the maleficent sorceress she had been, and how terribly her experiments had failed. She's committed a lot of atrocities, love. A lot of very terrible acts."

Tanithia absently plucked at a flower with her toes. "She has . . . I realize that now." She was silent again.

"Also, when Lyia spoke of the late baron who had died in the castle her words sounded wrong. I'd known the man and served him. I was suspicious of her, though there was little that I could point at directly. And it was obvious that I dared not tell you of my suspicions . . . you of all people." He held her close for a few moments more.

"Yet . . . we had all scoured the castle," commented Gort. "I don't understand how the evil managed to remain."

"It was my fault," she said, casting down her eyes with just a touch of shame as she clasped her hands together. "Near the end of the dungeons Lyia stopped me and proceeded to weave me, maze-minded, into her enchantments. It hadn't ocurred to me, I was so taken by her, until much later that I'd neglected to finish the exocism. What was in those remaining cells I can only guess. Yet it was in those final dark cells that the evil held its base, I think."

"So that's it," he said, idly playing with a strand of her long hair. "And of course there was Elijus and his men."

"Yes. How did they know I was at the castle, or even that I existed? They knew my name and my whereabouts, although they had many of the other facts rather confused." She smiled.

"Think, my pretty one. Wasn't it Elijus at the inn here when we were on our way with the soldiers? Wasn't it he who vanished as you danced?"

"Of course!" she exclaimed. "Of course. I thought his face seemed slightly familiar . . . I'd remembered him from the time of the revolution. I had seen him at a distance, briefly, when I fled from that bloody-handed hypocrite and made my escape."

Gort chuckled. "It's very hard in a shire as small as Drakenstane to keep secret the goings and comings of twoscore strangers. Particularly those who tend to aggravate others. Their holier-than-anyone attitudes set everyone's teeth to edge." He looked up at the leaves overhead, and at the pond nearby.

"When we came with all our men they'd tracked us to the castle and were lying in wait for you. Their scouts saw the soldiers leave and felt, logically enough, that only you remained. Others of their men had been to the local taverns and had heard talk of the evil sorceress and of the darkness which she'd set forth."

"I see," she said, running her hand along his chest. "They had heard of Lyia and naturally thought it was I." She threw back her head and laughed, shaking her long red-gold hair and swirling it with her hands. "How very,

very funny. So they set men to wait at the walls until they saw a woman, all prepared to sweep in and to abduct her. And just when I had raised the ire of the demon-creatures and angered them into hurling me into the garden pool . . . there they were. Waiting to rescue me." She laughed again. "How magnificently ironic . . . they wanted to kill me and saved me instead!"

"A strange set of coincidences, isn't it Tanithia?"

She kissed him briefly, and he returned her warmth. "So it seems, lover. But not so much as at first glance. I had done a spell when it became obvious that I couldn't escape from the castle . . . after I'd reached you through the mirror and called for help."

"Yes," he said. "The vision where I caught a glimpse of you in pain with your breast afire." He gently stroked her now-healed bosom. The soft skin above the open front of her dress now showed only the slightest of scars remaining . . . a welcome healing of the angry wounds that had disfigured her. "I came looking for you . . . being a shadow to those who were shadowing the castle, so to speak."

She held his hand to the softness of her breast. "Yes, I'd set forces in motion, since there was no direct way to escape, so that an indirect way would present itself. And it did." She leaned her head back so that her long hair tumbled golden over the grass, and thrust her breasts

at the sky.

"Ah, magnificent!" she said, and lay back on the ground again, laughing. "Come my love, and kiss me. The afternoon is warm and I'd like to go for a swim in that lovely pond. With you." She rumpled his hair and they kissed. "I feel happy again."

A few days later Count Waldmann and the rest of his men appeared once again. Tanithia came bounding down the hill to meet them, and joyously embraced and kissed each one of "her cavaliers". She threw her arms around the Count with a smile, and he swung her up onto the saddle.

"Well now . . . who is this homespun peasant girl that we see running so free through these woods? Or perhaps it's some lovely dryad." He gave her foot an affectionate squeeze, and she drew him close for a playful kiss. "Watch out, fair one, or perhaps a band of soldiers—this one, for instance—might carry you away to do some terrible deeds with you!"

Her eyes sparkled. "Promises, promises!" she gibed and hugged him, laughing.

She leaned forward on the neck of the horse and again greeted each of the men and talked of a dozen things at a time. With pauses for hugs and warm kisses.

"Ah, young Gort," spoke Waldmann. "I thought you'd be here and I prayed that she would be here also. How goes it?" Smiling broadly, they clasped hands and threw arms about each others' shoulders.

"Milord, her strength is back completely. We can be ready to leave tomorrow to finish that job at the castle. The one that didn't get done before." They had seen the innkeeper approaching and felt that further discussion needed to be done in private.

Toward evening they all sat relaxed and at ease over

tankards of ale in the inn's common-room. Tanithia was luxuriating in having her jewelled feet rubbed by two of the troopers. Gort was at her shoulder and occasionally brushed at her hair. He was certain enough of her affections now that his tendecy for jealousy had faded.

Her neck and breast now totally healed, and with a pack of clothes thoughtfully brought for her from his estate by Waldmann, she gratefully now again enjoyed wearing a fine silken dress draped as low and revealing as ever.

"So we can say, Lady Tanithia," Waldmann was saying, "that the demon-beings can't have grown so strong as they were before. We did grave damage to them in our earlier assault on the castle. And the magic with which you imbued our swords should be easily brought to maximum strength once again."

"Yes," she said. "And I feel that wc can move in and destroy them now. The sooner we get the job done the easier it will be. I can effect a more conventional rite of conjuration for your weapons," she smiled, "and I'm sorry, but as much as I'd like to do the slow, sensual charging as before, wc haven't the time to do it as we did the last time." There were good-natured words of disappointment from around the table.

"So we leave tomorrow," announced the Count. "We stop as before for a rite of charging and continue on. What's going to happen this time, based on your knowledge? What sort of a defense do you expect?"

"When I conjure otherwise there's no way they can keep the gate closed," she said with a trace of the old imperiousness. "I forsee it being much as before. It's possible they may try to intercept us en route physically, though they haven't had time to re-establish their influence over the weather as yet." She smiled confidently. "And I think they're out of tricks and deceptions this time."

On the urging of the entire troop she danced for them again that night and revelled in their admiration. The light dancing dress which she had improvised concealed little, yet her flying hair, flashing feet, the fullness of her bosom (her breast-band came unbound quite quickly, much to the approval of all), and the sight of her shapely legs as the gown swirled and spun away from her in the wild dance . . . these brought cheers and poundings on the table.

And, if the truth be known, brought back to her a greater measure of confidence in her own magnetism. A power which had been severely shaken by her recent mistakes.

She danced slowly and sinuously, danced wild and exhuberently . . . sometimes swaying slowly and seductively down to the board floor, to arch herself back as desert-women were wont to do, and to whirl once again into the heat of a wild and passionate dance.

Finally spent after a long and enjoyable evening of dancing, talking, food and drink, and dancing again, she begged off for the night and they all reluctantly left for their quarters as well. But they knew of her implicit magic within the dance, and they knew of the deeper meanings as well.

They rode out on the following day along a now-familiar, seldom-used road. And on the following night again the men stood rapt as the golden witch, clad only in her swirling, red-yellow hair, called forth the power of the old gods into their weapons and into themselves.

A circle of torches was about them; while she wore only jewelry, they were with chain mail and swords as she called Names which were unfamiliar to them, but which brought strange recognition deep within their minds . . . seeming to be memories which in this life they could not possibly know.

She looked at them all as she paused, then began the heart of the rite, chanting:

> *That we may best the Powers of Dark*
> *Shall we draw forth from all about us*
> *The pure white Power*
> *Which does pervade all the worlds.*

(Perhaps it was imagination, but the stars seemed brighter, and the ritual area seemed to glow.)

> *I draw the Power of Light*
> *Within us, as do you,*
> *Through every pore of our bodies*
> *And building a sunwise circle of Power,*
> *Growing stronger and ever yet stronger*
> *As the ever-waxing torrent*
> *Becomes a powerful vortex*
> *Linking earth and sky*
> *With ourselves, guiding the forces*
> *From the nexus-point*
> *Of vast and unworldly Power.*

(Tanithia seemed bathed in a white nimbus, which spread to all the soldiers. Suddenly, as if from far beyond the sky, brilliant beams of light seemed to arc downwards, curving through them, cutting through the bodies of all, in a feeling that was ecstatic to the point of pain. Tanithia obviously knew and expected it, but the men needed to keep a firm grip on themselves, for this strange, dazzling light seemed to be sweeping and rearranging their bodies, purifying and strengthening. Then, with the sound of a nearby storm, the sparkling, intense brilliance began to swirl faster and yet faster about them as she called, her arms raised high and her eyes on the stars.)

> *The pure Power of all which creates,*
> *Bringing forth and nurturing new life,*
> *Infinite and everlasting*

Beyond time and beyond space,
Vast matrix of Powers
Bearing true sentience,
Come within each of us
And build a Power of Life,
That we shall be clad in light
And radiant with Power.

(Rainbow hues seemed to fill the air and permeate those in the ritual, the brilliance now nearly blinding and the feel being one of pure, sensual ecstacy, yet with an exaltation of the soul and spirit. It seemed as though they were at the very center of a vast vortex which linked earth and sky, with themselves caught at the center. Undergoing a transformation and a strengthening that only the gods might know.)

The Power which we have called forth
Shall become ever stronger
And more vastly powerful
As time proceeds . . .
For the Gods have granted
Their Power!

The brilliance rippled down into her outstretched fingers to where she touched their blades. The irridescent Power leaped like flame from her hair, from her breasts, from her eyes that now were all glowing whiteness, from her womb, as the valkyr-being that had been Tanithia now called in a voice like thunder upon the ancient gods, and upon the magnificence of the ever-beautiful Witch-Goddess.

Finally the soldiers looked away, for they began to know what transcendent being had taken the place of their witch. And they could bear Her brilliance no more. Her Power flowed into their weapons and into them. Each knew that he could never be the same henceforth, and that their weapons would enter into legend when this task was over.

After a seeming eternity of unbearably exquisite whiteness, the coursing energies began to fade, and they heard, somewhere, Tanithia's voice concluding:

This rite of Power is ended.

Merry meet and merry part . . .

And suddenly it was over.

Tanithia, the torchlight glistening on her golden body, stood at the center of the circle with hands on her finely sculptured hips, and looked with amusement at her men.

"I know you're all very strong and excellent soldiers," she smiled, "But you don't realize just how ridiculous you look, sprawled all over the area like this. Get me something warm to drink, and let's relax for a while!"

"This is close enough, I think," said Tanithia, reining in her horse.

"The castle is less than an hour's ride from here, milady," said Waldmann, halting the column of horsemen.

"Yes. And there's a good bit of daylight still remaining. I feel that we should make our attack in the morning. Perhaps I can reconnoiter quietly on my own through paths that I know in this forest, and bring back what I can sense. We can plan accordingly and get the attack over quickly and easily."

"Alone?" asked Gort.

"Well . . . no. My dear Gort, will you accompany

me?" He smiled his assent.

"Count Waldmann," she said, touching his arm, "We'll be back shortly before sundown."

"Use care, my lady. I'd really rather that you took more men with you." The older man was concerned, and showed it.

"There won't be a problem, love." She took his hand briefly. "Gort and I have been through a lot, and we work well as a team."

"Very well, I envy him. Use caution, Tanithia, and may the Old Ones be with you."

Tanithia rode sidesaddle for now, wearing a long riding skirt which nonetheless was slung low about her bare waist. Her riding cloak had a high military collar, though it barely fell over the tips of her breasts, draping down her back below her waist. Its dark hue set off the tumbled red-gold mass of long hair which cascaded free down her back. Her arms were encased in close-fitting sleeves. The effect was at first glance a combination of both the demure and the wanton.

They had ridden better than a league beyond when Gort reigned up.

"What gives?" asked Tanithia, for her mind and her senses had been elsewhere.

"I don't know, Tanithia. But there are signs that there might be other riders in the vicinity. Wait here for just a little while as I scout on ahead."

"All right," she said. "I don't think that any of the creatures from the castle, winged or otherwise, are about. They all seem to be dormant in the daylight." She rubbed her forehead, trying to sort out her impressions. "They seem to be watching something and influencing something. But oddly enough, it's not us."

"Take care, my love," he said. "I'll be back as soon

as I've been able to scout carefully perhaps a league ahead." He drew close to her and she grasped at his breeches with her bare toes, leaned over, and kissed him. He reached under her traveling cloak and fondled her breasts for a moment. She smiled and ran her hand through his hair.

"Have a care, love," she said. "And get back as soon as you can."

He touched spurs gently to his horse and quietly disappeared down the trail.

Tanithia waited restlessly for a short while. Perhaps she should dismount and rest; this night and the next day were going to be very taxing indeed. But no. Perhaps if she moved just up to that high knoll a few hundred paces off in the forest she could get a clear view of the castle, and hence sense more clearly the forces that were shaping within it. She rode in that direction.

The way was longer and, due to dense brush and rock slides, considerably more roundabout than she had anticipated. Worriedly, Tanithia realized that she had come some distance from the old road where Gort would be returning.

Her horse snorted, apprehensive, and she reined him back. "What, boy? What is it?" She stroked her mount's neck.

From all sides the band of ruffians charged in. One massive fellow seized her reins, snatching them from her hands. Another grasped the bridle and jerked the horse down brutally as it began to rear. And yet others grabbed her ankles and pulled her unceremoniously from the saddle so that she fell into the dust . . . dishevelled, surprised, and a bit frightened.

"Who are you?" she looked around at them. "And what . . . other than the obvious . . . do you want with me?" She scrambled to her feet, readjusting her cloak and dusting off her skirt.

They ignored her for the moment. "D'ye think this is the girl?" growled one of the men. Another pulled her roughly around by the shoulder as she planted her feet firmly in the dirt and glared at him.

"Aye, there can't be any others like this wench . . . not the way she was described to us. Wait a moment . . . she looks familiar. I don't remember her face quite like this, but the rest of 'er . . ."

"Rob!" she gasped in surprise. Recognition also dawned in the surly face before her.

"The girl in the woods! Now I remember. My mates and I almost had you fair and squar'. Then this hoity lordship rides up and chases us away, and his peasants ran us well-nigh half a league to the river." He paused and looked over her body with a bold appraisal that made her cheeks burn red. "Quite a sword cut he gave me, wench. I'll get 'im for that, one of these days." He chuckled unpleasantly. "Well, I'll get ye this night and maybe get him when I gets back." Rob eyed her for a moment, considering.

"Wait a jot," he said slowly. "Could that noble what saved ye there be the same one wot ye're ridin' with now?"

He was close, she thought. Too dangerously close to the truth. Perhaps this thick fellow might not be able to link her with Waldmann, but if he talked with others they might be able to make the connection, and her good friend would stand to lose his life as well as his lands.

To her relief, another interrupted before Rob could question her further.

"Aye, a likely one indeed, " he leered, eyeing Tanithia's bare middle expectantly. "D'ye think his high mucky-muck deacon would mind if we . . ."

"Elijus!" she exclaimed.

"He minds everything," answered Rob. "I don't

see why we can't. No one misses a piece out of a cut cake."

"You're working for Elijus," she repeated.

"That's right," said one, running his finger under the front of her traveling cape to feel the hardness of her nipple beneath.

"Aye, we're servin' the one, true and only god. Of course it pays a little too." Several of them chuckled. "Since he lost his last band of men he hasn't been able to get together another big-sized bunch o' holy people like hisself. He's hired a few of us to do most of his dirty work."

The others gathered in close to her, and she felt that with this band of ruffians she would inevitably be raped, and shortly. Either she could fight it and expend the power she had been carefully building or . . . She smiled, catlike, and lowered her head to gaze challengingly at their leader.

"Do you dare touch me?" she taunted. "One of my men is near and pretty soon there'll be others looking for me here."

"Is that so?" His hands now roamed freely, clasping and fondling the full breasts that were bare beneath the cloak. "Boys, she's got friends about this place somewhere. Keep a sharp watch down the trail."

The others gathered close, stroked her hair, ran their hands over her slender bare waist and her firm belly.

"You wouldn't dare," she repeated in a breathless voice that was more an invitation than a warning.

"Hold her, lads," Rob said thickly as they seized her, dragging her back to arch her body as she resisted and protested. She did not beg, for with these crude oafs not much of an act was needed. She struggled enough against them to make it seem realistic, as she began shaping in her mind the patterns of force that these rough rogues could only but help to strengthen.

Rob threw her back further and tore her skirt up the side to the waistband. He pawed beneath, groping until she gasped, and he chuckled with coarse glee.

Forgive me, she thought to herself. Forgive me, Gort. Forgive me, Waldmann. Forgive me, my lovers . . . there's no way I can avoid this!

She cried out as Rob took her, grinding his heavy body into hers. A coarse and raw way of building power, but she had no choice, and the tables would turn shortly. Tanithia gasped and moaned, aroused in spite of herself, and looked hazily up as Rob ceased his ravishing and the next of his ruffians mounted her.

The power, she thought. Continue building the matrices of power . . .

Each of the rogues had his way, laughing coarsely and fondling her body, jeering as she obviously responded in spite of herself. Gasping in true passion at their grasping hands and their rough lovemaking.

Finally, spent and far more exhausted than they had anticipated, they lay scattered in the clearing and under the trees nearby. Tanithia, looking quite energetic though fully as dishevelled, stood leaning against a tree and breathing heavily as she caressed her battered breasts.

"Take the wench and let's go. Her soldier may be back soon," muttered Rob, weakly.

"Ahh, we can kill him!"

"No, she's got others around as well. Quickly now. The sooner we gets her back, the sooner we gets our money."

Resisting slightly, she was put onto the saddle in front of one of her captors. She hiked up her skirt and straddled the barrel of the horse with her golden legs, coldly amused at the admiring intakes of breath as she settled astride. Touselled, her cloak and torn skirt dusty and rumpled. But even so, tall in the saddle, confident, and sensuously strong.

They had a surprise coming, she mused. But they weren't going to like it.

They rode down one side trail and then another. Then, in a surprisingly short time, into the camp where they were met by a number of armed men. Both the amoral, cynical rogues and those with the sanctimonious, disapproving look she had come to know so well.

"You fools! You arrant fools!" A lean and wild-haired man came forth. Tanithia gasped in spite of herself. It was definitely Elijus, but his hair had turned totally white, and his face was scarred and lined.

"You idiots!" he shouted. "I told you to simply bring her back, not to rape her! She is devil-spawn, do you hear, devil-spawn! Only the Son knows what she can do since she has had you . . . ."

"Ha! She have us? I think it was the other way around, matey," said Rob. "Our agreement was payment on delivery of the trollop, and ye said nothing about ruffling up the feathers in the cookoo's nest." The white-haired man fumed, clenching and unclenching his fists in anger.

Tanithia looked closely at him. "Elijus . . . that *is* you?"

"Yes . . . queen of evil!" he snapped, looking up at

her. "Your pets, your hideous, unholy monsters . . . destroyed most of my men. Tore them to pieces as they fought and screamed. The things demanded to know where you were. Why, I don't know, for you must have been behind their attack, urging them on." His eyes had a haunted look which was not quite sane . . . as though they had seen far too much, and as though he had known too many nightmares.

"We killed many of them, yet many more came. And in the end only a few of us managed to flee for our lives." He fingered the ragged scar that disfigured his lined face. "I survived, but I shall wear this token of darkness long after you have been burned to ashes! *Ashes, witch!*"

He looked at her with a hatred made all the more fearsome by the sanity that flickered only weakly within . . . like a candle burned to its base and about to gutter out.

"I thought your Book and your Cross could protect you," she said with irony . . . and instantly regretted having gibed at him, for he struck her and sent her falling heavily into the dirt, the breath painfully knocked from her.

"Quiet, witch! Stay here in the dirt where you belong, for the Son and the God of the Sword will be our guide. And tomorrow we take your damnable castle," he stood over her, arms akimbo, glaring at her with a humorless smile, "With you tied to the lances that we'll be carrying. I'm having more of my men coming; they'll be here before the sun sets!"

"Ere the sun sets . . ." she repeated to herself and looked at the sky. The sun was indeed quite low in the sky. "Oh no," she said softly.

"Oh no!" Misinterpreting her, Elijus laughed . . . an unpleasant sound that made even the random rogues about him shy away. "Oh yes, witch. We'll keep you alive after we take and destroy your castle, putting the torch to it and to your pets. We will keep you alive long enough to get you to the capital where you shall be stripped and tortured. Tortured until you call for death as for a bridegroom." He put his face close to hers, and she flinched in spite of herself.

"Finally you shall be burned. Burned before the multitudes as you should have been three years ago!" He stood and gestured to some of the faithful.

"Take her away, but let only those of the Church guard her!"

Quickly, roughly, she was hustled off to a small tent at the center of the camp. She looked about, and her gaze fell on Rob, who looked somewhat the worse for wear, though still quite self-satisfied. She cast a long gaze at him to assure that she had his interested attention, and she significantly ran her fingers over the curves of her bosom as she drew in her breath. He saw and looked about, a gleam in his eye again.

Time passed all too rapidly. The sun was dipping down to the horizon and the others of the True Believers soon began to arrive. She could feel the Dark Forces gathering, and knew that time would be short.

There was a casual 'hello' outside the tent where she lay, bound hand and foot. "Hi there . . . take off for a nonce and say hello to your comrades, mate. I'll relieve you here for a short while. Just remember to hurry back, now."

"Thank you, brother," came the faint words as the footsteps of the other faded into the distance.

The tent flap was lifted, and the coarse Rob looked down on Tanithia. His eyes lingered over her bare thigh and legs, for the torn skirt concealed almost nothing . . . if she sat properly. Tanithia looked up at him with an eager smile.

"Aye, there's a wench. But such pretty feet shouldn't be bound." He took a knife from his belt, ran it down along her leg deliberately and slowly to enjoy her look of sudden apprehension. Then sawed the rope in twain and pulled it loose.

"And now, lass, ye should really be bound with your hands in front, rather than in back. Ah, the True Believers won't mind." He cut her arms free and, smiling warmly, she put her arms about him. For once Rob was startled. "What? I give ye my attentions and you come back for more?"

"Indeed," she said. "For how can I persuade you . . . rough thing that you are . . . that you're the closest thing that I have to a friend here." She ran her hand down the front of his shirt. He made as if to tie her hands, paused uncertainly, and threw the leathern thongs aside.

"Hardly a friend, wench." He ran his hand along her bare thigh. "You're a matter of business between that crazy one and meself. Nothing more. But I'd like to touch these fruits just once more to see if they're as soft and sweet now as they were before."

He pawed her roughly, and she closed her eyes to draw the most from his attentions.

Somewhere was building the sound of leathern wings, forbidding and ominous, though she was certain that only she could hear them.

He seized her roughly by the neck and shoved her to the ground again, mauling her with his pawing of her breasts, of the softness within her loins. She gasped . . . partly in pain, partly in pleasure at his passionate use of her.

Then he was arched over her, bowing over her as her hips moved rhythmically with his.

"Draw in the Power," she murmured. "Draw in the

Power from this wretch. And give the Power to me. Draw all Power. Draw . . . draw . . ."

"What power?" he gasped. "what power are you speaking of?"

"Yours," she purred, her slender arms like iron about his neck. "Yours!" she cried out in a half-painful, animal cry of ecstacy. He grunted and cried out as well . . . as though the soul were being drawn from him, though in pleasure rather than pain.

They paused and he rolled over, toppling from her.

"What's happened? I've never known such a grand feeling . . . but I can't stand. I'm too weak to even sit up!"

"But I'm strong," she said, rising to her feet and dusting herself off somewhat. "I'm sorry, but it had to be done." She looked with narrowed eyes at his frightened, dazed ones. "For a while I was a vampire of sorts, and I've drawn all your crude, raw strength within myself," she said.

She gazed at him, unsmiling. "I give you blessings. You're going to need them where you're going."

The sound of leathern wings was loud now, and all about. Hoarse cries filled the air as she opened the tent flap and quickly darted off to the side.

Nearly everywhere the dark, scaled, hideous monstrosities were attacking in the dim twilight. She observed them dispassionately. Here they had wings, while in the castle they did not. A small problem for any elemental being, and particularly for such strong ones. She scrambled for a place of relative security, though not really expecting to find one.

Up into this tree! The branches are thick. A slight chance not to be found . . . Hiking her skirt high about her legs, she climbed up into the tree, clinging to it and spreading herself flat against the limb.

She watched the slaughter below. The demon-

creatures spread in close, one or two of their number being hit by swords, and a few others being hit by what must have been somewhat concecrated crosses of the elements . . . falling to die and dissolve as others continued coming in and rending those on the ground.

The hired rogues broke and ran. She felt that perhaps some of them might possibly escape. The faithful stayed, presented their Books as shields. Shields that proved as insubstantial as the paper of which they were made. They fought . . . they died. Torn limb from limb, eyes plucked out, arms broken and severed. They fought, and took a surprisingly large number of the demon creatures with them. Perhaps, she felt, due entirely to their own strong wills, for fanaticism innately engenders strong will.

Yet before long the bodies of the faithful littered the ground just as thickly as the bodies of the demon-creatures.

Screaming defiance, Elijus launched himself at the largest creature, knowing full well that he was the last survivor. And being struck down cruelly, immediately. She heard his spine break as he was crushed underneath the clawed feet, crying for help from his desert god--for support which did not come.

Then the things began searching about, rending the bodies of the dead and the dying . . . snuffling and searching. It would be only a matter of time, she felt . . . they would find her.

And indeed, it happened. Inevitably.

A hoarse, almost obscene call rasped from the throat of one, and it pointed up with gibbering laughter at the woman in the tree. She tried to climb higher, but the creature came, half climbing, half slithering after her, to grasp her bare feet and drag her down so that she fell from the lower branches.

She picked herself up proudly, no trace of fear in

her eyes. With a certain arrogance she displayed her fine limbs and jutted out her breasts, challenging the creature that had dragged her from the tree.

With a low rasp the demon-thing came at her and rent her skirt fully up one side more. Then it threw her down and straddled her, hideously erect . . .

And then dissolved in flame, howling in agony.

For the massive Power which she had been storing within her body had lanced forth to totally destroy the creature. Another who came close to swing a clawed blow at her was caught by the same Power which she had called forth.

Tanithia laughed in taunting triumph, for the creatures could not touch her. In a travesty of human anger they shrieked and stamped and gibbered about. Another tried, and again a flare filled the clearing as its dying shriek echoed in the rills. The others withdrew in terror.

Finally the largest came to her, hatred in its scarlet eyes.

"Witch-woman, you've gained much strength since your escape from us. We cannot touch you . . . we cannot drain the Power from you with the strength that you have now. Yet we can harry you until you are exhausted." It gave a nightmare smile.

"Perhaps our leader will decide to let you go, you are so strong, eh? Come with us to the castle, witch-woman, and maybe we decide not to fight you. Stay here and fight us all night long . . . until Lyia and the Great One can come.

"Very well," she said with mock resignation. "I have Power, but I can't fight the waves of the dark sea. I'll go with you." They want a confrontation and they'll get it, thought Tanithia grimly.

"Do you submit?" came the rasp.

"I submit only if I must. But not to you!" she snapped. She walked forward, and there was a moan from her feet. Glancing down, she saw the horribly twisted body of Elijus in a pool of gore before her. The agony was fading as final shock began to glaze his eyes.

On impulse she knelt and stroked the sweating brow. Looking deep within the wild, fear-ridden eyes. "My friend . . . my dear friend . . . you must believe me now, for now your defenses are down and I can show you what is in me, as I know well what is in you." She stroked the wild, white hair into some semblance of order.

"You were wrong . . . you were terribly wrong." His hand reached, shaking, towards hers, and she took it saying, "I'm not that which you think, and the Old Ways can be as good as your own way. Accept it. For now you begin to see the other side of death, and you also see the truth to my words."

She held his hand up against her naked breasts, and then put it to her lips and kissed it.

"I give you blessings in the Name of the Goddess," she said softly. "I can't give you absolution, for you've sinned greatly against all those unfortunate people that you've destroyed for the sake of your god. You'll have to atone to them and make your absolution in lives to come. But for now, sleep. Sleep.

His eyes were on her. A hint . . . of a smile? No matter, his soul was gone, and his eyes were tortured no more. Closed.

Tanithia looked at Elijus for a long moment, then laid his hand across his broken chest.

She stood and straightened, as best she could, her stained and ruined garments. "Let's go," she said, standing cool and poised. "Only don't come too close, night creatures. You know my power."

Led by the demon creatures, she walked off into the darkness.

The route was long, and the road rough. The journey could have been the very essence of horror and nightmare . . . except that the horror and nightmare recoiled from the confident woman who walked in the midst of them.

As they approached the castle one of the creatures shambled before Tanithia and demanded that a rope be tied around her neck to show that she was submissive to their leaders. She made pretense of considering for a moment, the laughed scornfully. The ugly creatures involuntarily shrank back, snarling frustrated obscenities, and the matter was dropped.

She led the grotesque procession up to the massive, bone-white walls of the citadel. Smiling, she strode under the portcullis of the castle, dark and eerie in the moonlight, with no lights showing anywhere about.

The creatures, with their own stinking torches, led her into the great hall.

"We have brought her, Leader of Darkness. She is here!"

Lyia sat up on the high dais, in the antique throne chair. Tanithia admired once again the cool calmness and the perfect beauty of her adversary, and suddenly was conscious that her own feet were dusty and bruised, her own clothes torn and ruined, and her hair in disarray.

The witch-woman looked about. Off to one side sat a large, squat demon monster. This must be the senior one, she thought. The senior of her servants, and the one which had escaped her exorcism attempt. The only one, perhaps, which had managed to survive in the catacombs and the dungeon.

She stood, feet solidly spread on the flags, cloak thrown back to proudly display her naked torso, arms akimbo, fists planted on the low-slung loin strap of her skirt, where it draped over her hips.

Lyia was dressed in black, as beautiful as before. Her gown, as ever, revealing far more than it could conceal of her lovely breasts and slender waist. The breasts, Tanithia thought with a moment of regret, that she had touched with such affection in the past. And the beautiful dark hair that was so soft and long . . .

Stop!

Weakness was not to be tolerated. She had a mission, and the mission was all-important.

She had been doing a certain sort of magical breathing, drawing in more strength, throughout the entire walk. Actually, she had been drawing the force within her ever since being abducted, for she could not count on having her soldiers here on time. This task she would have to do, this battle she would have to fight, by herself. Of this she was certain.

"Tanithia, my love," said Lyia softly, showing her sharp white fangs. "I've been waiting for you. And I'm so glad to see that you came back. Even if you had to be, shall we say . . . persuaded."

"How could I stay away from you, dearest of the dear," Tanithia said with obvious sweetness.

"Pretty one, do you think that you're strong enough to simply walk back into my castle?" Lyia rested an elbow on the carven arm of her chair, and her chin on her hand. "And to think that you could merely cast us out?"

"Your castle, is it Lyia? No, it's not your castle and never has been. And never shall be." She began to build the Power within herself, stronger and ever yet stronger.

A glance showed her that the large demon-being was on the far side; she was certain that it would be unable to support its mistress in the first blow, and the others could not reach her in time to interfere physically.

Tanithia felt that she would be able to carry out her plan.

The Power within her waxed greater and ever yet greater as she gathered final strength. A faint glow began to appear around the tips of her nipples and the ends of

her fingers. It would be only a few moments now before they would sense the buildup and realize what she had planned.

"Tanithia, I loved you very much . . ." Lyia began, her voice softly ominous.

The witch felt the glow build. There was a faint swirl of light now visible around the power center of her womb. The massive Power was ready.

Lyia was continuing, " . . . And you were so ungrateful as to . . ."

"THERE!" screamed Tanithia, with a host-fettering cry. Hurling a crackling sphere of pure flame, glittering and brilliant, to impact Lyia full on her body. The vampire woman's shriek of agony permeated the air as she was blasted from the dais and hurled brutally into the opposite wall.

The small, ungainly creatures nearby chittered and screamed, fleeing in panic. Flames . . . real flames . . . licked at the tapestry.

Tanithia paused with a triumphant smile and walked leisurely across the broad stone floor until she stood over the fallen, senseless Lyia, who was now tattered, broken and bleeding.

"You fell so easily," commented the witch. "You broke with my first attack, vampire girl. Is this the true . . . what was the term . . . Leader of Darkness?"

There was a sudden deafening crackling, as of a too-close lightning bolt. The air seemed for a moment to be permeated with glowing red spider webs. Something hit Tanithia with a massive avalanche blow, smashing her thr through the air to fall crushingly against the more distant wall.

Every fiber in her body seemed to scream with pain, her breath gone, her entire being suddenly flooded with unbearable agony.

"No," came a rasping voice. *"This* is the 'Leader of Darkness', as you put it. You miscalculated again, witch-woman." A small part of her being that was not totally paralyzed in agony heard his unhuman chuckle as the large, squat demon-creature walked closer.

"You're not very good at figuring things out, witch. The vampire girl is my puppet, not I hers. She acted as my decoy; I knew that you'd strike at her, and that you can raise a lot of power. Enough to kill her." The un-human chuckling rose to an insane laughter.

"Well, I have you even more in my power than I did before." Desperately she tried to begin breathing once again, painfully trying to pull herself up on the leg of the ornate throne chair and the smoking ruin of the table that had stood next to it.

"Claw at that broken table if you will, beauteous one. Try to breathe if you will. Your powers are in abeyance with shock and counterspell. For a short while yet you're going to be as helpless as any trembling peasant." The hideous creature advanced on her, and Tanithia struggled to claw herself aright . . . gasping in agony and trying to force her breath to come again.

She had been decoyed . . . gulled. If only she could gain a few moments more to get her breath back and to get her wits back once more. But tears of pain filled her eyes, and her paralyzed lungs would not breathe. And it seemed as if all the soul-searing agony of the world had been battered into her body.

The monstrous being loomed over her triumphantly. Coolly, deliberatedly, accurately evaluating her helplessness, and how much longer it might last before she could begin to defend herself, its lipless mouth split in a travesty of a grin and it kicked her . . . and the pain seemed to burst anew as she sprawled limply with the blow.

Tanithia grimly clung to consciousness as the agony seemed to wash over her very being. As if in a haze she saw its massive arms raised over her, perhaps for a bone-crushing blow or more likely to loose a lethal burst of dark power into her supine form. To blast her once more, perhaps, and with her defenses down to reduce her body to pulped flesh and splintered bone . . .

Light flared brilliantly, blindingly. A crackle as of thunder split the air.

Flame burst against the side of the creature, slamming it down crushingly against the stone floor as parts of its repellent form seemed to crack and splinter. A brilliant flare of intense heat caused tapestry and woodwork to explode into flames nearby.

The beast shrieked unhumanly, cringing and wailing for a seemingly endless moment as the fetid smell of its burnt flesh filled the air.

And yet, impossibly, it clawed itself up from the floor, its bellows of agony giving way to thunders of wrath.

Tanithia looked around, her agonized breath beginning to come, gaspingly. Lyia! It was Lyia. The vampire girl had used the energy, the Power, which she had been storing within herself. The Power which she had been drawing from Tanithia's own veins, and that which she had retained from her better days.

And now, for whatever reason, she had hurled it at the creature which had so tormented her since her fall.

But the creature staggered to its feet and turned, a terrible malevolence in its eyes, and hurled its power full at Lyia with full force. The vampire girl shrieked in terminal agony as the dark flame impacted her slender form, hurling her like a rag doll across the great hall to hit with an audible crackling against the opposite wall.

But for a moment the creature had completely spent its energy, partly in surviving her attack, partly in being hit and radiating its energy in an uncontrolled gout as it was hit, then in its demonic wrath, hurling all which remained at the hapless Lyia, who now lay in a broken heap at the far, flaming wall.

Tanithia pulled herself unsteadily to her feet, breathing deeply, if raggedly, and forcing the ache in her body to recede as she focused her mind sharply and ever yet more sharply. The demon-creature stood, looking away from her towards Lyia's body, its shoulders bent and its clawed hands opening and closing spasmodically.

She drew the Power within herself, more and more strongly, and walked silently towards the creature. She began changing, altering her form.

The demon-being turned at her. Flame leaped from her fingers as she jabbed them directly into its strange eyes, and they burst in foul green slime. It shrieked in unholy agony as she then thrust her talon-sharp fingertips, fire licking off them, into its throat in a sudden, superhumanly strong and fast thrust. She drew back her clenched fist, tearing away the ichorous flesh as tentacle-like veins, severed and quivering, sprayed a nauseous black vileness.

For Tanithia had called within herself far more than the strength of a human. Light built around her head and her body, and swirled irridescently from the power centers of her body.

Her eyes flashed a glowing blue luminousness as she again thrust, screaming a host-fetter call. Her hand now thrust into the very chest of the gruesome creature, splintering bone, and dragged forth the slimy, dripping black protuberance which passed for a heart.

The being, still peternaturally and evilly alive, clawed for its heart. Tanithia laughed loudly and coldly, and hurled the pulsing, veined organ to the floor. And slammed her heel down on it with all the force she could muster. Power burst momentarily through and around her foot, and the stone under the heart was suddenly crazed and splintered. The organ itself burst like a boil, and dissolved into repellent ichor.

The demon-creature staggered back with a scream, its massive body folding in on itself and dissolving into putrescence. With a final shriek that tore away the rest of its throat, the thing fell, and dissolved.

There was a sudden uproar from the direction of the main gate . . . the clash of swords, the unhuman howling of many demon creatures, and the strident yells of men. The clamor grew louder and yet more louder, and the soldiers came sweeping in, blades swinging and chopping at the smaller creatures that swarmed to attack them from chambers and corridors throughout the castle.

An unhuman din filled the air as the scaled beings died in wailing screams before the glowing weapons of Count Waldmann and his men . . . terrified and yet compelled to rush to their doom in the mindless evil which served them in lieu of souls. The soldiers, grinning and yelling in the terrifying exultation of battle, advanced steadily in a tight diamond formation with shields overlapping, each man carefully covering his comrades as they moved forward through the hazy smoke of the great hall.

Then all was quiet, save for the crackling of the flames that were reaching for the high-vaulted wooden ceiling. A last demon creature ran in shrieking, only to have its ugly body transfixed by three glowing blades. Only a few moments later it was putrifying into shapelessness as it became indistinguishable from scores of other rapidly decomposing corpses strewn inside the hall, and perhaps hundreds outside.

Tanithia was leaning, bone-weary and aching everywhere, against the shattered ruin of a table, still staring blankly at the very large and very foul-smelling corpse that had been the largest of the demon-creatures. With an unsteady hand she wiped the sweat and grime from her forehead and made an attempt to brush back the tangled hair which hung over her face, though with no noticeable effect.

Waldmann gave a brief order and the men formed into a defensive perimeter, their weapons at the ready and scanning the flame-lit smoke for any other attack. But the huge hall remained empty, save for the slowly spreading flames.

Waldmann pulled off his helmet and wiped his sweating face with a gauntleted forearm as he strode to her. Gort was at his side, dusty and spattered with black blood but, like the rest, unharmed by the battle.

"My Lady, you're all right?" Waldmann's eyes were concerned as he scanned the battered and ragged figure before him. Gort ran to her.

"No problem . . . no need to worry. I'm quite well, my Count, really." Strange words, considering her multitude of scrapes and bloody scratches, and the agonized expression as she limped towards them, embracing first Gort and then the Count.

Waldmann held her trembling, exhausted form and stroked her hair. "My sweet Lady Tanithia, with all due respects . . . you look like hell!"

She leaned back and smiled at him wanly. "My dear Count, I'd really be feeling excellent . . . if every fiber in my body didn't feel like it had a toothache!"

They eased her to a sitting position on the broken dais. Gort swabbed her face and bosom with water from a pouch-flask as Waldmann spoke to her. "It took a good while for Gort to track where you'd wandered. We joined him as he searched. When we found signs of your abduction we felt that it must have been the doing of these . . . things . . . from the castle, so we came here. Quite a battle before the gate and in the courtyard it was; just as before, all these creatures were drawn to us. And just as before, the spell on our weapons made it simply a matter of hacking our way through." He looked around and stroked his grey moustache reflectively. "Our assumptions were wrong, but our actions were right."

"Yes milord," said Tanithia, rousing somewhat with the coolness of the water, "I felt that would be the case, and you'd be here for that very reason. But I felt, though, that I'd have to handle this job myself." She coughed and then rubbed at her arms with a grimace. "By the gods, I feel like a whole cavalry troop has charged over the top of me, and then come back again. If it weren't for my powers I'm certain that I'd be little more than carrion right about now."

She suddenly looked about, eyes wide, searching the flame-lit smoky redness of the hall. "Lyia!"

Swiftly she made her way across the hall, the thickening smoke making all of them cough more and more, to where the vampire girl lay. To her surprise, Tanithia found a small spark of life yet remaining. As the others came up alongside her she knelt at the piteously broken body, clasped the other's soft hand to her breasts, and then kissed it. Lyia opened her eyes slowly and looked up at her. No pain remained in the eyes, only a soft darkness.

"I loved you. I really did."

"I know, pretty one. I know," said Tanithia, tears streaking her face.

"You must believe me. In spite of all I did . . ." Lyia

coughed, and dark blood welled forth. She gagged and coughed again. "In spite of it all you brought back some semblance of warmth and joy to a life which had been . . . been ruined and become totally hideous." Her breath came harder now. "And love. Most of all you brought back love."

Tanithia stroked Lyia's hair gently. The dying girl's expression told the truth of her words, and told more than mere words. Lyia smiled weakly.

"Cast your spells for me, O witch woman . . . witch lover . . . that we may meet again in the worlds beyond, and that . . . under better circumstances in our lives to come, we shall meet as sisters or as lovers. And practice the great rites together."

"I'll say my prayers for you, dear one," said Tanithia as the spark of life faded from Lyia's broken frame. For a long moment the tableau remained in the dim, flame-lit hall. Tanithia sobbing quietly over one who had, in spite of all, meant much to her. Lover, betrayer, antagonist, and yet, in the final twilight, an ally and a friend once again.

"My Lady," said the Count softly, "We had best be leaving. The main structure of this hall is afire, and it's going to spread to the rest of the castle very rapidly. We'd better all be going. As few as we are we couldn't hope to contain these flames."

"Yes . . . yes, we must. Yet, help me with her body. I would that she were given a good funeral . . . with all the chants of the Old Ones and of the Goddess."

Flanked by the soldiers, they made their way out of the burning castle as flame and smoke waxed behind them. Cleansing and consuming all in pure, scarlet fire.

As dawn spread across the horizon the soldiers stood as a guard of honor while the flames of the pyre consumed

all that remained of Lady Lyia. The chants had been spoken, the spells had been cast.

On a hill overlooking the scene, in an archaic and pagan manner, Tanithia lay in the arms of Gort, naked, as they watched the smoke rise to the sky.

"She's gone. My tears are gone with her," said Tanithia softly.

"My love," murmured Gort. "Come with me. Be mine. The land is clean at last." He looked towards the glow of the flames which were still rising from the ruin of the castle. "You know my feelings for you." He kissed her gently.

She smiled tenderly at him and ran her hands over his face as he bent low over her again. "My love, my dear Gort. Don't you see? Even though I love you and you love me, there's a difference between us that's greater by far than castles and demon-creatures. And vampiress noblewomen." She raised herself for a moment and kissed him.

"You're a hearty young man of the fields and the mountains and the streams. I am a witch and a sorceress . . . a seeker of mysteries. Our ways may touch from time to time but, at least in this lifetime, they will always diverge. Neither of us can change our ways long enough or deep enough to make a permanent change. And neither of us, in the long run, would be happy." She ran her fingers gently over his temples and his lips. "We're all too different, my love. Too different."

"Perhaps we . . ."

"No," She interrupted gently. "We cannot work it out, as you were about to say. Believe me, dear. Listen to my words. Leave with the new day. Go forth to your village, you'll be the leader there now, I understand. And the Count has chosen to appoint you as Baron of Drakenstane. The whole province . . . it's a good position,

remote though this land may be."

She smiled and embraced him closely, shutting her eyes to feel his closeness all the better. "Find yourself a lovely, sweet maiden who loves you dearly and desires you passionately. Make her yours . . . and in times to come, when you so desire, I can see that someone will come out of the forest to train her, or to train you both, in the Old Ways. It's best, my love, to mould and to fashion your own High Priestess."

They lay silently together for a long time. Then he kissed her again, long and lovingly. And words were not needed.

The moon had turned through its phases one more full time. Tanithia had returned with the Count and his men. They consoled her, which she appreciated in her sadness, for she needed their jovial company, their warmth, and their attention.

Yet eventually she felt that the time had come for her to leave Count Waldmann. Clad as she was when first he found her, in a simple peasant dress and barefoot, she kissed him one last time and walked off into the autumn forest, alone.

He looked after her for a long, long time. Then turned and walked away, for he too, understood.

ALONE again, save for a few elderly servants who were sleeping at this time of the night, she sat in the study of her remote estate, lost far among the wooded hills beyond the Count's lands. She reclined on a velvet-cushioned couch and gazed at the large black mirror which covered nearly all of one full wall. Books were scattered about, and her eyes were bleary with lack of sleep.

She waved her hands in a slow, careful pattern and flickers of light seemed to drift across the mirror face. Random patches swirled and ebbed and flowed across the blackness, and finally shaped into the silhouette of a woman's head, becoming more and more clear as they talked. Shaping more distinctly into the image of an elderly woman, advanced in years but kindly and wise.

"My Vala," said Tanithia, "The task is done. The shire is scoured, the castle destroyed, and new seeds have been planted which will be far more vital than the old ones."

"You did well, my daughter." The words seemed to drift from the mirror. Perhaps only Tanithia heard them; perhaps had there been others in the room they too might have heard the words. Or perhaps they might not have seen or heard anything . . .

"I released young Gort."

"Yes, I know. And your decision was wise."

"And I released the good Count Waldmann."

"That too was wise, my daughter. He was beginning to fear you, and fear would in time have affected his love for you. But he's a wise man with a good heart, and you can rely on him."

I know, my Vala. I was done. I had known much love and yet I'm alone . . . so alone . . . once again."

"But you did well, Tanithia," came the voice of the older one. "You scoured Drakenstane Shire before it attracted the attention of those who would destroy our people."

"Indeed, Mother. I was worried that Elijus and his men could have been the vanguard." She paused. "But no, it seems that the central government and the regents there felt him to be merely a fanatical fool. They ignored him and paid scant notice to the loss of his people, feeling merely that they had marched into the mountains and been destroyed by an avalanche during a thunderstorm." There was silence for a while.

"How strange." Tanithia smiled sadly. "Poor Elijus."

"He shall suffer for his actions in lives to come," reminded the voice from the shadowy figure in the mirror.

"I know, Mother. I'm sorry for him, yet I don't forgive him."

"And our own valley," said the Elder one, "is more secure than it ever has been."

"Yes. Because Drakenstane, now as in the past, guards the approach to our own valley of the Old Ways. Of course no one there knows it now." Tanithia considered. "Though in time Baron Gort may come to realize it. Eventually, I think he'll become one of us."

There was a long period of silence, and finally Tanithia spoke again.

"It wasn't all the doing of Lyia, was it?"

"No. She was evil and she did much wrong. Yet there was evil implicit as the counterpole of this new cult of the One Great God. It's brought evil throughout the land, as any unbalanced fanaticism will do. And, in other worlds and other dimensions, it triggered her own evil into something that she could not control. Yes, what she did and what she became is linked inextricably to what Elijus and his men have levied upon the land. Ironic, isn't it?"

There was a long period of silence, and the image flickered slightly. Tanithia spoke softly. "My Vala?"

"Yes daughter?"

"Where is my lover? The one who was with me when I was queen?"

"Tanithia, you realize as well as I that you must not know that. For you must not go to him, nor he to you. You must stay where you are. For you, my daughter, are still the spear-point of the Old Ways."

"You mean my researches."

"Indeed. You're the only one with the mind, with the inclinations, and the magical contacts in this lifetime, to search for what we need. The portals to the Rainbow Lands . . . the elvish kingdoms . . . are what we must find, and where we must go." The elderly face in the mirror looked pained. "This world is no longer for us.

They will have their struggles, they will have their bloodsheds, they'll have their enemies . . . but it must be without us. We belong to an older era, and perhaps our time will be gone forever. But I think perhaps our ways may come again. It will be something fresh and new for the people of a future era. For now, though, we must leave. And you, my daughter, must show us the way."

Tanithia sat quietly for a long time. "One last thing, Mother. My child . . . how is she?"

"She's beautiful. She'll be as lovely as her mother."

"Please, when she gets old enough, would you train her so that she can talk with me over the mirror?"

"Indeed, dear one. And remember . . . we love you always, completely and totally."

"I know. Thank you for reassuring me."

"Farewell, and may the Goddess be with you."

"Farewell, and blessed be, Mother."

The mirror grew black again as the image faded. And for a long time Tanithia sat alone in the dimness of her study, her head bowed.

Seven Short Essays
by Ed Fitch

On the Reality of various matters underlying

THE CASTLE OF DECEPTION

CONCERNING THE REALITY OF DEMONS

"The sky, like the sea, is not innately evil, but it is terribly unforgiving of any omission of vigilance, any ignorance, or any misjudgement."

—Aviators' saying

"Nothing is originally good or evil, except that men make it so."

—Anonymous

"... A fountain poisoned at its source, foredoomed to tragedy and to disaster."
—"The Dutchess of Malfi", A Jacobian drama, ca 1650

"Don't spit into the wind."
—Folk saying.

Demons come in three basic types: good, bad, and indifferent. People generally like to take personal credit for the doings of the first group, ignore the last, and to get justifiably upset about the middle category.

In ancient times demons were viewed as being merely forces within oneself or out in the universe at large, since it was a tenet of philosophy that the human reflected the world, and the world the human ... "As above, so below" ... a belief which, taken symbolically, can still be quite valid.

Socrates typified much of the classical view when he commented that his personal demon had suggested that he go to an elementary school to learn music with the children in their own classes. In his case the "demon" was a part of his own mind, and he obviously viewed it as such. (He went to the school, by the way; much to the amusement of the children.)

Yet in that era it was felt that the mind could have effect on the world, and vice versa, so that a demon ... or a god ... that existed within the mind would exist beyond the mind as well, having its most perfect existence on the realms of intellect and emotion. The myth and legend of that era was marvelously rich in all manner of non-human powers and beings. Few were notably good or remarkably bad: most were an interesting mixture of behavior and intentions which could at times seem much like ourselves in moral makeup.

In many other cultures this is still the case. The fearsome-looking demons of the Tibetan culture are viewed as being inextricably linked with the mind of each human being, and yet a part of the external world as well.

Similarly, the demons of the Buddhist cultures from Vietnam to Japan and Mongolia: They're not good or bad, but manifestations of natural forces ... though one would be advised to avoid provoking them unnecessarily! This view is reflected in Africa and in Polynesia and in the native legends of the Americas. The Amer-Indians' nature spirit and demigod Coyote met with scores of elemental being types, and only a small handful of them were malignant. (The truly evil ones were also stupid, which aided the shrewd Coyote in his destruction of them.)

A mountain or a river is neither good nor is it evil. It is merely *there*. And its power and beauty are very impressive to us humans.

But a mountain or a river can be polluted: through lack of care or more likely through avarice and thoughtlessness they can be imbued with poisons which can last a long, long time. In such cases as these a force of nature can become deadly to that which encounters it. Wild carnivores can become so used to feeding off garbage dumps that they forget their parents' skills of hunting, or are too sickly to stalk game in the wild, and instead begin to prey on domestic animals. And eventually on humans. Dogs trained to fight and to kill in lucerative but highly illegal pit contests are indeed veritable demons when they accidently get loose in a residential neighborhood or near a school.

There are examples in mythology. The Norse god Loki was not bad originally. A jokester and a mischief-maker, he slowly and by degrees became bitter and drawn within himself, until near the end of the Norse legend cycle he had become almost totally destructive. There were numerous prior causes and circumstances which seem to have nudged him in the wrong direction, but the end was the same: he in time brought about the destruction of Valhalla, the holocaust of Ragnarok, and the end of the Gods.

And of course the teachings of magic in all cultures and all eras are that thoughts and emotions become physically manifest if they are strong enough and maintained for a long enough time, and that a locale can retain such manifestations for quite a long while. Properly (or maliciously) begun, they can draw strength and sustenance from the fears and anxieties of those who encounter them, then by manifesting can create more fears to feed on, and so forth.

The original intent need not be evil for the end result to be deadly. The Golem of Prague was designed and magically animated by the Rabbi magicians to protect the Hebrews of that medieval city. Yet once it began using its vast strength to protect its people, the creature became impossible to control and devastated much of the city until a brave Rabbi finally halted its ravages.

Call the phenomenon "magical pollution" if you will, or perhaps "astral poisoning", demons of the bad variety can be quite real. Aided by a populace inculcated for generations in the belief (even if it's not valid) that the world is naturally evil, and that anything not specifically of heaven is derived from hell, an emanation of nature which is only slightly dark can be made as black as the Abyss. Thus the active negativism of deliberate evil can be shaped by a trained mind to have being and shape; it can then gain strength and perhaps even a physical manifestation through years of ignorance and fear.

But it can be destroyed, though such is not always easy. In whatever culture and in whatever era the expulsion of entrenched evil will become a hard, dangerous task. But such expulsion and such exorcism is the stuff of which heroic tales . . . some of them true in fact, and all true in intent and concept . . . will grow and be an inspiration for others.

And this inspiration benefits us all, for evil must always be opposed.

VAMPIRISM — THE DARK FASCINATION

The popular belief in vampires has existed in all times, in all cultures, and in all lands. A nineteenth-century writer ... I can't recall the name at present ... commented that if consistency of belief were any measure of truth, then the existence of the vampire could be considered as proven.

There has been a remarkable resurgence of interest in such things during the latter part of the twentieth century, stemming perhaps from the reshaping and modernization of the Dracula legend by Bram Stoker about a hundred years ago.

The original from whom Stoker drew his story, one Vlad Dracul, was a nobleman from the Transylvania region of what is now Roumania. Even for his time he was remarkably cruel and harsh, though considering that his lands were on the marches of the vast and fearsome Ottoman Empire ... hardly known for its gentleness with non-Muslims ... one can accept that he had to be known as very terrible in order to merely hold his lands and to survive. Historically, Vlad Dracul seems to have been fair and a good administrator as far as his people were concerned, though one can imagine that his concept of justice was one that forgave very little. Dracul (meaning "dragon") did not acquire the curious reputation of being a vampire until long after his death. This reputation is, by the way, almost unknown in modern Roumania, where "Comrade Vlad" is a nationalsitic hero and indeed viewed much the same way that we view George Washington!

Although in all folk cultures the vampire was (and is) known as extremely plebian and unpleasant, Stoker and the Irish writer LeFanu reshaped the old legends, retaining most of the Central European traditions and yet also adding a cold, icy, elegant image of old, cruel nobility. Evil most definitely, but also with a hint of being lonely and tormented.

The image has proved to be very compelling, touching perhaps on some dark Jungian archetype in its power and fascination. The host of books and motion pictures which resulted, and which continue, are not considered the best examples of literature although they have a durable popularity. There have been some memorable portrayals of the dread Count in motion pictures, including those by Bela Lugosi, Christopher Lee, Frank Langella, and even a deftly humorous portrayal by George Hamiltion.

It is not widely known, but Sheridan LeFanu's "Carmilla" preceded and perhaps influenced Bram Stoker. The heroine/villainess which LeFanu created is herself a strongly compelling individual ...of the ancient nobility (of course), sensual, beautiful, darkly erotic, and with a preference for women. But LeFanu's work is only a novelette, and regrettably not as well crafted as Stoker's novel. Still, several quite interesting films have been made with Carmilla as the main character, and it is quite certain that we have not heard or seen the last of this cruel and yet fascinating lady.

As mentioned earlier, both Dracula and Carmilla seem to touch a very deep, compelling image within the dim subconscious, an image which frightens and yet fascinates, joining paranormal powers, immortality coexisting with death, cruelty, and dark, intense sensuality. Both seem possessed of the knowledge of the ultimate secrets of death and life.

Implicitly, the stories treat the nobility of both Carmilla and Dracula in an interesting way that was a part of the ancient pagan German culture: their noble lineage seems inferred to be archaic ...non-human in origin, either from some supernatural source or from some race which existed before humankind, or both. Their backgrounds and earlier existences have only brief, ominous mention: the reader assumes that whatever their earlier lives, and the intervening states of being, their experiences would have been piercingly different from anything we could comprehend. Alien, definitely. Horrible? That might depend on your viewpoint. Tormenting? Quite possibly. Lonely? Most definitely. But the deep, unhuman wisdom, the vistas of centuries of time; one wonders whether these might not lead to some strange, "dark transcendence"?

The reader may muse over these questions, but the answers are not forthcoming. Nor does it seem likely that anyone lives who could give the answers ...

The ancient Greek playrights knew that audiences are invariably fascinated with those who are larger than life, whether good or evil: Kings, nobility, heroes, and so on. In the ancient world those of such exhalted status had to have greater learning, greater wisdom than most, and thus be "closer to the gods." Subliminally this belief is still general today.

Perhaps Stoker, LeFanu, and the most talented who have followed them took the old folk legends and restored them to their original, archetypal fearsomeness by making them "larger than life". Certainly such compelling, intense characters are much more interesting than the brutish, mindless vampires of Russian and eastern European folk legend (typical also of African and Asian legends) who would cause occasional perplexity to the living until progressive decay eventually made it impossible for their semi-reanimated bodies to leave their unconsecrated graves . . . or until some priest or village wise-woman firmly pinned them down with a stake of (usually) rowan wood, one thing which could break the fragile matrix of "lifeless life", and/or seal the grave with a consecrated symbol of the Earth. This would be a cross, usually, since from time's beginning nearly all cultures have had the symbol of the earth as an equal-armed cross or a circle intersected by an equal-armed cross. This would, of course, be similar to the traditional Celtic Cross.

And of course the reader always wonders, "How is it done?" What is the secret which gives such a strange sort of potentially immortal existence? Fascinating narrations exist in ancient literature about then-current beliefs. Witches in Thessaly in Roman times were said to have the power to temporarily raise the dead. In Aupelius's "The Golden Ass" there is a most interesting description of a rite in which a priest temporarily re-animated a corpse so that the man in question could name his murderer. (Upon being so awakened he was very ill-tempered. The body had obviously been rendered untenable for his spirit and soul to have vacated it, and two or three days more in the Mediterranian summer had certainly not improved its condition!).

In the stories, of course, blood sustains the villainous being. Such could be a part of it (though not necessarily so), for occult traditions aver that blood is extraordinarily rich in the non-material essence of life. Even a living body tends to run down after a few decades: infusions of pure life force can stem or reverse this process for a period longer.

But how, one might ask? What is the exact process? That, I'm afraid, is a secret which perhaps only a few adepts might possibly possess. Or perhaps a secret which might take decades of study by an extraordinarily gifted person.

However, like the Priestess Magessa Lyia of a more recent novel, such investigators would tend to be quite silent about such things. And, like her, they might find that the side-effects and social implications of such knowledge could be, shall we say, rather unfortunate! ,

RITUAL MAGICK

Magick is essentially the manipulation of events, objects, and probability by means of powers residing in or keyed by the subconscious mind. This deep part of the human psyche is as yet shadowy and little known both in content and in capabilities. The great psychologist Jung pioneered the mapping of the subconscious in a manner which gives some understanding of how such things as racial memories and paranormal phenomena would occur, and a study of his works is a must for anyone seriously interested in this subject.

The subconscious is both primitive and primal. It must be trained, aimed, and triggered . . . yet communicating with it and motivating it is the great problem. Mere words do not affect the subconscious, as it is far too primitive to comprehend them. Hypnosis can probe the depths of the subconscious and can be a valuable therapeutic tool as well as familiarizing one with some of the vast reaches of the subconscious mindscape.

The subconscious seems to understand strong primal imagery, powerful emotions, and experiences, whether real or theatrical. It can be trained over a long period of time with a regular exposure to a mental/physical conditioning such as yoga or the martial arts. It can become active and potent with the proper stage-setting and a carefully channelized buildup of intense, focused feelings. For the working of magick the training and conditioning of the mind is of great importance, using meditation exercises, visualization which is very vivid, and what can only be described as "magic thinking". (There is no room here to discuss what the latter means. The interested reader is advised to study some of Robert Graves' works for an understanding of magical thinking. Particularly, "The White Goddess" and his novels are recommended.)

After the mind training has become routine comes the setup for the ritual itself. The costume should be unique and "magical" to the wearer. The setting for the rite must be a fully harmonious stage setting of which every aspect is directed towards the ceremony and towards that which is sought. Like the setting and costume, the words to be spoken must be a comprehensive part of the drama which will be undertaken to affect the subconscious and to trigger the happenings. (With more and more practice there is less need for these special measures, as the mind has learned intuitively how to function magically. Even with the adept, however, the form and substance of an esthetically and magically perfect rite has the soothing and yet elevating effect which is so rewarding to the participants.) A ritual can act out that which is needed or desired. Since certain physical objects such as jewels or weapons or statues can attain and hold a considerable charge of magical power, as told in countless legends from all nations, these can be alternately used as a focus to accomplish results. And in many of the ancient legends there are mentions of magical "names of power" which can also be so used. It is interesting that these styles of magic seem to be so constant throughout the world and in all eras.

Chants or singing, with the participants in a hypnotic or alpha state, is a method for performing magick which is worldwide in scope. Particularly interesting anthropological studies have been made of this method as used by Siberian shamans and by the Australian aborigines. Such chants or songs are repeated long and steadily, or with a long, powerful buildup to a cathartic peak.

Studies have also been made quite thoroughly on shamanic trance-working, wherein the witch or sorceror places the self in a deep trance and leaves the body to go out into other dimensions to accomplish the goal which is sought.

There are "formula" ceremonies which are what we normally think of as ritual magick. Numerous styles exist or have been described in the writings of the ancients. Perhaps a few of the most interesting might be mentioned.

The Quabalistic method is based on Hebraic metaphysical documents which seem to reflect a system from about the time of ancient Babylon, though it is impossible to tell at the present. The earliest Quabalistic texts still existing are Medieval grimoires or spell-books. Although this is essentially a Hebrew system it seems that nowadays the system is worked more often by gentiles, though the critical parts of the liturgy are still written and spoken in Hebrew. The Society of the Golden Dawn, a hundred years ago, pioneered the rennaissance of the Quabalah, and its influence is still quite wide even in the present.

Elemental or naturalistic magick is that which has always been used by witch and pagan groups, and nowadays is an emotional, poetic, and esthetic system. That which is needed is specified in a poetic manner, after requesting the presence of elemental forces and the powers of Nature.

Seid (pronounced "Sei*th*', with *th* as in *then)* was the ancient Norse and Germanic system. Probably originally from Siberia, where many such magical systems and traditions seem to have originated, it used chants or "runes", out-of-body workings, and god-form evocations. It is discussed at length in the Elder and Lesser Eddas and was still extant at the time of the most recent Edda, about a thousand years ago and numerous runes are carefully recorded. Apparently, though, this powerful tradition is no longer a living system.

Dance magic is perhaps a form which can be considered to be a type of ritual magic, if one expands the definition a bit. As the name indicates, dance magic expresses that which is desired in dance mime, and in using the dance to call on god-forms or elemental beings to request that it be done. Either the magical power generated by the dancers can be channelized through a god-form or elemental/natural power to accomplish the goal, or the dancer can endeavor to effect the event directly.

All primitive societies seem to have used dance magic for hunting purposes, and there seem to be indications of using dance to express some rather sophisticated philosophical and theological meanings even twenty or thirty thousand years ago, if we can judge from the cave paintings in parts of Europe.

In the Middle East, prior to the incursions and takeover by the tribes who became the present-day Arabs, dance magic seems to have been regularly practiced at the temples of the goddesses Fortuna and Venus, those goddess religions which had existed there since before the dawn of history. Apparently, dance priestesses would perform their magic to work for fertility of the land, the waters, and the people. What we now call "belly dancing" is the descendant of this once widespread and very highly regarded magical art.

There have been a lot of ways for working ritual magick. They've all been interesting.

SOME THOUGHTS ON ANIMAL COMMUNICATION

When I was not much more than a year of age my parents bought a puppy. He of course grew and matured far faster than I, and what began as a pair of infant playmates became in time a relationship wherein I was still the toddler and he became the mature supervisor, mindful of his responsibilities.

Shep had, it so happened, that marvelous combination of strong, intelligent genetics and loving care which made him a genius and natural leader in the canine world. As soon as he became mature he assumed leadership of the farm's varying pack of hunting dogs, and remained the leader for the rest of his long life.

As a small child I was most impressed by the pack's skill at tracking and hunting, at herding cattle and even chickens back to the pens, and awed at the quick, brutal skill they showed in the dangerous task of locating and killing poisonous snakes. I tagged along with the dogs as they would occasionally rove through the forest near the farm, imitating their mannerisms and trying to do what they did so well . . . and feeling frustrated because my shape was not so fast as theirs, nor my nose as sharp.

Their communication fascinated me even at that early age . . . the look of an eye, the drop of an ear, expression of the face and the bearing of the body, the tone of a whine, bark or a growl, the wrinkling of a nose . . . all these were part of a rather efficient system of communication which sufficed for nearly all everyday affairs, and which indeed could have considerable subtlety to it. My child's efforts to mimic them was greeted with friendly amusement by the canines, who treated me (once we were in the wood and away from the human world of the farmyard) with the gentle patience reserved for any puppy.

Perhaps one of my first experiences with the mystical inner world of animals came on a night when the moon was bright and full, and the pack was at the edge of the dark forest, gathered for a group howl. Wrapping myself in a pelt that had been stored in a shed, I joined them for what was a truly remarkable experience of oneness, of closeness, of magic and mystery. Perhaps it would not be so for an adult, for the intrapersonal relationships were important and mayhap something that only a small child could have been accepted into. There was, I discovered, the experience of feeling something far more archaic and strange than would normally be expected of domestic animals on a very prosaic Virginia farm.

In later years I was to live on a ranch far back in California's Siskiyou Range, and came to know coyotes in the wild. This time the relationship was, regrettably, one of adversaries rather than of friends. Yet it was fascinating to observe these extremely wily and intelligent animals . . . far smarter than our dull domestic canines . . . and their use of teamwork and almost military-style tactics to locate and to bring down deer and weakened or ill cattle. Although deadly in their hunting, they would at times show sparkles of humor in what could only be called their practical jokes on the rancher and his dogs.

(It has been more than a generation since that time, and on my yearly returns to camp near the ruins of the long-abandoned ranch, I sometimes am fortunate enough to hear their magnificent group howls . . . far more musical and magical than our farm dogs ever managed. I also observed, and verified with a few of the old-timers in the mountains, that the three major packs or clans of coyotes that I remember picking out as a boy, based on three great mountains nearby, are still there. They have been existing as social units for at least a major part of this century. Perhaps they have been there much longer, though there is no way of knowing for certain.)

Many who are involved with the magical arts will state unequivocally that their pets as well as other animals have a goodly capability for mind-to-mind communication, and use it often. I personally have had good success in giving telepathic commands to dogs, and having them obeyed, or having a cat pause and gaze significantly into my eyes, then realizing spontaneously what the animal was communicating. Perhaps most of this is expected reactions with an animal that one knows well, based on a mutual understanding. Perhaps part of it is subtle body language and expression.

But perhaps it's more than that. I tend to think so.

SHAPE-CHANGING

Shape-changing is an ancient part of our common folklore which seems to possess an everlasting fascination. It has been the staple premise for quite a few motion pictures and television thrillers, most of which manage to be mediocre at best, though even so are better quality than the innumerable novels and comic books which repeat the theme ad infinitum.

Most people don't seem to realize that shape-changing, often called were-change or lycanthropy, is a vivid part of early folklore in every society on this planet. The histories of all lands seem to indicate legal action or worse against those who practiced this mysterious art, though in some societies the changing into the shape of wolves or of other creatures was an accepted part of the order of doing things.

In the northern part of ancient Greece, for example, there was an order of priesthood in an agrarian and livestock-raising province, whose function it was to assure that the wolves in that area did not attack the sheep and cattle. We unfortunately know nothing of the religious tenets or of the meditation and training which the priests followed; history only relates that once every seven years one member of the Order was chosen to become a werewolf, and thenceforth ran as a wolf with the mountain packs, leading them away from the livestock of the settled areas and into wilderness places where there was game aplenty.

The shamans of the Siberian steppes were usually instructed in were-change by their masters while still in apprenticeship, and used the technique often in seeking personal enlightenment and understanding as well as in their tribal duties as healers, exorcists, and in escorting the spirits of dead clan members into the Afterworld. Perhaps in most primitive societies where the shaman or sorcerer or magician is a legitimate member of society with his or her own assigned duties, the art of shape-changing has been an accepted method of accomplishing their work.

Where there is no longer a place in a society for the magician, the sorcerer, or the witch this art falls into disrepute and often gains a sinister reputation. It has become an arcane and disturbing fragment from an earlier civilization, and perhaps something to be feared.

In Thailand there are no wolves, but there still are tigers in the jungles and in the mountains. Were-tigers are feared even to this day by the villages in remote northern provinces. It is not unknown for Buddhist monks, well-trained in the magical arts of their culture in monastaries which specialize in such training, to be dispatched for nighttime sweeps through the rice paddies and the rain forest, carrying torches and silver-tipped spears. Any tiger which is more than twelve feet in length from nose to tail is viewed as a more-than-mortal being . . . either a magical animal-magician of its own kind, or as a human who has become a shape-changer. Either way, if they become man-killers they must be dealt with in a magical way, or their spirits and mana will remain to haunt the area, and perhaps even to become vampiric.

And of course the legends of the werewolf were once a dark part of European backwoods folklore. The Inquisition and assorted witch-trials relate many cases of various unfortunate beings brought to trial for the ecclesiastical offense of shape-changing (after all, the gods and religious establishments of one era become the devils and satanic cults of the next era. Shape changing and the Old Gods were no exception.)

There seemed to be two major types of shape-changing. The easier, and the one most quoted in the Medieval trials, would be for the shaman to put his or her body into a deep trance and exude an animal form which would roam far afield on various errands, to meet with others of like talents, or merely for the learning experience of becoming some other kind of being. Such a magical operation could only be accomplished at night, for the sun would be harmful and perhaps even fatal to this exuded form . . . an interestingly identical belief with the Spiritualists' theory of ectoplasm today.

The more difficult would be a complete alteration of the physical structure of the body, something which apparently could be accomplished by a trained adept. Obviously, it would not be an easy technique to master, but the change would be total and could perhaps only be detected by another trained magic-worker. The Eddas, the legends and literature of ancient Norse, speak frequently of witches being able to accomplish this difficult feat.

But is it possible? It is for real? Is it done today? ·

The answer is interesting, for in remote areas and even in some very urban areas of Europe and the US it is said that the art is still practiced by folk-magicians in backwater provinces and by displaced country folk and sophisticated witches and magicians of the urban middle class. Quite discreetly, of course.

How? That's another story, and perhaps the subject for another book.

SEX MAGICK

The using of sex to accomplish magical goals is perhaps as old as the art of magic: that is, probably considerably older than the human race itself. Much has been lost in our histories due to periods of puritanism and revisionism, but there are indications that sex magic may have been known, used, and regularly taught at temples of Pan and Aphrodite in pre-classical times. Certainly in the Far East there is evidence of a Goddess-oriented precursor to Buddhism ("Bon") which has long taught sex magic through the Tantric method. These techniques of Tantric Yoga have been re-introduced into the Western world, though they are still not well known nor widely practiced yet, perhaps a hundred years or so after the translation of the system into the languages of the West.

Basically, all sytems of metaphysics teach that there is a vital energy or force field which pervades all things living and non-living, and which extends to every part of the universe. This Power or Force can be generated in many ways, though living beings can give rise to it in vast quantities. We are all one with this life force, it works through us and we through it. This *Kundalini, Ki,* or *The Force* is the source of magical power.

The sexual and more subtle sensual aspects of the human psyche and body are easily the most natural and powerful sources of Kundalini or Ki that we have. But such Forces are like fast, deep rivers which must be properly channelized and controlled to accomplish results. Additionally, when such flow can be generated, the magician absolutely must keep it controlled and modulated or risk grave physical and emotional damage. Definitely, it's "life in the fast lane"! Like a river, one's sexually-derived powers are not easy to control, though once mastered they can accomplish great things.

The basic conditioning for such workings should involve intensive study of a discipline such as Yoga or the martial arts, with much time spent just learning the basics and making them second nature. A thorough inculcation is needed into the theories dealing with the flow of Ki through the body, learning to generate and to direct this power according to conscious will. Months or even years of such conditioning would be recommended before then taking up the study of Tantric Yoga or one of its Westernized derivitives.

While involved in this long and deep conditioning, it is well to study what is available on the theory and practice of sex magic, and to begin practicing with a partner who hopefully has similar interests and inclinations, and with whom a mutual strong physical attraction and emotional bonding exists. Put the theory and the yoga/martial arts conditioning into practice, learning mutually how to establish and practice the linkages involved in generating and directing the Ki or Kundalini through sexual means. There are many aspects to it, many of which are quite subtle.

Effectiveness increases with practice, and in learning which objects to work for . . . even magic cannot work against strong improbabilities. One must learn to flow with the stream, and to divert it in a "soft" manner.

Every detail of preparation for the "Great Rite" of sexual magick can and does contribute to its effectiveness. The selection of goals and discussion of them for a deep mutual understanding, a long long buildup for the key rite, gradually increasing the potential as a dam gradually builds a deep reservoir, and perhaps preparatory rites with one's close partner and lover . . . all these are important.

On the final, key evening every part of such a rite must be carefully set up to build the power with full atmosphere and setting, bearring more and more strongly in mind not only all of the sensual rite before you, but every aspect of the goal or goals to be accomplished.

Then . . . catharsis. Holding and directing with the best of conditioning and technique the flow of the energies so generated.

It works, and works well. But it takes a lot to do it properly.

WITCHCRAFT — ECHO OF THE PAST,
PRECURSOR TO THE FUTURE

A religion, a philosophy, and a magical system far older than our recorded history, is making a comeback in this country and at this time. It is quiet, for the prevailing majority religion long ago began attempts to exterminate this archaic creed and world-view. It is near-invisible, unless one knows where and when to look.

It is known by many names, the most common being the Craft, the Old Religion, Wicca, and Witchcraft. Those within it often prefer to refer to it be either the homy short "Craft" or by the ancient Saxon word, "Wicca", which means "Witch", but lacks the latter noun's late-show connotations.

The Craft is based on the evocation of ancient archetypes both within and without the practicioner's mind. It sees the universe, nature, and humankind as all part of the same intimately interlinked continuum, and magic as a relatively effective way of getting things done. It presupposes a close spiritual link and especially an emotional syzygy between its prime deity, the Great Goddess, the God, and the Witches themselves.

Modern scholars who have become familiar with it have asked whether the Craft is indeed of ancient and unbroken lineage (and if so, for the proof), whether a modern reconstruction of an ancient system of belief, or whether it might be a do-it-yourself offshoot from the sociological, political, and spiritual eccentricities of the 1960's.

A part of the answer is easy; the writings of Gerald Gardner, Justine Glass, Doreen Valiente and others indicate its presence in the 1950's and before. Folklore and mythological sources mirror many of its festivals, spells, and magical techniques in many countries and far back in time. Whether or not an exact mother-to-daughter linage exists, provable directly, is more difficult to ascertain.

There have been many infusions of old and modern material into the Wicca as it exists today, much taking place in the last thirty or forty years. Ten and fifteen years ago many groups were making

claims of great antiquity, though to my knowledge no proof of unbroken lineage was ever put forth that would satisfy a scholar from
Harvard, the University of Southern California, or the Library of
Congress. Evidence existed that the best known branch of the Craft,
the Gardnerian, seemed to be derived from something older, and
that there seemed to be folk traditions of some sort in such places
as the Great Smoky Mountains, in Pennsylvania, and other locales.
There was an undeniable antiquity to American Indian religions,
African-derived Voudon, and Mexican Brujeria, though . . . and these
all had interesting similarities to Wicca.

But on the everyday level a realization has been coming to
exist that perhaps even though eventual proof would be interesting
and important from a scholar's viewpoint, there is something of
much greater immediate value.

It works. It gets results. That in itself is a very significant fact.

To step back for a moment, and set a few definitions. Paganism, as it has come to be understood in this country and in Britain,
is an overall view of the universe, stressing a oneness with Nature in
all her aspects. Witchcraft or Wicca is the "cutting edge" of Paganism
nowadays, consisting of investigators and magic-workers who seek to
make things happen, using traditional or traditionally-derived
methods. Of the Witches there are some whose investigations have
pushed even further, so that these adepts have established elite
Mystery Orders to investigate far into the nature of things, attempting to gain a deep understanding of some of the fundamental questions
of life, of time, and the structure of existence.

Witchcraft is a descendant, either directly or by reconstruction,
of the ancient Mystery cults which were of such fame up through
Classical times, and whose members included many of the most
famous thinkers who founded the beginnings of our civilization.

With the coming of the Christian era, however, these groups, at
Delphi, Ephesus, and elsewhere, were suppressed as being non-
Christian. Old folk beliefs continued for a long while afterwards, and
Mystery cults existed for some time afterwards in Northern Europe,
in the schools of the Valas and perhaps elsewhere.

They faded though, as a well-organized Christianity, allied
with the most vital political cultures of its day, gradually expanded
to eventually take over all of Europe and much of Asia Minor. The
old Pagan beliefs, some of considerable depth and value, changed
their surface coloration and continued. (I'd suggest a careful reading

of Jakob Grimm's "Teutonic Mythology", all four volumes, for an appreciation of just what has remained.)

Where did the Valas go, and what happened to the surviving Mystery schools? There's no answer that I know of. They simply haven't been mentioned anywhere during the last thousand years or so. I don't think they're around, but . . . who knows?

But interest began coming back as the strength of Christianity slowly began to fade. The Romantic Era of the last century brought back a renewed interest in mythology and folklore, as well as some beautifully Pagan art and music.

Deriving its inspiration and much of its working material from Egypt and the Middle East, the Society of the Golden Dawn brought the concept of operative magic back into the West about a hundred years ago, attracting some of the top minds of that time. Yeats and others used the Golden Dawn techniques within the framework of Irish, Scots, and Welsh folklore, initiating a return to the rich folk traditions of the Celtic lands.

Now several generations of investigators have followed, informally and without much fanfare. Our past has proven to be a mine of immense value and cultural richness.

The formal renaissance of the Craft began with Gerald Gardner during the 1940's and 1950's in Britain, with an eventual spread to the United States. Infusions of lore and inspiration have come from Middle and Eastern European, Welsh, Irish, Amerind, and backwoods American folklore and mythic sources. Magical techniques have been adapted from a wide variety of folk practices, with rituals and spells reconstructed from the past's fragments and shards. A rejuvenation of American folk traditions has similarly resulted, and is continuing.

The material and the researches which will fit our archetypes, which makes things happen, and which generates and continues that unique closeness of the Wicca with their gods and with Nature, this is what is accruing. A building for the future is continuing.

And what of the future? One of the key traditions of the Craft is that "From the stars ye came and to the stars ye shall return." Interesting and perhaps a significant statement during a time when the Old Religion seems to be joined by an increasing number of high-technology adherents, and those oriented to working for an improved future and perhaps an ultimate expansion to the stars themselves.

The richness of the past, the depth and breadth of the human mind, and the promise of an infinite frontier. These disparate and yet harmonious aspects illuminate the Witchcraft of today . . . and of tomorrow.

STAYING IN TOUCH

On the following pages you will find listed, with their current prices, some of the books and tapes now available that may interest you as a reader of this book. Your book dealer stocks most of these, and will stock new ones as they become available.

However, to obtain our full catalog, and to keep informed on the new books and tapes as they become available, you may write for our bi-monthly newspaper/catalog. A sample copy is free, and it will continue coming to you at no cost as long as you are an active mail customer. Or you may keep it coming for a full year with a donation of just $2.00 ($5.00 for Canada and Mexico, $10.00 overseas, first class mail).

Stay in touch! Included are news and reviews of new books and tapes, words from our authors, articles about New Age subjects, news, advertising of products and services, etc.

THE LLEWELLYN NEW TIMES
Llewellyn Publications, P.O. Box 43383-COD
St. Paul, MN 55164-0383, U.S.A.

TO ORDER BOOKS OR TAPES

If your book dealer does not have the books or tapes described on the following pages readily available, you may order them direct from the publisher by sending full price in U.S. currency plus $1.00 each for postage and handling within the United States, $2.00 each for surface mail outside the United States, or $7.00 each for foreign airmail, except as otherwise indicated. Credit card orders are accepted (VISA, MasterCharge, American Express, Diners Club). Charge card orders may be phoned free by dialing: 1-800-THE MOON. Mail orders to:

LLEWELLYN PUBLICATIONS
213 E. 4th St., P.O. Box 43383-COD
St. Paul, MN 55164-0383, U.S.A.

FANTASY JOURNEYS
Narrated Quests of the Mind and Spirit by Ed Fitch

In this series of guided imagery sessions, Ed Fitch takes you on inner journeys to some very real realms of Magick where your Mind and Spirit explore and learn, create and enjoy, and come back enriched.

These tapes are based on Ed's extensive knowledge and years of practice and teaching. They combine aspects of Jungian Psychology, Qabalah and Magick, and the Pagan World Views into a composite of high technological application to fulfill your need for guidance into new worlds of consciousness.

TAPE I

SIDE 1: THE ARMOR OF LIGHT. You will be led on an adventure during which you will find your personal suit of armor, constructed with your own hands out of resources from the inner world. Here is an adventure with real meaning in your explorations of other dimensions.

SIDE 2: AUDIENCE WITH THE SEA QUEEN. Moon Magick, Ocean Magick, the Lady of the Skies, the Lady of the Ocean Depths. Meet Her, explore Her Realm and gain the powers that contact with this Archetype alone can give.

TAPE II

SIDE 1: JOURNEY TO THE LAND OF YESOD. Within the Qabalah's Tree of Life there is a strange world ruled by the Moon. It is an Astral World with its own laws and strange powers you can learn to wield as you adventure through it with Ed's guidance.

SIDE 2: DRAGON RIDE. The Dragon is an age-old symbol of the active Female principle: creation embodied in a horrific and strange beast. On this quest, you will search out the dragon, understand it and harness its energies . . . or will it do the same to you, instead?

TAPE III

SIDE 1: VISIT TO THE ELVISH HILLS. The true Lords of the Night are the Elves and Fairies. Meet them, understand them, and know their power. You will be rewarded, and you will never be quite the same again.

SIDE 2: THRONE OF THE GOLDEN AGES. The Tree is huge and powerful, old and venerable . . . its roots sunk deep into being. Climb the great Tree and discover the throne of a Demigod. Take Its place, and know Its power yourself.

TAPE IV

SIDE 1: BUILDING AN ASTRAL TEMPLE. From materials of the astral world: astral wood, stone, air and fire, you build a temple of the soul. Your design, Your power, Your Symbols of Being are all incorporated into this mighty structure, built and filled with the power of your magick.

SIDE 2: VISIT TO THE CAVE OF APHRODITE. Journey to the beginning of Creation, walk with the spirits of Aphrodite's world of beauty and power. Here is the inner home of the True Pagan.

Each tape cassette is 60 minutes in length, priced at $9.95, or $32.00 for the set of four. To order direct, please add .50 handling per order, and .50 per tape for postage. For airmail postage outside U.S.A. add $3.00 per tape, or $10.00 for the set of four.

Travel Beyond This World with Ed Fitch

You've read CASTLE OF DECEPTION and journeyed into the fog-shrouded past. Now, through these incredible tapes, you can journey into mankind's infinite future!

Ed Fitch is uniquely qualified to be your guide on these journeys: Well known as the head of the pagan movement in America, editor of the extraordinarily beautiful magazine of Pagan Magic, THE CRYSTAL WELL, writer of one of the most startling magic/adventure series ever to be published, Ed Fitch, using another name, is a highly respected space scientist and consultant to NASA!

On STAR VOYAGE I, Side One, **Ocean World**, you will explore an incredible undersea world, meet its inhabitants and experience the marvels and dangers of this exotic kingdom.

On Side Two, **Dead Civilization**, you will touch the remains of a civilization as old as man, learn the awesome powers of their sciences, learn why they ceased to exist—except in the deep recesses of your own mind!

Through STAR VOYAGE II, Side One, **Primeval World**, you will walk the dark earth of a world filled with life forms long thought extinct. But, are you walking in the past— or the future? Learn the secrets of this primitive, exciting world and know the truth of your own origins!

On Side Two, **Advanced Civilization**, you will travel to the end of time, to a world of incredible technology, new dangers and astonishing discoveries. Learn where we are headed as a civilization and what your part will be in this Brave New WORLD!

STAR VOYAGE I, Ocean World and Dead Civilization, 60 minute cassette, EF005, $9.95

STAR VOYAGE II, Primeval World, and Advanced Civilization, 60 minute cassette, EF006, $9.95

OTHER BOOKS FROM LLEWELLYN

Llewellyn's Astrological Calendar. America's oldest—published for over 50 years by the oldest astrological organization in the entire Western Hemisphere. More than a calendar! 64 large 10" x 13" pages, illustrated, with monthly calendar pages giving not only date but Moon's Sign & Phase, Planetary Aspects, and Sun's entry into the signs—with Best Planting & Fishing Dates indicated. Also includes complete Daily Ephemeris, Personal Birth-Sign Forecasts with Favorable & Unfavorable Days, and World Predictions for each month. Additional pages give complete guidance to the meanings of the Planets, Signs and Aspects; the Influence of the Moon through the Signs; Casting a Solar Horoscope, and using Planetary Predictions; Interpretations for the Birth-Signs; Transits & Aspects; Gardening by the Moon; Planning daily activities by the Moon; Holidays—American, Canadian, Mexican, British, Christian, Jewish, Pagan; Astrology for Health with Herbs; Flower Remedies & Recipes; Astrology for Relationships, in Business, in Fashion, and At Home. Published in August for the following calendar year. **0-87542-414-7, $5.95**

Llewellyn's DAILY PLANETARY GUIDE. A complete pocket guide to practical uses of astrology, with complete Daily Ephemeris & Aspectarian, week-at-a-glance calendar/diary, guidance to planning actions by astrologically stable & unstable times each day and the active Lunar Hours, Ruling Planet Readings for each Birth-Sign and Personal Forecasts, and an extensive listing of planetary rulerships and magical correspondences for each planet. 352 pages. 4¼ x 7, Published in September for the following calendar year. 0-87542-415-5, $2.95

Llewellyn's MOON SIGN BOOK. Planting by the Moon—this oldest astrological almanac in the Western Hemisphere is a complete guide to the best dates and times for all types of Farming & Gardening activities, including special needs of different plants. In addition, it's a complete guide to choosing the best time for nearly every kind of activity—from buying & selling to job-hunting & signing documents to romance & marriage to Fishing, to Setting Eggs, Breeding Animals, Destroying Growths & Pests, etc. Also includes Birthsign Forecasts, News and Markets, Weather Forecasts, and much more. Nearly 400 pages. 4¼" x 7", Published in September for the following calendar year. 0-87542-413-9, $3.95

PRACTICAL CANDLE BURNING RITUALS, by Ray Buckland. Magick for fun, Magick as a Craft, Magick for Success, Love, Luck, Money, Marriage, Healing, to stop slander, to learn Truth, to heal an unhappy marriage, to overcome a bad habit, to break up a love affair, etc. Magick with nothing fancier than candles and the 28 easy rituals in this book—given in both Christian and Old Religion versions. 189 illustrated pages, 5¼ x 8, softbound. **0-87542-048-6, $5.95**

MAGICAL HERBALISM, by Scott Cunningham. This is the magic of amulets & charms, sachets & scented oils, simples & infusions, incenses & ointments—a special art that does not use the medicinal or chemical powers of herbs, but their subtle vibrations that touch the psychic centres in the brain and stir the astral light to affect the causal level behind the material world. Here is step-by-step guidance to the gathering & preparation of over 100 herbs, their compounding and their use in easy rituals & spells for every purpose—from attracting love & success to protection from harm & unwanted attentions. Index, tables, 256 pages, 5¼ x 8, softbound. **0-87542-120-2, $7.95**

ASTROLOGY FOR THE MILLIONS, by Grant Lewi. The classic introduction to easy casting of the Birth Horoscope, and to predicting your future based on Planetary Transits to the Birth Chart. Special tables and text enable you to set up and read the birth chart in just a few minutes for any person born between 1877 to the present, and then to project it into the future—up to 1999. Gives understanding to the past, and enables you to plan for the future. 300 pages, 6 x 9, hardbound. **0-87542-441-4, $10.00**

WITCHCRAFT FROM THE INSIDE, by Ray Buckland. An understanding of the Old Religion from pre-historic times to now, the history of its persecution and its revival in modern America, an explanation of sympathetic and ritual magick, a description of Initiation and the Sabbats. Illustrated with photographs and drawings. 158 pages, 5¼ x 8, softbound. **0-87542-085-0, $3.95**

THE LLEWELLYN PRACTICAL GUIDES
by Melita Denning & Osborne Phillips

THE LLEWELLYN PRACTICAL GUIDE TO ASTRAL PROJECTION, Yes, the Out-of-Body Experience can be learned, safely, by anyone. Consciousness can move in Time and Space, free of the physical body—experiencing the "Life Without Death" state. Step-by-step guidance and progressive practices lead naturally and easily to this new reality—which can be extended to include another person in the bliss of sexual union on the astral plane. Illustrated with photographs, and with unique 'puts-you-in-the-picture' drawings that aid the learning process. 239 pages, 5¼ x 8, softbound.   **0-87542-181-4, $6.95**

THE LLEWELLYN DEEP MIND TAPE FOR ASTRAL PROJECTION, Inducing the Out-of-Body Experience. A powerful new tool combining guided Mind Programming techniques with specially created sound and music to evoke deep level response in the psyche and the psychic centres for controlled development, and successful projection. This tape supplements the book listed above. 90-minute cassette tape.   **3-87542-201, $9.95**

THE LLEWELLYN PRACTICAL GUIDE TO CREATIVE VISUALIZATION, Mentally create fulfillment of your desires, and then bring them into physical world reality with this program of training in the technique and development of the psychic power. Step-by-step guidance and progressive practices train you to tap the limitless Energy/Matter potential of the Universe and channel it to meet your needs. 265 pages, 5¼ x 8, softbound.   **0-87542-183-0, $6.95**

THE LLEWELLYN PRACTICAL GUIDE TO THE DEVELOPMENT OF PSYCHIC POWERS, Psychic Powers are real, and are natural and inherent. Everyone can—and should—develop them. Without them we function at very low levels compared to our Human Potential. Full guidance to ESP, Astral Vision, Divination, Prophecy, Telekinesis, Psychometry, Dowsing, Scrying, Mediumship, Telepathy. Includes an inner development program of meditation, breathing, visualizing, chanting as well as instructions to testing your talent and progress. 265 pages, 5¼ x 8, softbound.   **0-87542-191-1, $6.95**

THE LLEWELLYN PRACTICAL GUIDE TO THE MAGICK OF SEX, "Sex Magick" unites not only Man and Woman, but the different levels of Mind and Soul to bring about true Spiritual Oneness. Exercises in psychic awakening and in Fantasy, Massage and Ritual lead to Rites of Sex Magick for Material Success and Abundance and the Eight-Day Ritual for the Conception of a Child with all the Glory and Blessing of Divine Power! These are dimensions of Love and Sex rarely experienced. 250 pages, 5¼ x 8, softbound. **0-87542-192-X, $6.95**

THE LLEWELLYN PRACTICAL GUIDE TO THE MAGICK OF THE TAROT. This book gives you guidance to using the Tarot Cards in Divination—to learn the inner truth about a situation and its predicted outcome, and then to use a special technique of reversal and magical dramatization to change the future to meet your needs. You can also use the power of the Tarot Cards, in special arrangements and with directed magical power, to bring about desired effects. Approx 250 pages, 5¼ x 8, softbound.   **0-87542-198-9, $6.95**

THE LLEWELLYN PRACTICAL GUIDE TO PSYCHIC SELF-DEFENSE AND WELL-BEING, This book shows you how genuine psychic attacks, as well as ordinary psychic and mental stress, hurt you. It then gives you full instruction, and guided exercises, to build up and energize your AURA into a powerful defense shield, AND a source of psychic strength for success and well-being. Includes the Rite of the First Kathisma using the PSALMS to invoke Divine Blessing. 250 pages, 5¼ x 8, softbound.   **0-87542-190-3, $6.95**

Also by Denning & Phillips

VOUDOUN FIRE: THE LIVING REALITY OF MYSTICAL RELIGION. This book explores the meaning, the actual practices, and the spiritual reality of the Voudoun religion. Authenticated, full-color, photographs taken during actual religious rites in Haiti show true psychic phenomena—the Astral Fire, the Astral bodies of Damballah and Ayida Weydo, Descent of a Fire Serpent, Possession. 39 full-page color plates, nearly 100 black & white photos and drawings. Complete glossary of Voodoo words. Text describes the origins and history of the religion, the nature of its ceremony and initiations, the reality of its power. 182 pages, 8½ x 11, softbound.   **0-87542-699-9, $9.95**